Science of Mind in Daily Living

by DONALD CURTIS

Here is a practical approach to self-improvement for those who want to lead a richer, fuller life. In it are collected the tried and tested methods that have worked near-miracles in the lives of thousands of people throughout the world.

This book contains scores of specific techniques for conditioning the mind to accept health, happiness, success, prosperity and all the spiritual and material rewards of life.

Amply illustrated with actual case histories drawn from the author's many years of teaching and counseling, this book contains over thirty-three treatments for personal thought control, development, conditioning, and discipline.

These treatments cover a wide field of human desires—from attaining better health, wealth and happiness to becoming more creative and acquiring new friends. They are designed to help the average man break through the barriers separating him from his inner consciousness, and find the fulfillment of his desires as he learns more about himself.

Written in an easy-to-understand and down-to-earth style, this profound work is filled with the wisdom of the ages, wisdom that will help people of all ages, interests and backgrounds.

Business and professional men will find new and exciting ways for making the right decisions; understanding and cooperating with the people they work with; and creating the proper personal image in the minds of others.

Moreover, this guide shows how to improve personal relationships—how to make friends of enemies and of total strangers. In addition, it contains special treatments to help resolve marital problems—social problems of single men and women—and problems between parent and child.

Also, there are treatments for unleashing the hidden skills and talents within each one of us. This book shows you how to develop these skills and create greater self-confidence, more energy and enthusiasm for living, and a new, more lucrative career.

In addition, this book gives an excitingly bold explanation of the origins of the Universe and of Universal Power. It shows how to use this, the greatest of all forces to create changes for the better.

Students of effective prayer will find this book an indispensable guide to their studies, and a valuable document on the success of the Science of Mind philosophy.

But essentially this is a practical, straightforward handbook for solving problems and getting results through scientific prayer. It tells the reader exactly how to prepare, what to do, what to say, and when and how to say it.

Rich and poor, young and old alike will benefit from this carefully designed plan for getting the most out of life. All will find it a source of inspiration that will not only tide them over the rough days in life, but will release the dynamics of the inner potential, and lead the way to richer, fuller living.

by Donald Curtis

An outstanding leader in New Thought and metaphysics for over twenty years, Dr. Donald Curtis is the senior minister of the Unity Church of Dallas where he ministers to thousands in person and through his regular radio and television programs.

In addition to his major books,
Your Thoughts Can Change Your Life
Human Problems and How To Solve Them
Daily Power For Joyful Living
Science of Mind in Daily Living
New Age Understanding

he is the author of many inspirational booklets which are widely read by Truth students everywhere. He has written hundreds of articles which have appeared regularly over the years in **Science of Mind, New Thought Quarterly,** and Unity periodicals. He is a District President of the International New Thought Alliance and speaks and teaches regularly at the INTA Congress each year.

Dr. Curtis speaks and conducts classes at Unity and other metaphysical churches throughout the United States and abroad. His seminars based upon his books are widely attended everywhere.

His writings are used as textbooks in healing, meditation, and spiritual education at many churches and centers. Dr. Curtis' sales and executive and leadership training seminars are popular in the business and professional fields, and he is in great demand as an after-dinner and convention speaker. He appears regularly before service clubs, speaking on his favorite theme, "The Unlimited Potential Within You." He presents techniques for developing this potential, releasing the free, full flow of life through the individual as his consciousness expands and he experiences richer, fuller living. Through the Spiritual Unity of Nations and other organizations throughout the world, Dr. Curtis works tirelessly for human understanding, international cooperation, and world peace.

He carries on a large correspondence with readers, teachers, and students all over the world. An extensive traveler, he has spoken in England, Switzerland, Germany, Ghana, South Africa, Greece, India, Japan, Hawaii and in the Caribbean Islands. A deep student of world religions, Dr. Curtis has studied with the yogis and holy men of India, spending time in their ashrams, as well as seeking out the counsel and instruction of Buddhist monks, and Tibetan lamas. In Japan, he studied Oriental techniques of healing, studied Zen, did research in the traditional older religions, and spoke at the centers of many of the "new religions" there, including an extensive lecture tour for Seicho-No-Ie founded by Masaharu Taniguchi.

Dr. Curtis' broad background and universal approach to spiritual matters make him welcome by religious groups of all denominations.

Science of Mind in Daily Living

Donald Curtis

Published by
Melvin Powers
WILSHIRE BOOK COMPANY
12015 Sherman Road
No. Hollywood, California 91605
Telephone: (213) 875-1711

TO MY SON DANNY

© Copyright 1975 by Dr. Donald Curtis
ALL RIGHTS RESERVED. NO PART OF THIS
BOOK MAY BE REPRODUCED IN ANY FORM
OR BY ANY MEANS, WITHOUT PERMISSION
IN WRITING FROM THE PUBLISHER.

LIBRARY OF CONGRESS
CATALOGUE CARD NUMBER: 69-11732
ISBN 0-87980-299-5
PRINTED IN THE UNITED STATES OF AMERICA

By the Same Author

Daily Power for Joyful Living

Your Thoughts Can Change Your Life

Human Problems and How to Solve Them

How This Book Can Work for You

WE have all said, "I could write a book about that experience!" or "The problems I have had would fill a book!" or "I have a whole book full of questions which I would like answered."

Here is that book.

This book is about you, about me—about all of us who are involved in the adventure of living this life with its joys and its pains, its problems and its rewards, its needs and its fulfillments, its challenges and its accomplishments.

This book deals with your favorite subject—you. Who is the most important person in the world? You are. You'd better believe it. Everything that concerns you starts with you. You and you alone are responsible for you.

This book deals with that responsibility and what to do about it.

THIS BOOK WAS WRITTEN FOR YOU

As you take charge of your own life, every moment is an adventure. We make many discoveries about what we know and what we don't know. Sometimes we need others to answer some questions and to show us the way.

That is why this book was written. I wish to share with you not only some of the answers which I have found from years of study and experience, but a working technique of personal thought control and discipline —*The Science of Mind*—which is the science of accomplishment through conditioning, re-conditioning, developing and building your inner consciousness, which is the cause of all good things in your life.

This book has been written for you to give you a practical working knowledge of this science that has shaped my life, and has helped me help many thousands of others re-shape theirs through the technique of Science of Mind Treatment.

This book is an adventure in total experience. This is your book. Every word is about you. Every Treatment is for you. As you immerse yourself in the Science of Mind treatments in each chapter, you find your thoughts clearing, and you break into a constructively higher, purer stream of consciousness which will not only give you an exhilarating new experience, but one which when constantly repeated as taught in this book, will entirely transform you.

THIS BOOK ANSWERS YOUR QUESTIONS AND HELPS SOLVE YOUR PROBLEMS

We learn by asking questions. We grow by solving our problems.

The answer is inherent in the question when it is asked. The questing mind is the expanding mind. The progression is from information, to knowledge, to wisdom, to understanding, to demonstration.

This book is dedicated to self-understanding. This understanding comes not so much from being given answers, as in being led to ask the right questions.

You already have the solutions or you wouldn't have the problems. Science of Mind Treatment does not free us from the appearance of problems, but it is the means by which we receive the solutions.

We will always have problems, but the great thrill of life comes from not getting hung up on the same old ones, but in moving along to bigger and more beneficial ones.

Who minds problems when he knows that he knows how to solve them? That is what this book is about.

Science of Mind Treatment is the process by which we claim and accept our good.

HOW THIS BOOK CAN CHANGE YOUR LIFE

Your life has already been changed as you glimpse the great promises which this new and abundant approach to life extends to you in this book. It will continue to change for the better as you move progressively through each chapter and make Science of Mind Treatment your way of life.

You are now upon the Upward Path which is the Golden Bridge to greater and more abundant and satisfying experiences. There is no limit to what you can be, what you can do, and what you can have.

Whatever you claim henceforth within yourself must appear in your experience.

Science of Mind Treatment is the process of establishing and strengthening this inner claim in consciousness.

The Creative Law does the rest.

HOW TO MAKE THIS BOOK YOUR CONSTANT COMPANION

This book is not just to be read, but to be absorbed, identified with, and lived with.

Let its ideas infiltrate into your subconscious. Follow the techniques and suggestions given. Repeat the treatments over and over until they become the very structure of your consciousness.

A new life is yours now. And so it is.

DONALD CURTIS

Contents

Part I—WHAT THE SCIENCE OF MIND IS

1. HOW TO UNDERSTAND YOURSELF 3

   Are you a stranger to yourself? Cooperate with life • Attaining self-understanding • Who Am I? Your link to the Infinite • A new technique for personal effectiveness • How treatment works • Patience makes things possible • Where did I come from? A new approach to evolution • Involution and evolution • Why am I here? The business of life • Life is a school • A program of action • What is treatment? How to get your new way of life • How to use treatment

2. HOW TO UNDERSTAND GOD—SOURCE OF ALL GOOD   14

   Where is God? The inner God • Experiencing God • How to look within yourself • Becoming God • Be still and know • God-like qualities • "If there be any virtue and if there be any praise, think on these things." Science of mind develops God-awareness • Finding God through treatment • The three Omni's • How to know God is all there is

3. HOW TO UNDERSTAND THE UNIVERSE 24

   How you can understand the universe • The starting point • How to contemplate the Infinite • Questions and answers • The Infinite One • Infite Being • The Intelligent Universe • Laws of the universe • The law and our choice • How law works • Universal inhabitants • Man—the knower • Natives of eternity • Infinite Intelligence • Wonders of the universe • The story of creation • Crea-

tion is consciousness unfolding • Seven "days" of creation • Treatment expands the mind

4. HOW TO UNDERSTAND THE WORLD WE LIVE IN   36

The world we create • How a marriage was rescued • One world vs. many worlds • How consciousness creates all • Change yourself—change your world • Individual consciousness • How a broken man formed his new world • What is consciousness? The secret of the ages • Treatment reforms our world • The world in true perspective • What a heart attack taught Arnold • Maintain and sustain dominion • Treasures not of this world • The abundant life • Real and unreal • Fact vs. truth • Science of mind and the world • Thoughts are things • Challenges from the world • Consciousness is the only reality • Purpose of treatment

Part II—HOW THE SCIENCE OF MIND WORKS

5. HOW TO USE THE POWER THAT WORKS WONDERS   51

The basic principles • The anatomy of mind—intelligence • One mind • Spirit • Substance • Law • Science • Your invisible power • Individual mind • Self-consciousness • The eternal secret • The secret doctrine • The way to achieve your true potential • Infinite potential • The creative principle • Our true potential • How treatment releases potential • Principles of the creative process

6. THE POWER WORKS FOR US BY WORKING THROUGH US   64

The only problem • Basic principles of the science of mind • The human mind • Conscious mind • Surface mind • We live in mind • Choice and selection • Decision • Subconscious mind • Your creative mind • How your "Personal Computer" works for you • It works for you by working through you • Change yourself—change your life • Conditioning and habit • How to build constructive patterns • Treatment: consciously creating circumstances

7. THE CREATIVE PRINCIPLE IN YOU   76

The garden of your mind • I. What nature plants • The perfect seed • Your freedom to choose • How to learn to use our power • How to plant personal thoughts for benefits • II. Conscious planting • Mental discipline • The secret of success • The builder • Weeding and replanting • III. Unconscious planting • Unrelenting guard necessary • Science of mind for the sick and the well • He forgot before he remembered • How to monitor your planting • Dangers of mass thought and race mind • IV. Subconscious memory • Your storehouse of the eternal • What the Will of God means • The science of constructivity • Building good karma • How to know the real power in yourself • How conscious and subconscious reciprocity work

8. HOW INDIVIDUAL MIND EXPRESSES UNIVERSAL MIND 91

Your divine spark • How to remove your personal interference • How to reverse negative thought • How to unlock your prison • How Jim found himself • How to break hypnotic suggestion • The science of mind frees us • How problems blind solutions • The best time to start beating problems • Wake up and live—now • An example of how science of mind showed the way • How to treat for truth • How to use your full mental capacities • The mental process • Thought • Will • Concentration • Attention • Imagination • An example of creative imagination • The power of unlimited imagination • Visualization • The film in your mental camera • Two types of visualization • Treatment is using your mind constructively

Part III—WHAT THE SCIENCE OF MIND DOES

9. HOW THE SCIENCE OF MIND MAKES YOU HAPPY 104

The dilemma of success • Laws of life • What is meant by the loving heart • How hate produced ulcers • The practical science of love • Evolution toward love • Attaining grace • Dare to live by love • How to recondition for happiness • The importance of accepting treatment as workable • The kingdom of happiness is always within you • Treatment instruction

10. HOW THE SCIENCE OF MIND MAKES YOU HEALTHY 118

The path of a falling star • How new life took place • How the healing power of mind works • Health means wholeness • Healing the whole person • The healing consciousness • Science of mind for healthy people • Real physical health • Emotional health • A mental healing for physical health • These were healed • Your key to healings • The quality of radiant wholeness

11. HOW THE SCIENCE OF MIND MAKES YOU WEALTHY 128

What real values are • Inner reality • What true prayer does • The law of the inner awareness • How to profit from problems • Mental alchemy effective • Self-concept • How consciousness of worth works for you • Let the power use you • How to draw on your inner resources • How the plus factor brings results • How to get subconscious agreement • How to turn liabilities into assets • Love: the coin of the universal spirit

12. HOW THE SCIENCE OF MIND MAKES YOU WISE 139

Universal Mind: Source of all knowledge • The anatomy of mind • Thought • Knowledge • Information • Ideas • Concepts • Opinions • Convictions • The power of conviction within • Attitudes • Change your attitude; change your world • Wisdom • Understanding • Importance of discrimination • Empathy • Your infinite potential • Treatment develops understanding

Part IV—HOW YOU CAN USE THE SCIENCE OF MIND

13. HOW TO USE THE SCIENCE OF MIND IN BUSINESS 153

Principles of successful living • The attitude of success • Your attitude toward yourself • Don't look where you are; look where you are going • The technique to solve your problems • How a change of attitude saved a business • How to bless your business • Why you should love your business • What does work profit you? What the science of service means • The true meaning of salesmanship • How to participate in life's profits • How to treat for success

14. HOW TO USE THE SCIENCE OF MIND IN PERSONAL RELATIONSHIPS 164

How to change other people's opinions of you • How to

get along with others • How to get along with yourself • Where your greatest love should rest • How to approach your neighbor • The single standard • True forgiveness • Love is active doing • The golden rule • Love heals all

15. THE PRACTICAL TECHNIQUES OF SCIENCE OF MIND TREATMENT 174

Individual personal application • Healings of health from treatment • Personal problems respond to treatment • Treatment solves financial matters • Treatment effective for achievement • How treatment changes consciousness • Treatment integrates the mind • Functions of treatment • Treatment conditions you by changing your consciousness • Treatment is true prayer • What treatment is not • Your personal treatment • Talking to God • Spontaneous treatment • Use treatment regularly

16. HOW TO DEVELOP YOUR DESIRED FULL POTENTIAL 187

Development from within • How to get realization and fulfillment • Your infinite potential • How God is individualized in you • The anatomy of mental action • Vision • God's vision • Imagination • Spiritual imagination • Activating imagination • Reality of imagination • Intuition • Direct knowing • Developing intuition • Inspiration • How good shines through you • Meditation and contemplation • Communion • Union • Realization • Inner contact • Voice of the silence • How to achieve your greatest experience • The mystical way • Meditation is listening prayer • How meditation clears the mind • Attunement • Vibration • Awareness • The invisible universe • Attaining self-development • Enlightment • Self-improvement through self-unfoldment • The upward path • Illumination • The one light

EPILOGUE 207

The way is clear for you • The key you can turn for all good • What do you need to be free from? Self-realization and true awareness • Your life without limitation

Personal Science of Mind Treatments in This Book

1. Treatment for Self-Discovery	6
2. Treatment for Self-Understanding	12
3. Treatment for God Receptivity	19
4. Treatment to Understand God	22
5. Treatment—Being	27
6. Treatment—Becoming	34
7. Treatment to Create My World	40
8. Treatment to Understand the World	46
9. Treatment to Comprehend Universal Mind	56
10. Treatment to Develop My Individual Mind	62
11. Treatment for Personal Awakening	65
12. Treatment for Personal Power	73
13. Treatment for Planting My Mental Garden	81
14. Treatment for Conscious and Subconscious Agreement	89
15. Treatment for Creative Achievement	97
16. Treatment for Intelligent Action	104
17. Treatment for Love	114
18. Treatment for Happiness	116
19. Treatment for Healing	121
20. Treatment for Health	126
21. Treatment for Abundance	130
22. Treatment for True Wealth	137
23. Treatment for Wisdom	146
24. Treatment for Understanding	149
25. Treatment for Personal Success	161
26. Treatment for the Success of My Business	162
27. Treatment to Get Along with Myself	170
28. Treatment to Get Along with Other People	172
29. Treatment:	
A) To Correct	179
B) To Construct	179
C) To Direct	180
D) To Maintain and Sustain	181
30. Treatment for Self-Realization	185
31. Treatment for Personal Growth	204
32. Treatment to Express My Full Potential	205
33. Treatment for Your Life Without Limitation	210

Chapter 1

How to Understand Yourself

THE first object of our study must be the one person about whom we know most—and least—ourselves.

There is only one place and one time to start this momentous study—right here and right now.

If we are to really understand ourselves, we must probe the mysteries of the inner kingdom. From deep within ourselves come the answers which we seek. These answers give us understanding. Understanding leads to power, power leads to effectiveness, and effectiveness leads to productivity. Productivity is the result of setting the Creative Law into operation and sustaining it in its natural action.

ARE YOU A STRANGER TO YOURSELF?

Have you ever had the feeling that you don't know yourself at all? Have you ever looked into the mirror and found a stranger staring back at you?

This was Joe's problem. He was always a stranger to himself—mixed up and confused as to who and what he was. Whether he was looking into the mirror, or anywhere else, he could not find himself. He tried many remedies without avail—until one day he looked within himself and made a great discovery.

"I have discovered that there is something within me that I would like to know more about," he told me in one of our counseling sessions one day after we had been working upon his basic problem for some time. "You know, Dr. Curtis, I'm a person just like everyone else."

"No, Joe," I corrected him, "Not just like everyone else. You are yourself, therefore unique. We are all the same in that we are people, but beyond that we are all different individuals with our own traits and characteristics. Our business in life is to start from this beginning and go on to make the most of ourselves."

This is what Joe did. Once he came to know himself he could cooperate with life instead of fighting it.

COOPERATE WITH LIFE

When we cooperate with the natural creative action of life, all good unfolds in and through us. We experience health, happiness, success and prosperity, freedom, peace, self-expression, and all of the good things that make life pleasant and worthwhile. Understanding ourselves is the first step toward releasing our true potential so that we may justify our reason for existence, achieve our purpose, and live the good life.

ATTAINING SELF-UNDERSTANDING

It took some time for Ella to learn to understand herself, just as it does for many of us.

She seemed to be a misfit. A naturally tall child, her rapid growth made her awkward and ungainly. She was unable to keep pace with the other children on the playground, and her clumsiness was a source of great humiliation to her. This frustration carried into the classroom and she lagged far behind in her studies, barely managing to get by. Her ineptitude led to great inner suffering, which in turn became a chronic hostility and rebellion which stayed with her well into adulthood.

Finally, after continuing unhappiness which included two broken marriages, Ella finally came to self-understanding, and through a series of steps such as we will present in this book, she not only came to understand herself, but to develop faith and self-confidence. When she stopped fighting and resisting life, she, too, came to understand herself. The adventure of self-discovery led to the unearthing of a tremendous talent for painting. She came to understand herself and what she could do, and today she is both a successful artist and a successful person.

Ella and Joe have both achieved what each one of us can and must—self-understanding.

Self-understanding is something which we must achieve by ourselves. Others may help us, inspire us, and lead us out of the dark land of problems, through the confusion of turbulent emotions. They may teach us to overcome ignorance and indecision, but no one can enter into self-understanding and self-mastery except we ourselves.

WHO AM I?

Am I my body, or do I have a body? Am I my feelings, or do I have feelings? Am I my mind, or do I have thoughts, ideas and concepts? Am I my habits, conditioned responses and actions, or do these merely form patterns which have settled upon me? Am I my experiences, my actions and my achievements, or are these also subordinate to the fact of my greater being?

It would seem that we are greater than the sum total of all of our parts. We need a larger focus of identification. Let us think of ourselves not as *becoming*, but as *being*. Let us think of ourselves not as a human being struggling up an evolutionary pathway toward some kind of achievement, but as a spiritual being going through human experience for the purpose of growth and development.

YOUR LINK TO THE INFINITE

The idealistic philosophies of the ages have taught that man is an eternal being, embodying a spark of divinity of which he is sole custodian and over which he has personal individual responsibility. The Science of Mind is the present-day expression of the great religious, psychological and philosophical teachings of the ages, unified by scientific methods of thought and behavior. The Science of Mind provides techniques of constructive mental and emotional conditioning which make us capable of receiving instruction from the Infinite Intelligence within us.

We are making contact with Divine Mind right now as we ask questions and receive answers through a process that is greater than personal thought—more efficient and reliable. Through introspection, insight and intuition, we have revealed to us the secrets of our Greater Being—that which we really are—a Self which overshadows the self. Once we make contact with our own Soul, because that is what this Inner Self is, and when we learn to sustain and maintain this contact, we add greater dimension to our lives. The mystics of the ages have known and practiced this through various techniques of introspection, contemplation, prayer and meditation. But always this practice was reserved for the few, while the masses, lacking the techniques for attaining higher understanding and wisdom, have struggled through the trial and error labyrinth of their own misdirected thoughts.

A NEW TECHNIQUE FOR PERSONAL EFFECTIVENESS

The Science of Mind presents a space age technique for attaining personal effectiveness. It is called *Treatment*. We will deal with this basic technique throughout this book. Personal scientific Prayer Treatment is the essence of the Science of Mind. The basic treatments which are given in each chapter are for your personal use. Go over them diligently, absorb them wholly, and your entire life can change. Here is your first treatment.

Sit quietly and go over this treatment, reading it first and then just thinking about its statements of truth and positive affirmation. Know that these statements are true about the real you whether they seem to be so or not at present. As we let these ideas work, we will have ourselves revealed to us.

Personal Science of Mind Treatment for Self-Discovery

Quietly and calmly, I release myself from all outer concern as I go upward and inward to the center of my own being. I am free from the petty details of daily living as I align myself with the harmonious life of the Infinite Oneness. I go forth to discover my Self.

Where God is, I am. Where I am, God is. We are one. God is all of me. I am that part of God which I can understand. The true nature of my being is revealed to me as I let go and let God reveal himself to me as what I really am. My life is God's life in me. I individualize the Infinite. I express the Divine. I am one with all that is good. I recognize this Truth and live by this premise. I approach the facts of life from the highest point of view.

I am in this world but not of it. I do what is normal, natural and right for me to do. I use what I am given to use—my mind, my soul, my body, my senses, my thoughts, my feelings, and all of the material and spiritual blessings of God's abundant universe. But I am greater than the sum total of all of these.

I am more than I appear to be. "I am fearfully and wonderfully made."

I discover myself in the commonplace as well as the unusual aspects of life. All are an out-picturing of my inner consciousness. I discover who and what I really am as I go to the center of my being and let God reveal himself to me there. There is One Life. This Life is God. This Life is Whole. This Life is Perfect. This Life is my life now.

There is only perfect God, perfect man and perfect being. This Truth is revealed to me as I travel the Pathway to Self-Discovery. I find myself today right where I am. And so it is.

We have now made a start with our first treatment. There will be two in each chapter throughout the book. Take each one in order and work with it as it comes. This book is designed to bring about a complete change for the better in our lives. If at first you do not notice any change, keep at it. Open up your mind to the flow of these positive ideas. They will change your life.

HOW TREATMENT WORKS

Treatment is not just a magic wand which you wave to bring about whatever you may want. Treatment is a technique of prayer which frees the self from error and false belief so that true expression and demonstration may take place. It is not a matter of getting something or making something happen; it is the process of *being that which causes desirable good to come about*. There is no limit to our development of our true potential when we systematically and regularly practice Science of Mind Treatment. The results which follow are the natural result of the working of the law of cause and effect. Good results are the inevitable effect of good causes.

Patience makes things possible

Bill is eloquent evidence of the effectiveness of treatment. He had somehow secured my first book, *Your Thoughts Can Change Your Life*, which was my first major work on Treatment and the principles of the Science of Mind. He came storming into my office and practically threw it at me.

"This doesn't work!" he shouted. "I've been trying to do what you say and nothing happens. It sounds good, but that's as far as it goes."

"How long have you been working at it?" I asked.

"Three whole weeks."

"Three weeks of treatment, as compared to—?"

"What?"

"How old are you?"

"Forty-two."

"Three weeks of treatment to correct forty-two years of problems? Perhaps we should be a little more patient."

Bill agreed and kept up his study of the principles and the practice of Treatment. Soon he noticed that things were changing in his life just as they will in yours. He started giving thanks for the small blessings as they appeared, and soon larger ones were on the way. It wasn't long before most of his major problems were under control. He is continuing to work on the rest of them with these techniques that always bring results.

WHERE DID I COME FROM?

Even though the question, "Where did I come from?" may not be as important as the unmistakable fact that we are here now, in our thoughtful moments the question invariably arises. Do we really come from God as the mystic poets state? Undoubtedly so, because the Bible says we are sons of God ("Beloved, now are we the sons of God...." [I John 3: 2]), and that we are actually gods ("... 'Is it not written in your law,' I said, 'Ye are gods'?" [John 10: 34]).

What does this mean? Is there anything in this concept which will help us to be more effective right now? That is what we are primarily interested in, isn't it? Certainly the higher the self-image we hold, the better the person is who emerges. This is simple cause and effect. Therefore it follows that the higher origin we are aware of, the clearer the picture we will have of who and what we really are.

A NEW APPROACH TO EVOLUTION

Of course, we cannot ignore the scientific principles of evolution. The development of man from lower forms of life has been unmistakably proved. Indeed, our ascent from the one-celled amoeba can be very clearly traced—on the physical level. But what about the real man? Where did the real me come from? I am willing to accept the evolution of my body—even my functions, senses and processes, but what about the essence of me? This surely did not emerge from the primordial ooze. I know that there is that within me which has always existed and will always exist. From whence did that something—which is more than it appears to be—come from? "What a piece of work is a man! how noble in reason! how infinite in faculty! in form and moving how express and admirable! in action how like an angel! in apprehension how like a god!"

(*Hamlet,* Act II, scene 2)

INVOLUTION AND EVOLUTION

Where did this creature come from? "... from God who is our home?" Let's assume so. If this is true, then we must have come from both the lower and the higher levels. Physically we have evolved; spiritually we have been involved. The god which we really are indwells the creature which we seem to be. The Higher Presence has descended so that the lower form may ascend. Browning calls this the "imprisoned splendor ... the spark that animates our clod."

Doesn't this clear up many of the questions which you have asked? Doesn't this explain our deep inner memory of glorious prior existence and the feeling that we really don't belong here—that we are strangers in a foreign land—that we are weary travellers seeking to return home again—that we may be in the world, but are really not of it? If all of this is true, then

WHY AM I HERE?

Haven't you often asked yourself this eternal question? Since we ask it so often, perhaps we are here to find out why we are here. Let us assume that there is a purpose in life—that it has meaning and significance—that individual existence is sacred and important. Everything within us either affirms or hopes that this is true. To the degree that we believe it is true, it becomes true for us. Once all of the nagging questions are settled, we can go about the business of living with direction and enthusiasm.

THE BUSINESS OF LIFE

The business of life is to accomplish that for which we came here. Jesus called this "... My Father's business" (Luke 2: 49), and early in His life He was able to define his reason for existence: "... for this cause came I into the world, that I should bear witness unto the truth...." (John 18:37) Your business and mine is exactly the same, because Jesus represents the prototype for all mankind. We reveal Truth by self-development and achievement. From within ourselves we find the motivation for what we do, and wise is the person who follows the admonition: "Whatsoever thy hand findeth to do, do it with thy might...." (Eccl. 9:10)

LIFE IS A SCHOOL

Some of us build better mousetraps, some paint more beautiful pictures, others dig deeper ditches or climb higher mountains, either because they are there, or because we feel a compulsion. Life lives itself through each of us in terms of our own capacities, abilities, consciousness and dedication. We are here, then, to do our work, express ourselves, help others and to grow in the process. Life is more of an internal unfoldment than an external development. Life is a school in which we learn lessons on every level: materially, physically, socially, emotionally, mentally and spiritually. There is no limit to what we can accomplish and learn if we make life an adventure and approach it from the larger viewpoint. We are not only ascending from below, but we have also descended from above. We are not just man, but also God in man. This is the key to the entire matter. The Science of Mind teaches that man is divine as well as human.

We are not just human beings trying to be good, but we are spiritual beings going through human experience on the way toward fulfillment and self-unfoldment.

A PROGRAM OF ACTION

What shall we do about all of this? A sensible and systematic program of action is essential if we are to make a success of this business of living. The Science of Mind provides this program of action. We have already started. At the beginning of this chapter we suggested that you:

1. Start where you are.
2. Look at yourself honestly.
3. Take a personal inventory.
4. Be willing to change.
5. Do something about you.
6. Undertake a sensible and systematic program of action.

The first step in this program of action is to understand yourself. This chapter has provided true guides to introspection and self-understanding. From this basis we are ready to move along in the next few chapters into extended areas of understanding, but first we are ready for another Science of Mind Treatment.

WHAT IS TREATMENT?

Treatment is the *practice* of the Science of Mind. Treatment is the technique by which we change ourselves mentally, emotionally and spiritually. Treatment is the means by which we condition ourselves to receive and accomplish desired goals and objectives. As you make a practice of repeating these statements, meaning and believing them, they become true in your life.

HOW TO GET YOUR NEW WAY OF LIFE

The Science of Mind is a way of life. In this book are the keys to wisdom and the techniques of personal application which will change your life. Read the book carefully. Take your time and master each section and step before going on to the next one. This book provides the structure for a practical working program and the techniques for personal application and practice which lead to rich, full, effective living. There is no limit to where you can go as you make the Science of Mind your way of life.

Miracles may well appear in your life from the moment you start reading this book and giving your first Treatment. However, it is to be stressed that the benefits of living by the Science of Mind reach far beyond mere immediate demonstrations or healings. The main benefits are those which come from that inner growth and unfoldment which moves us along the pathway of self-realization.

HOW TO USE TREATMENT

The Science of Mind works if we work it. This book provides a working technique for your personal use. Follow the steps as given, and you will experience a new life. In working with the two treatments given in each chapter, always relax first, then repeat the treatment as given with an attitude of assurance and expectancy. Every statement of Truth is true about you as you believe it. Read the treatment first, then repeat it with conviction. Then think about it and meditate upon it quietly, letting it sink deep into your subconscious, then release it and let it happen.

Every treatment in this book is about you. Make them your own. Return to them frequently to accomplish the purpose for which they are designed. Apply yourself to mastering this technique of building yourself and your life by expanding your consciousness. You may want to write the treatments out in longhand, in addition to saying them out loud. This helps them penetrate the subconscious. Or you may wish to read them aloud in unison. You discover the ways which are most beneficial for you. But above all—use two or more of these treatments each day of your life. The benefits will be so obvious that you will make this approach a permanent part of your daily life.

When the time comes, and you will know it when it does, you will want to free yourself from these treatments which I have written and speak or write your own. But first, begin at the beginning and let the steps unfold one at a time.

Personal Science of Mind Treatment for Self-Understanding

As I relax and release myself from all outer concerns, my mind is free to move upward and inward into greater areas of awareness and insight. My thought is free from all negativity and confusion. I am attuned to inner instruction. I am led into greater understanding.

In understanding myself, I do a better job of living. I approach this inward journey with confidence and faith. I know that there is revealed to me that which I need to know. I know that God is all of me, and I am that part of God which I can understand. I am beginning to understand now.

I start where I am and I look at myself honestly. During my personal inventory I discover who I am, because I have a clearer understanding of where I came from, why I am here, and where I am going. All answers are revealed to me as I reside quietly at the center of my being and let the understanding unfold. As I grow in understanding, I get a clearer picture of myself the way I really am. I understand that I am much more than I appear to be.

My new self-image emerges from my new understanding. A

perfect pattern emerges from within me. Truth is revealed. As I understand myself I understand something of the great areas within and beyond myself. My unfolding understanding moves me inward, upward and onward into greater awareness of all things.

And so it is.

CHAPTER 1 SUMMARY

1. Deep within us are the answers we seek.
2. When we cooperate with life, life cooperates with us.
3. Self-understanding is the first step in releasing our true potential.
4. Get a clear and true self-image and you will reach higher levels of expression and experience.
5. Think of yourself not just as a human being struggling through life, but as a spiritual being going through human experience for the purpose of growth and development.
6. Make contact with your inner being, and you will add great dimension to your life.
7. We have evolved from lower levels of life. We have been involved from higher levels of life.
8. Life lives itself through us in terms of our capacities, abilities, consciousness and dedication.
9. Life is a school—more of an internal unfoldment than an external development.
10. The Science of Mind helps you understand yourself.

Chapter 2

How to Understand God—Source of All Good

"G_{OD}! Everybody's talking about God, but I have yet to find anybody who has actually seen Him. Have you seen God, Dr. Curtis? Tell me the truth! Have you seen God?"

Conrad was trembling as he grasped the edge of my desk and leaned imploringly across it toward me, his voice and entire body tense with excitement.

"Perhaps not in just the way you are trying to see Him," I conceded, "But yes, yes, I've seen God. In fact, once you learn how, it's hard to see anything else."

"How is that?" Conrad asked, and immediately became still and attentive as he sensed that perhaps there was a way to God which he had never thought of. It was obvious that he wanted to find and understand God more than anything else in the world.

I proceeded to cover some of these points which helped Conrad understand God, just as they will help us as we ask the right questions and look in the right places in the right way.

In endeavoring to understand God, the ancients concluded, "To name Him is to limit Him; to define Him is to defile Him." However, just as man has always done, we continue to seek God, and at stages along our search we name Him and venture definitions.

WHERE IS GOD?

Part of the difficulty in endeavoring to reach a clear understanding of God comes because we look in the wrong place and in the wrong way.

The tendency is to look outward with a three-dimensional consciousness and find nothing but intensified involvment with our own confusions, inadequacies and anxieties. Inevitably, our outer search ends up with our projecting ourselves upon the universe, and we settle for an anthropomorphic God that is merely an amplification of ourselves. We are even more terrified of this God than we are of ourselves, and we end up with a religion that teaches fear and superstitition, and a form of worship that is taken up with appeasement and begging. The outward method of seeking God is obviously not the answer.

For ages man has been endeavoring to breathe life into graven images, while, all the time, the God of our own Infinite Potential lies waiting to be awakened from within our own being.

THE INNER GOD

The time has come to look inward and let the fourth and fifth dimensions reveal the true God to us. This is the first step which will lead us into the infinite dimension of the Spirit and bring us not only the understanding but the experience of God. "In my Father's house are many mansions; if it were not so, I would have told you." (John 14: 2)

The Science of Mind leads us into these "many mansions" within ourselves until we find that we do not need to seek God. We merely need to learn how to "Be still and know that I am God." (Psalm 46: 10)

The True Self within each one of us is God. God constitutes individual consciousness. You are a point of light within the Mind of God; you are a point of love within the Heart of God. Each of us is a cell of awareness, intelligence, action, feeling, and manifestation of being, within the Great Being which is God. We might well say, "God is all of me; I am that part of God which I can understand."

EXPERIENCING GOD

Our personal understanding of God comes from our individual experience of God. We can see God, we can hear God, we can feel God—not with eyes, ears or touch, but with an inner intuition and perception, which is actually God experiencing Himself—in and through us.

> Speak to Him thou for He hears,
> And Spirit with Spirit can meet.

> Closer is He than breathing,
> And nearer than hands and feet.
> (Tennyson, "The Higher Pantheism")

God instantly comes to life when we look for Him in the right way and in the right place.

"God Lives in My Heart," is the title of a modern sacred song.

"Behold the kingdom of God is within you" (Luke 17:21), Jesus taught, and went on to explain: "I and my father are one." (John 10:30) "He that hath seen me hath seen the Father. Believe me that I am in the Father, and the Father in me." (John 14:11)

There can be little doubt that true understanding of God can come only through the development of personal insight and awareness.

Lao-Tze, many years before Jesus, said, "There is no need to run outside for better seeing, nor to peer from a window. Rather abide at the center of your being, for the more you leave it, the less you learn."

In a more modern day, Robert Browning echoed the same instruction: "Truth is within ourselves. There is an inmost center in us all where the Truth abides in fullness. And to know, rather consists of opening out a way whence the imprisoned splendor may escape, than in effecting entry for a light supposed to be without."

HOW TO LOOK WITHIN YOURSELF

Wally was what would be classified as an extrovert. Actually he was loud, agressive and overbearing, as well as miserable. Nobody liked him, and as we talked together it was obvious that he didn't like himself.

"I've even asked God to help me," he admitted, his loud manner stilled. "I've prayed by the hour, but I doubt if there is anybody there to hear me—or *anything*. At any rate, nothing has happened."

"Where did you think God was that you could shout loud enough for Him to hear you, or where did you think He was that no matter how softly you spoke he could fail to hear you?" I challenged him.

"I just don't know," he pondered. "But I do know that if I can find God I'll be all right. Maybe not completely, but I'll be on the right track."

"Exactly. Let's start by looking inside instead of outside."

Which we did. Wally applied himself to learning treatment and meditation, and even though his stubborness and unpleasant personality seemed to block the way for a long time, he kept at it until he began to change.

When he learned to look inward instead of outward, he saw something bigger than he was. *This is what changed Wally.* We always become what we contemplate.

BECOMING GOD

Obviously, the way to understand God is to let Him reveal Himself to us. It is not so much *what* we look at as *how* we look and *with* what. In our search for God, we can well heed the observation of Dr. Ernest Holmes: "What you are looking for, you are looking at, and you are looking with." It seems then that the only way to find or understand God is to *become* God. That is, to develop within ourselves, those qualities which are God-like—compatible with good, because God is good—The All-Good. God is neither an entity nor an abstraction. **God is.** God is neither a concept nor a manifestation. **God is.** God is none of these things —*but* is *all* things. God is greater than the sum total of all things. He is the original First Cause of all creation, but at the same time indwells each atom of Its creation with Itself. God is the great No Thing, but is *everything*.

BE STILL AND KNOW

God cannot be comprehended by conventional methods. Think about Him and He eludes you. Talk about Him and He evades you. Pursue Him and He escapes you, but become still and invite Him in, and He fills you and envelops you with His Presence and Power. We must practice the Presence of God until we become God-like. We perceive Him through what we are. It becomes a matter of being what we really are—sons of God, and becoming all that that implies—whatever infinite potential it may be.

Jesus said, "Beloved now are we the sons of God and it doth not yet appear what we shall be." (I John 3:2), and the Scripture proclaims, "I have said, ye are Gods." (Ps. 82:6)

GOD-LIKE QUALITIES

How are we to bridge this obvious gap between what we seem to be and what we really are? First of all, we must *do* something *about* ourselves and *for* ourselves that will develop our finer, or God-like qualities. Paul admonished:

> Whatsoever things are true,
> Whatsoever things are honest,
> Whatsoever things are just,
> Whatsoever things are pure,
> Whatsoever things are lovely,
> Whatsoever things are of good report;
> If there be any virtue, and if there be any praise, think on these things. (Phil. 4: 8)

The mind that is filled with truth, honesty, justice, purity, loveliness, and good reports is certainly more likely to know God than one which is filled with their opposites. The mind which is filled with truth cannot know error. The honest person cannot know deviousness. The just code will not condone unfairness. Purity of mind, heart and soul dissolves contamination. Loveliness is the absence of ugliness, and the Gospels themselves are the "good news" that "The kingdom of God is within you" (Luke 17: 21). These qualities are of God, and the development and practice of them not only make us better and happier individuals, but move us closer to our goal of understanding God.

"IF THERE BE ANY VIRTUE AND IF THERE BE ANY PRAISE, THINK ON THESE THINGS."

This is our instruction, to look for virtue and goodness in everything, because isn't God the Ultimate Virtue? If we see It, we become It. If we become It, we see It.

"If there be any virtue, and if there be any praise . . ." Start where you are. "Better to light one candle than to curse the darkness." If the virtuous and praiseworthy are not readily discernible . . . look for them, encourage them, nurture them, until they blossom into God-recognition and expression. If we would understand God, remember that He reveals Himself in and through us, and in and through all people and all things. "Beauty is in the eye of the beholder." God sees only God. Self-purification and self-development are the first steps toward understanding God.

"Think on these things." Thinking is the process which we employ in the first stages toward God-realization. Whatever we are to know must be known either initially or eventually in the mind . . . hence the Science of Mind. The major goal of the Science of Mind is to help us understand God. If we understand God, we understand everything.

> Flower in the crannied wall
> I pluck you out of the crannies,
> I hold you here, root and all, in my hand,
> Little flower—but if I could understand
> What you are, root and all, and all in all,
> I should know what God and man is.
> (Tennyson, "Flower in the Crannied Wall")

SCIENCE OF MIND DEVELOPS GOD-AWARENESS

The Science of Mind helps us develop both our intellectual and our intuitive faculties so that we may come to understand God both through reason and by insight. It doesn't matter which approach we use. One blends into the other. All roads lead to God. We may start with thought and progress to awareness, or, with the mystics, we may start with realization, and thereby transform our minds. "Be ye transformed by the renewing of your mind." (Romans 12:2) The Science of Mind helps you accomplish this. The renewed mind is prepared to understand God. The mind which understands God is automatically renewed.

FINDING GOD THROUGH TREATMENT

In the Science of Mind, when we want something, we treat for it. Sometimes it seems as if we are getting no results whatsoever, but then we become aware of changes within ourselves—changes that either lead us to the demonstration of the original desire or to unfoldment or change that is much greater than that which we conceived in the first place.

Personal Science of Mind Treatment for God Receptivity

"I have conscious Divine Intelligence. I individualize Omniscience. I have direct knowledge of Truth. I have perfect intuition. I have spiritual perception. I know." (Emmet Fox)

I know that I know. I open my eyes and I see inward and upward. I recognize the God of my being. He speaks to me, and I speak to Him. There is no place where God leaves off and I begin. "He who hath seen me hath seen the Father." (John 14:9) God is in me and I am in God. I behold the Presence and the Glory of God in all things and in all persons. That which I see in myself, I see everywhere. That which I see everywhere, I see in myself. "I and my Father are One." (John 10:30)

I think on the true, the honest, and the just. My heart is filled only with purity and wholesomeness. My eyes see only the beautiful, and my ears constantly receive the good report that "the Kingdom of Heaven" is at hand. My soul is edified by the good that I see in Nature and in my fellow man. I behold the Christ in you. My eye is single, and my whole body is full of light.

I sing the praises of God with my heart, and my voice proclaims the Word of God. "So shall my word be that goeth forth out of my mouth; it shall not return unto me void, but it shall accomplish that which I please, and it shall prosper in the thing whereto I send it." (Isa 55:11)

God understands me, and my mind learns its lessons well. I am receptive to the influx of Truth as it fills my entire being. As I receive, I grow in my awareness and understanding of God.

"I have conscious Divine Intelligence. I individualize Omniscience. I have direct knowledge of Truth. I have perfect intuition. I have spiritual perception. I know."

And so it is.

THE THREE OMNI'S

The Science of Mind teaches the Omniscience, the Omnipotence and the Omnipresence of God. The three together indicate the Nature of God and assist in our understanding. "Omni" is the Latin prefix meaning "all." God is All in All.

Omniscience—Since God is all, He knows all. There is nothing to be known except That which knows all that is to be known. There is One Mind, the Universal Mind, the Mind of God. This Mind is in everything and everything is in Mind. God is Infinite Self-Knowingness, therefore He is knowing himself in us. What God knows, we know, **if** we know we know it. Paul said, "Let this mind be in you, which was also in Christ Jesus." (Phil 2:5)

Omnipotence—Knowledge is power. Therefore, All-Knowingness leads to All-Power. Is there anything that God can't do? Of course not. Is there anything else that does anything? Of course not. "I speak not of myself; but the Father that dwelleth in me, He doeth the works." (John 14: 10)

"In the beginning was the Word, and the Word was with God, and the Word was God. The same was in the beginning with God." (John 1: 1,2)

The All-Power which is God is available to us. "If ye have Faith, as a grain of mustard seed, nothing shall be impossible unto you." (Matt 17: 20) "With God all things are possible." (Matt. 19: 26) There is no power except the Only Power.

Omnipresence—There is no presence except the Only Presence. "Whither shall I go from thy spirit? Or whither shall I flee from thy presence? If I ascend up into heaven, thou art there: If I make my bed in hell, behold thou are there." (Ps. 139: 8,9)

Emerson said, "God is that which peoples the lonely places."

Empedocles said, "God is a circle whose center is everywhere, and its circumference nowhere."

Brother Lawrence, the simple monk who lived in the seventeenth century, provides an example for all to follow in his "Practicing the Presence of God," which describes in detail how the individual is transformed by the simple discipline of seeing God in everyone and in everything. The mystics and the saints have always made this the focal point of their lives. This is what we teach and practice in the Science of Mind.

Conscious awareness of the onmipresence of God is the key to understanding God. The moment we *know* He is there, He reveals Himself to us. He never appears in part. That would be impossible because He is All. To see Him is to know Him. To Know Him is to understand Him. To understand Him is to become One with Him—All.

HOW TO KNOW GOD IS ALL THERE IS

James R. was a minister, sincere, dedicated and devoted to his calling. He spent long hours in study, prayer and meditation each day. He loved God and put forth every effort to know more about Him. He was faithful in the discharge of his duties, and he set the highest standards for himself and others.

Understandably, he became impatient when he seemed to make little progress toward experiencing closeness with God.

"I'm so busy with outer duties that my own spiritual life suffers," he complained to me one day. "I seem to be making very little progress toward understanding God."

"But you are making progress. Perhaps you should not be so impatient with yourself," I suggested. "Ease up a little, let yourself enjoy your tasks, and you will actually find God at every turn, because God is all there is. Knowing that is the great secret."

"I do know that," he countered. "But I seem to forget."

Rev. R's problem was the same as everyone's. *We forget.* Treatment is a time set aside specifically for remembering and knowing things of Truth and Good. As we are regular in its practice, we find that our inner change brings about outer results.

As we treat to understand God, we begin to know Him. This makes all the difference.

Personal Science of Mind Treatment to Understand God

God is All. God is Truth. God is Love. God is Oneness. God is Wholeness. God is.

God is the Father-Mother Principle of Being. God is active and intelligent. God is creative activity and fulfillment. God is the Source of all things. God is the One—the First Cause from which all things come:

> Oh, Thou, who giveth sustenance to the Universe
> From whom all things proceed,
> And to whom all things return,
> Unveil to us the face
> Of the true Spiritual Sun
> That we may know the Truth
> And do our full duty
> As we journey to thy sacred feet.
>
> (*The Gayatri*)

God is Omniscient, Omnipotent and Omnipresent. God is the Supreme Beingness. God is All. God is all of me. I am that part of God which I can understand.

There is no place where God leaves off and I begin. I and my Father are one. In Him I live and move and have my being. My mind is my use of God's Mind. My thoughts are the expression of God as Intelligence. My ideas are God's way of communicating with me. I keep my mind ever attuned to the Infinite Mind. Understanding comes to me as I learn to understand.

Love comes to me and I learn to love. I attune my feelings to God, and become purified in the envelopment of His Infinite Love. My feelings of well-being, joy and enthusiasm come from God who is my very being.

As I think thoughts of God I am one with God in my mind. As I feel the Presence of God, I am one with God in my soul. As I do God's work, I express God in my body and in all that I do. As I practice the Presence of God, He reveals Himself to me.

Truly, I am one with God now and forever.

And so it is.

CHAPTER 2 SUMMARY

1. God is all of me; I am that part of God which I can understand.
2. Our personal understanding of God comes from our individual experience of God.
3. It is not so much *what* we look at, as *how* we look and *with what* that helps us find God.
4. The only way to find and understand God is to develop God-like qualities within ourselves.
5. Self-purification and self-development are the first steps toward understanding God.
6. Whatever we are to know must be known either initially or eventually in the mind.
7. If we understand God, we understand everything.
8. The Science of Mind helps us develop both our intellectual and our intuitive faculties so that we may come to understand God both through reason and by insight.
9. God is All-Knowing, All-Powerful and Ever-Present.
10. The Science of Mind helps you understand God.

Chapter 3

How to Understand the Universe

When Thomas Carlyle said, "I don't pretend to understand the Universe—it's a great deal bigger than I am," he undoubtedly was summing up a very common point of view, but still we hear Robert Browning challenging us, "Ah, but a man's reach should exceed his grasp, Or what's a heaven for?" ("Andrea del Sarto")

We know that we have within us the capacity to understand all things, because we are intuitively aware of our oneness with all things. The outer manifestation of the Universe inspires and has always inspired us: "O Lord, how manifold are thy works! In wisdom has thou made them all: the earth is full of thy riches." (Psalm 104: 24) But when we want to understand that which we behold, we go within and ask the questions, seek the answers, and formulate conclusions.

> When I consider thy heavens, the work of thy fingers, the moon and the stars, which thou hast ordained; what is man, that thou art mindful of him? and the son of man, that thou visitest him? For thou hast made him a little lower than the angels, and hast crowned him with glory and honor. Thou madest him to have dominion over the works of thy hands; thou hast put all things under his feet.
>
> (Psalm 8: 3–6)

HOW YOU CAN UNDERSTAND THE UNIVERSE

If we have been given dominion over the works of God's hands, and if all things have been put under our feet (our understanding), then there is no reason why we should not accept our potential of understanding the Universe. As we glimpse this potentiality, we have already gained more understanding because our mind and entire consciousness has expanded and encompassed new areas of comprehension. We are proving that the unit has the qualities of the whole and that in the recognition of its infinite capacity to grow and its decision, discipline and dedication to do so, it becomes one with the whole. As the individual embraces the Universal, the Universal expresses itself in the individual.

We are the Universe in miniature. If we understand ourselves completely, we will understand the Universe. As we understand the Universe, we understand ourselves. "As below so above; as above, so below."

THE STARTING POINT

Where do we start? This book and the Science of Mind teaching are for the purpose of helping us understand ourselves, live with ourselves, and express ourselves effectively. In order to do this, we must extend our vision.

The obese lady had visited her physician several times in one week, and at each visit demanded a prescription.

Finally, the doctor lost patience. The patient was overdoing it. "Mrs. Smith, what are you doing here again? I saw you just yesterday."

"But, doctor, I need a prescription."

"I'll give you a prescription!" he grunted exasperatedly as he scribbled hastily on a pad and handed it to his persistent patient.

"Take one trip to Niagara Falls!" she exclaimed. "What kind of a prescription is that?"

"Just once I would like you to take a look at something bigger than you are!"

HOW TO CONTEMPLATE THE INFINITE

This is sound wisdom. If we are to expand and improve ourselves, we must rise above ourselves and grow beyond ourselves. Since the self cannot rise above the self, how are we to do this? If looking at a large conformation of rocks with a lot of water going over them could help to heal the fat lady, just how much do you suppose we will be helped by looking at the Universe and into the Infinite? The answer is obvious: *What we contemplate, we come to understand; what we understand, we become.*

As we contemplate the infinitute, beauty, order, harmony, and perfection of the Universe, we awaken the same qualities, and demonstrate the same conditions within ourselves. I say "awaken" advisedly, because if we did not already have infinitute, beauty, order, harmony, and perfection within ourselves, how could we be aware of them elsewhere?

Actually, there is no "elsewhere." It is only "everywhere," because God is omnipresent and All-in-All. Since the Universe consists of the totality of things, it would seem that "God" and "Universe" are synonymous and identical, which indeed they are. Universal Mind and Intelligence is the Spirit of God; Universal Power and Law is the Soul of God; Universal Manifestation and Form is the Body of God.

Since man is made in the "image and likeness of God," and since God and the Universe are One, we are made in the image and likeness of the Universe. "Things which are equal to the same thing are equal to each other."

QUESTIONS AND ANSWERS

This should settle the question of atheism once and for all:

"Do you believe in God?"
"There is no God."
"Well then, do you believe in the Universe?"
"Of course. I can see the Universe."

Or that of the agnostic:
"Do you believe in God?"
"I don't know if there is a God."
"Do you believe in the Universe?"
"Of course. I am in the Universe."

And the position of the man of faith:
"Do you believe in God?"
"Yes, I do."
"Do you believe in the Universe?"
"Of course. They are the same."

THE INFINITE ONE

Universe, of course means "One." There is only One God and One Universe. Since there can't be two of anything which is "One," they must be identical. So we prove by logic as well as by intuition that God *is*—the Universe *is*, therefore, we *are*, because we can understand this.

We need not understand all *about* the Universe to understand that there *is* the Universe. Once our consciousness accepts this conviction, we only need then to be true to our own nature, which is to be man—"the knower" —and we will know God—the Universe. This book is written to assist us in this unfoldment into Universal Beingness.

INFINITE BEING

We are what we think—what we know. As we are aware of being, we express being. As we are aware of Being, we express Being. So great is the capacity and potential of the human mind that it is capable of identifying and expressing the attributes of Divine Mind. The main attribute of the One Mind is Infinite Being. As we become aware of Infinite Being within ourselves we are one with all Being.

In this Treatment, release yourself from all awareness of the little self and let yourself flow with the stream of consciousness which will blend you with the Great Self. These statements are for the purpose of engaging your mind with thoughts and ideas of infinite proportion. Let them take over.

Personal Science of Mind Treatment—Being

The Universe is everywhere. I am in the Universe; the Universe is in me. As I look upward into the heavens and outward into space, I experience the infinitude of the Universe. As I travel outward to the farthest reach of limitless space, I am also travelling inward to the great height, depth and breadth of my own being. I understand myself as I learn more about the Universe. I understand the Universe as I learn more about myself.

I am at the center of the Universe. The center of the Universe is within me. All is One. I am an integrated unit in a universal system which is the totality of all things. I am one with everything that exists. God is expressed in and through the Universe. The Universe expresses as Life—Life abundant, omnipresent, and eternal. The Universe is Infinite—without beginning or end. There cannot be any more or any less of that which is All. I am One with the All. There can be no less of me; there can be no end to me. I am. That which I know I am is always expanding to be that which I AM—One with the Universe.

I am a universal being in individual form and expression.

I am one with all time and space, but I am free from any limitations of time or space. I experience the free, full flow of Infinite Intelligence as it unfolds itself into universal creation. I am in orbit with the planets, tracking my cycles through eternity, maintaining a rhythmic and harmonious accord with the Infinite rhythm and harmony. I sparkle with the stars, raying out my light throughout all the Universe. The stellar galaxies range out into Infinity from within my consciousness. I expand with and into the constantly expanding Universe.

I do not know large or small—here or there—I only know to be. I am aware of my own being, and so I am aware of all Being. I think. I know. I perceive. I am aware. The Universe within me expands into greater and greater areas of knowing and being.

The Universe is my father, my mother, my brother, my Self. The Universe is my origin, my home, my life. I release all into the Mind and Soul of the Universe. Infinite Creative Law is ever in action through me, creating and evolving me into the expression of my Infinite Potential. I am One with God, One with the Universe, One with All Being. I am upon an Infinite Pathway of becoming that which I already am.

And so it is.

THE INTELLIGENT UNIVERSE

Science has long investigated the question, "Is the Universe fundamental or accidental?" We have no intention of entering into or even recognizing this controversy because it only arises when the Universe is thought of solely as a physical system or material structure. This is to see only the outer effect, forgetting that as the Universe is One, it must also be Cause—containing within Itself the One First Cause of all Creation. We can no more look at the outer manifestation only and say, "That is the Universe" than we can look at our own body and say, "That is I." Intelligence precedes all Creation and must have a medium through which to work.

This medium is Mind, both at the Universal and at the individual level. Therefore, we see that the nature of the Universe is Spirit—Intelligence. It creates through Soul—Law, and produces Body—Form. Love is the constructive cohesiveness that holds the whole system together and keeps it operating. "Love is the fulfilling of the Law." (Romans 13: 10) Love is the Universal Law, the process by which the One Perfect Cause (God) flows out into perfect Creation.

LAWS OF THE UNIVERSE

The Laws of the Universe are laws of harmony, balance and order—Laws of Love. These are automatic. As Emerson said, "The Universe is begirt with Laws which execute themselves." The law of gravity is one such example on the physical level. The law of the transmutation of energy, which says that no energy is ever lost, but merely expresses itself on other levels and in different forms, is another.

We are more aware of laws on the physical and material levels because their operation is more readily discernible, but all laws are based upon Spiritual Principles which have their origin and existence in the Intelligence of Universal Mind. The Universe is One of Law and Order. Law is the way it operates. Everything in the Universe must maintain and sustain cooperation and harmony with the Law. Again, on the Universal level, this is automatic. Nature maintains its own balance.

THE LAW AND OUR CHOICE

Only man is capable of breaking the Law, because we have the power of choice. We can act other than with Love. When we do, we are out of harmony with the Creative Law of the Universe and must suffer accordingly. When we break the Law, the Law breaks us. It appears to be working against us, but is really not. The Law is merely pursuing its perfect course and is bringing all things into harmony with it. This results in correction on the individual level. If we do not correct and keep ourselves in tune with Infinite Law consciously and willingly, the Universe deals with us on its own terms.

Life is a school in which we have the privilege of learning how to cooperate with the Law through Love. The Science of Mind is one of the courses of study.

HOW LAW WORKS

Since the Universe is Infinite, the Universal Laws are also Infinite—both in number and in scope. The Laws cover every facet of Being on every level—cosmically, universally, spiritually, mentally, emotionally, physically and materially.

The cosmic, Universal and spiritual Laws are The Law, and execute themselves. The mental and emotional laws are the Law working through us individually in the areas where we learn intelligent choice and personal control.

Natural laws on the physical and material levels are evidence of the automatic action of Universal Law, but there are other laws set up on these levels governing every phase of human endeavor—social law, civil law, governmental law, financial law, and many others—all for the purpose of regulating and controlling the actions of individuals in our relationships with each other. When man-made laws are in harmony with the Law they work beneficially; when they are not, they do not work at all.

The working of the Law in our personal lives is the running theme of this book. The Science of Mind teaches how to live by Law and Love.

UNIVERSAL INHABITANTS

That the physical Universe is the macrocosm which is made up of an infinite number of worlds, planets, stars, nebulae and stellar galaxies—myriad universes within the Universe, is well known. The structure of the physical Universe alone defies comprehension—and it is still expanding. Each split second of time there are energy explosions in outer space which bring into manifestation new galaxies and new systems of such magnitude as to make our own solar system infinitesimal by comparison, and our own earth but a speck of cosmic dust whirling through space.

Space and time factors are of such magnitude as to render all efforts to measure them completely ineffectual. Science has long since concluded that there is really no space at all as it is ordinarily thought of, because it is only the property of apparent extension and separation of images, and exists primarily in our own consciousness. A more accurate name would be Time, and time is Now. So the Universe which is described as All Time and All Space, is really no time and no space—just Being.

MAN—THE KNOWER

At the center of all this is man—man the knower, who is capable of self-conscious awareness of his own being, and through this awareness—

aware of Cosmic Being. This revelation alone should be enough to remove all limitations and restrictions from our minds. This is exactly what is happening. Our penetrations into outer space have come about because of our penetrations into inner space. The fact that we haven't gone very far in either direction is obvious. So far, our explorations into the Spiritual Universe of both inner and outer space have been meager, but we are on our way!

If we can attune ourselves to the Universal Law of Love, we will be able to comprehend more of the wonders of inner space and, in turn, think of our explorations into outer space in larger terms than just to gain military or temporal advantage. And we will be able to use the secrets of atomic energy and power, not destructively, but as the means by which the Divine Plan of freedom may be realized.

NATIVES OF ETERNITY

We are all travellers through space, but we are not "lost out here in the stars." We are natives of eternity, and each center of consciousness has its place in the Universe. We are evolving through progressive cycles until we reach total awareness of the Universe. When we say "we," we must include levels and expressions of life that extend far above and beyond that which we know on this planet. Ours may actually be a very limited expression of life compared to that now expressed by the other waves of evolving life which have passed this way before.

Just as our planet earth is peopled with human beings on various levels of consciousness, so the Universe is populated with an infinite number of evolving beings. The ancients taught that the heavenly bodies—the planets and the stars—are actually great Beings who occupy positions of great authority and importance in the Universe. Each is the center of its particular orbit, just as you and I are in our more limited areas.

INFINITE INTELLIGENCE

There is a Cosmic Will that created and holds this entire system together—an Infinite Intelligence of which we are a part, and which dwells within the vast inner space of our own consciousness. As we gaze into outer space, we are inspired by the glory of the heavens. As the stars look down upon us, we somehow feel a clarion call to our own magnificence, and are moved to nobler thoughts and higher aspirations. Emerson said that if the stars came out only once every thousand years, it would be an event of such importance that we would do nothing except to gaze upon them and let ourselves be filled with their inspiring message of Infinity.

WONDERS OF THE UNIVERSE

We take so much for granted. Dante said, "Pricked out with less and greater lights, between the poles of the universe, the Milky Way so gleameth white as to set very sages questioning." And yet we take the wonders of the Universe so much for granted that we even neglect to look at them, and the challenges of space fail to move us. Christian Huygens said, "If 25 years are required for a bullet out of a cannon, with its utmost swiftness, to travel from sun to us, such a bullet would spend almost 700,000 years in its journey between us and the fixed stars. And yet when in a clear night we look upon them, we cannot think them above some few miles over our heads."

THE STORY OF CREATION

We cannot even begin to understand the Universe until we give some thought to Creation, how it started and why, and what happened. Science has advanced many theories as to the origin and nature of the physical Universe, but even though many have conjectured about it, no one has satisfactorily explained the mysteries of Time, Space, and Intelligence which are the essence of the Great Plan that gives one glimpse of itself as the manifest Universe.

Perhaps the most accurate realization would be that God thinking within Himself, upon Himself and about Himself, created the manifest Universe. "In the beginning God . . .," introduces the first chapter of Genesis, which tells an allegorical story of the Creation which is magnificent in its scope and imagery. Beautiful though the story is, however, it has failed to explain the creation of the Universe, simply because scientists and thinkers cannot take it literally, and fundamentalist religionists insist upon doing so.

Man is in the position of not being able to ignore the Genesis story, but in not being able to believe it either. Therefore we must assume that it is an allegory which contains veiled truths and principles.

CREATION IS CONSCIOUSNESS UNFOLDING

Let us assume that the "God" of the Bible is Infinite Intelligence or Consciousness, and that the story in Genesis is an exposition of how this Consciousness unfolds itself through the process of eternal Creation into manifestation. Since this Consciousness is infinite, the Universe is the material expression of this infinitude, and since it is eternal, the process of creation is still going on. Since every particle of the Infinite possesses the attributes of the Infinite, then Creation eternally continues to take place through every part of itself. This, of course, must include man, who possesses self-conscious intelligence and is therefore a co-creator with Absolute Intelligence. In a very real sense, the Universe is continuing to be created through us. As we expand, it expands, and as it expands, we expand.

SEVEN "DAYS" OF CREATION

The "seven days" of the Biblical story of Creation obviously do not refer to days as we know them, or even time the way it is now measured. Each "day" represents the period of time necessary for that particular stage of development to take place, which might be forever, and undoubtedly is. Remember, we are dealing with infinite concepts.

Let us think, then, of the Seven Days of Creation as seven steps through which Intelligence unfolds as it progresses from unknowing through awakening, consciousness, decision, power, self-awareness and self-realization. These steps are constantly unfolding through both the Universal and the individual. Therefore, Creation is an eternally progressive process through which the Infinite Beingness is expressing itself. We are an integral part of the process. We are on the eternal pathway of Being and Becoming.

TREATMENT EXPANDS THE MIND

In the first Treatment in this chapter, we developed an awareness of our own Being. In the following one, we move steadily along with the process of Becoming. As usual, relax and release. Speak these statements out loud and let your mind absorb them. Great ideas expand our minds and enable the free full flow of Creation to take place in and through us.

Personal Science of Mind Treatment—Becoming

"How great Thou art! How great Thou art!" I am on the Infinite Pathway of becoming that which I already am. I am an individual particle in an Infinite Universe. I am one with the Whole. My true nature is Infinite. I let my consciousness expand to become one with all Being.

I am free from the restrictions of time, space, place or thought. I move upward along the Golden Bridge of Becoming, toward the mountain top of Universal Self-Awareness. I am free from all inhibiting ideas and negative influences. There is nothing good which I cannot be. I am already all that is wonderful, beautiful and eternal, and I am becoming a channel through which all wonderful things are expressed. Creation is eternally taking place through me. My true being is whole and perfect. Throughout eternity I unfold through a process of becoming that which is.

"In the beginning God . . ." The story of Creation is told over and over as "the Unbegotten is always begetting the only begotten." I am an expanding, unfolding action of God, but in the bud. It does not yet appear what I shall be, but I know that the I AM within me is God. I am becoming That which I AM.

The Infinite lies stretched with smiling repose, being Itself in awesome splendor. I release all personal effort as I contemplate the Self within. As I orbit into Inner Space, I am free from all factors which may have kept me from becoming one with my real Being.

The free, full flow of eternal life is surging through me now. The processes of evolution and creation are assisted by my Self-Awareness. I contemplate Spirit and let it have its free, full way with me. The mysteries of Life are unfolding through me. I am becoming Being.

And so it is.

CHAPTER 3 SUMMARY

1. We have within us the capacity to understand all things.
2. As we glimpse our true potentiality we gain more understanding.

because our mind and entire consciousness expands and encompasses new areas of comprehension.
3. We are the Universe in miniature.
4. If we are to expand and improve ourselves, we must rise above ourselves and grow beyond ourselves.
5. What we contemplate, we come to understand; what we understand, we become.
6. Since the Universe consists of the totality of things, God and the Universe are synonomous and identical.
7. Mind is the medium through which Intelligence flows into Creation.
8. The Nature of the Universe is Spirit—Intelligence. It creates through Soul—Law, and produces Body—Form.
9. The Laws of the Universe are laws of harmony, balance and order—Laws of Love.
10. Life is a school in which we have the privilege of learning how to cooperate with Law through Love.

Chapter 4

How to Understand the World We Live in

There is a legend which tells of a group of angels who were meeting with God about the affairs and destiny of the world. One angel complained about the sad state it was in. God silenced the discontented one by saying, "If you don't like the world the way it is, go and make a better one."

THE WORLD WE CREATE

The point is unmistakable. If we don't like our world the way it is, only we can change it. No one can do it for us—for a very simple reason: *We created it*. God created the heavens and the earth—the Universe—but we create our own world. The earth is the planet upon which we live. The world is what we have made of it. Each of us creates his own world. Therefore, the world not only looks different, but **is** different for each one of us.

How a marriage was rescued

Jane and John seemed to have everything it took to be an ideal married couple. Handsome, charming and intelligent, everyone thought they were ideally mated, and hailed their marriage as a blessing.

However, it wasn't long before signs of trouble appeared. Signs of strain were easy to detect, and the young couple seemed irritable and uncomfortable with each other. They couldn't seem to agree on anything, and their devotion deteriorated into moody silences and ignoring each other. They tried to find the answers to their difficulties, but had great difficulty in talking things over together.

When they came to me with their problem, it was easy to see that they were actually living in different worlds, because they believed different things, had different backgrounds, and actually looked at things in different ways. When they came to see that these differences could be dissolved and consolidated into an area of mutual sharing which would still give leeway for individual points of view and uniqueness so that they could live in the same world, they were able to handle their problems and their marriage.

As they entered into the game of understanding each other, their two worlds met in mutuality and compatibility.

One world vs. *many worlds*

The world in which we live is the projection of our thoughts, feelings and attitudes—both collectively and individually. We live in a group world and an individual world. What we project individually becomes part of the whole. The phrase "one world" is literal and accurate up to a point—but within the one world there are as many worlds as there are individuals who comprise it. The world is manifestation—form, but behind its solid outer appearance is that which caused it—consciousness. That is why Jesus said, "Judge not according to the appearance, but judge righteous judgment." (John 7: 24)

HOW CONSCIOUSNESS CREATES ALL

The consciousness of God—perfect and whole—created the heavens and the *earth*. The consciousness of man creates the *world*. With the exception of natural creative evolution and progression, the **earth** remains the same because it is part of the manifestation of the One First Cause—God. The *world*, however, is in a constant state of flux, because it is constantly acted upon and formed by the changing currents of group and individual consciousness.

The *earth* is characterized by unity—the world by diversity. The earth is permanent—the world transitory. The earth offers peace; the world often presents problems. But we can overcome the problems of the world, when we realize that they are of our own making—the outgrowth of our thoughts, feelings and attitudes. Certainly, if we do not like our world, we can change it. Jesus said, "In the world ye shall have tribulation: but be of good cheer; I have overcome the world." (John 16:33)

CHANGE YOURSELF—CHANGE YOUR WORLD

The world was a constant threat to George M. He faced it each day in an agony of apprehension. He felt that people were against him and that he could never find his place in the world's confusing maelstrom of work and activity. To George the world was a monster which terrified him. He withdrew from it and contemplated it in solitary despair. However, his natural desire to find his place in the world drove him to seek help.

He was able to find it—within himself, when he came to realize that he created his world out of his own consciousness. When we change inside, the outside world changes.

INDIVIDUAL CONSCIOUSNESS

We create our own world, and we are responsible for what we create —either to change it or to maintain it. We have dominion: "And God said, 'Let us make man in our image, after our likeness: and let them have dominion over the fish of the sea, and over the fowl of the air, and over the cattle, and over all the earth, and over every creeping thing that creepeth upon the earth.'" (Gen. 1:26)

The key to this dominion is our consciousness. It is through consciousness that we establish our particular personal world on this earth. The earth is given us as a proving ground—a laboratory in which we work out the experiments of life. It is a garden figuratively and literally, in which we can plant an infinite variety of growing things which produce the crops which comprise the world. The one big garden is the group world made up of the many individual plots or personal worlds. In short, we live in a world of our own making. Our world is formed by the projection of our consciousness.

How a broken man formed his new world

Wilton illustrated this perfectly. Once a happy, healthy and successful man, he became a near-derelict, broken in body and spirit, dependent upon others for his livelihood, and completely out of step with the world.

"What happened?" I asked him.

"I don't know," he answered. "It just happened. All of a sudden everything fell apart. Nothing seemed to work out, and before I knew it I hit bottom."

Further discussion revealed that it didn't "just happen." In a very real sense, Wilton "happened" it. First, his wife had died, leaving him shocked and grief-stricken. He turned bitter and resentful against the world, and brooded over his loss. Friends and associates sustained and comforted him for a long time, but finally became alienated by his self-pity and bitterness, leaving him alone in his crumbling world.

It wasn't easy for Wilton to find his way back into the world. For a time he seemed to want only to wallow in his problem. Finally, he put the principles of the Science of Mind into practice and started on his way back. A new world began to form around him. He not only regained the world he had lost, but he formed a new one from within himself.

WHAT IS CONSCIOUSNESS?

Consciousness is simply what we are: mentally, emotionally and spiritually. The clarity and insight of our thought, the strength and wholesomeness of our feelings, and the attunement and inclusiveness of our awareness blend together to form the essence and content of our being. This beingness is our consciousness.

We are responsible for our own consciousness, therefore, responsible for the world that we create. We all have the potential of a perfect world by developing a high state of consciousness. This is known as "wholeness" or "holiness," and is described variously in the Bible as "The Kingdom of God," "The Kingdom of Heaven" or simply as "The Kingdom," or "Thy Kingdom." The "Kingdom of God" is the state of Whole Consciousness or perfection. We are told that it is within us: "Behold, the kingdom of God is within you." (Luke 17:21)

THE SECRET OF THE AGES

Jesus gives us the secret of forming our world: "Seek ye first the kingdom of God, and his righteousness; and all these things shall be added unto you." (Matt. 6:33) When he says "My kingdom is not of this world,"

(John 18: 36) he is indicating that it is only through building a consciousness of the larger scope of things that we can realize our true potential in this world. When in the Lord's Prayer we pray:

> Our Father, which art in Heaven,
> Hallowed be thy name;
> Thy kingdom come;
> Thy will be done in earth, as it is in heaven. (Matt 6: 9)

we are expressing our understanding that our world is formed in this earth out of our inner consciousness, and that the higher and more harmonious our consciousness (heaven), the better will be our world. As someone has said, "This world seen rightly **is** the Kingdom of Heaven." The challenge is to make our life—our world—"heaven on earth."

TREATMENT REFORMS OUR WORLD

Since consciousness is infinite in potential, this world offers limitless possiblity for expressing and experiencing good. The Science of Mind teaches these principles and shows us how to develop and raise our consciousness to bring about the greatest personal and collective good in our world.

Treatment is the technique by which we develop our consciousness. The repetition of positive, scientific statements of Truth forms our consciousness on a solid, constructive basis from which unfolds the creative action which shapes our world.

Personal Science of Mind Treatment to Create My World

The kingdom of God is within me. Heaven is the state of my consciousness in which I perceive this kingdom. As I experience the kingdom of Heaven, I am one with God, and all things of good are possible in my world. My world is my expression of the kingdom of God. As I make my will one with God's will, my world comes into perfect form.

I go busily about the business of creation today. I am building my world. I start where I am. If I don't like my world the way it is, I build a better one. I clear my consciousness of all negative and imperfect thoughts, feelings and attitudes. I dissolve all unworthy desires and unwholesome habits. As I establish dominion over myself, I automatically have dominion over my world.

I am my consciousness. My consciousness is my world. Therefore I am my world. My world is an expression of me. If I don't like my world, I must change myself. As I change my inner self into the image and likeness of God as I was created, my world becomes the Garden of Eden, the kingdom of God on earth.

As I become aware of the Infinite Potential within me, I see the limitless possibilities of my world. I plant the earthly garden with the seeds of mighty endeavor. I cultivate worthy qualities. I align myself with noble purposes and ideals. I invest my God-given talents in projects which bring great dividends to all people.

I walk with God in my world. I look out upon my world and I see it is good. I give thanks for my world as a wonderful place.

And so it is.

THE WORLD IN TRUE PERSPECTIVE

As we develop an understanding of our world and how it is created, it comes into focus and we see it in its proper perspective. We realize that we are in the world but not of it. It is an experience we are going through because we need it for our growth. We live in it, we use it, and we either enjoy it or suffer through it, but we must never lose sight of the truth that our real being is not of this world. Our true identity is of a higher nature:

> In him we live, and move, and have our being—
> For as much then as we are the offspring of God,
> We ought not to think that the Godhead is
> like unto gold, or silver, or stone,
> graven by art and man's device. (Acts 17: 29)

What a heart attack taught Arnold

Arnold F. was a dynamo of energy and activity. He was always busy doing things for himself and others. If anyone wanted anything done, they asked Arnold. He was always capable and willing. He was completely involved with the world's business, and had little time to spend for himself.

He was only in his early forties when it hit him the first time. His coronary knocked him out of action for six months, with a recommendation from the doctors that he rest for another six months and then completely change his pattern of life. However he was soon back to his old habits immersed completely in business and service activities, with sports and heavy weekened activity as the only variety.

When it hit him the second time, he had plenty of time to think during the eighteen months he was inactivated. I saw him many times during that period, and Arnold was an apt student. He came to understand that there was more to life than what he **did.** He discovered that what he **was** inside was important too. He devoted himself to the exploration of inner space, and when he got back to his world he made it an entirely different one.

Today Arnold F. lives a happy, healthy, balanced life after surviving two extreme physical incapacities. He is grateful for being granted a new lease on life in this world, and he is living it fully—but in a different way.

MAINTAIN AND SUSTAIN DOMINION

The challenge is to maintain dominion in our world and to live actively and creatively in it without becoming too involved in it. This threat of wordly absorption is ever present:

> The world is too much with us; late and soon,
> Getting and spending, we lay waste our powers:
> Little we see in Nature that is ours.
> (William Wordsworth, "The World Is Too Much with Us")

Nature, the Good Earth, the Garden of Eden, the Kingdom of Heaven, are all around us representing our true habitat, but wordly illusion blinds and imprisons us. As Jesus said, "Ye have the poor always with you." (Matt. 26: 11)

TREASURES NOT OF THIS WORLD

But the Master also gave instruction as to how to avail ourselves of our divine heritage while we are living in this world. When the rich young man, uneasy of the world, asked Jesus what he should do to have "eternal life" (true happiness), the Master instructed, "Go and sell that thou hast, and give to the poor, and thou shalt have treasure in heaven: and come and follow me." (Matt. 19: 21)

In other words, we are admonished to free ourselves from the inferior life of worldliness and materialism in favor of that of Inner Reality. However, the rich young man of Biblical times lacked perspective then, just as we still lack it. We mistake appearance for reality and fact for Truth, and do exactly as he did when ". . . he went away sorrowful; for he had great possessions." (Matt. 19: 22)

Jesus went on to point out how too much worldliness and materialism separate us from ourselves: "A rich man shall hardly enter into the kingdom of heaven—It is easier for a camel to go through the eye of a needle, than for a rich man to enter into the kingdom of God." (Matt. 19: 23, 24)

THE ABUNDANT LIFE

Bear in mind that these statements are not against money or wealth, as they are often misinterpreted. Jesus never taught poverty or limitation. On the contrary, He said, "I am come that they might have life, and that they might have it more abundantly." (John 10: 10)

Now we must understand exactly what constitutes the abundant life. Can the world give it to us, or must we seek something else. Scriptural instruction is clear: "A man's life consisteth not in the abundance of the things which he possesseth." (Luke 12: 15) We have established in the most real sense that our world is the form which our life takes. We must not allow our lives to be governed by the world. Again, the great teaching of the Christ shows the way:

"Lay not up for yourselves treasures upon earth, where moth and rust doth corrupt, and where thieves break through and steal.

"But lay up for yourselves treasures in heaven, where neither moth nor rust doth corrupt, and where thieves do not break through nor steal:

"For where your treasure is, there will your heart be also." (Matt. 6: 19–21)

REAL AND UNREAL

It would seem that the secret of living harmoniously in the world lies in our ability to distinguish the real from the unreal. This is not as easy as it seems. The tangible, solid world *seems* real but is really illusion, while the ephemeral, invisible realm of the Spirit seems illusory, but is actually the Real. There is a great difference between fact and Truth.

The Truth is a fact but all facts aren't Truth. War, disease, poverty and suffering are facts in this world, but there is no Truth in them. Neither is there any Truth in ignorance, stupidity, selfishness and greed, but they exist. Could it be that as we develop our understanding, we become free from the snares and delusions of the world? Jesus taught, "Ye shall know the truth, and the truth shall make you free." (John 8:32)

FACT *VS.* TRUTH

The world is real as fact but not as Truth. The world is solid fact which has congealed from the stream of our consciousness, which has acted upon the Universal substance from which all things are made. Our individual consciousness is our personal use of the Infinite Consciousness—God—"which created the heavens and the earth."

God's consciousness is perfect, since He is all-knowing. Individual consciousness is imperfect because we know only in part. Therefore, God's earth is perfect. Nature is perfect, while our world is the imperfect use of Nature. Behind this imperfection, however, awaits the Divine Pattern, ready to be called into expression. "The finite alone hath wrought and suffered. The Infinite lies stretched in smiling repose." (Emerson)

SCIENCE OF MIND AND THE WORLD

The spiritual and mystical teachings, and the idealistic philosophies of the ages teach man to rise above the world by conquering himself and discovering his true inner nature. The Science of Mind teaches mental and spiritual techniques to accomplish these purposes.

As you study this book step by step, follow its suggestions, and use the exercises given, you will find that you are living in a new world—a world in which you express freely and joyously, and in which you experience health, happiness, prosperity, peace and fulfillment. You will become aware that the things, events, places, and often persons in your world have changed. When we change, our world changes. Consciousness is cause; world is effect. The more good in our consciousness, the more good in our world. "The former things are passed away—Behold, I make all things new." (Rev. 21: 4, 5)

THOUGHTS ARE THINGS

Thoughts are things—literally. Our personal, physical and material world is made up of all of the things which have been formed from the world of our thoughts—or consciousness. The world in which nearly four billion human beings live is the aggregate. Therefore, each of us lives in two worlds, the individual and the group world. This explains why we are often caught up in wordly circumstances and events for which we do not feel responsible.

What are we going to do about that? The only thing we can do: what Jesus did—"overcome the world" by changing causes within ourselves. The moment we do this, our personal world changes, and we contribute to the good of the whole world. "And I, if I be lifted up from the earth, will draw all men unto me." (John 12: 32)

CHALLENGES FROM THE WORLD

Each moment we are confronted with the challenges of life. These often objectify into what we call world problems, but from what we have come to understand in this chapter, we see that this is inaccurate.

There are no such things as problems; they are merely the outer symptoms of imperfect causes in the inner consciousness of the individual or the group. Of course, these outer manifestations create appearances with which we must deal. This we must do in the most practical and efficient way possible. In doing this, however, we must remember that "all they that take the sword shall perish with the sword." (Matt. 26: 52)

CONSCIOUSNESS IS THE ONLY REALITY

Outer, or worldly methods alone are not sufficient. Consciousness is the only reality. Deal with all things first and continuously in consciousness. As you live in and deal with your world, adopt an attitude of "Divine indifference" toward it. Enjoy it and learn from it, but do not give the world power to move you. **You move it.**

When, with the Master, we learn to "Render to Caesar the things that are Caesar's, and to God the things that are God's" (Mark 12: 17), we will be able to say with Him, "In the world ye shall have tribulation, but be of good cheer; I have overcome the world." (John 17: 23)

This is understanding the world.

PURPOSE OF TREATMENT

We are now ready for another treatment. Are you practicing regularly the ones you have already been given—going over them carefully and thoughtfully, and gradually starting to frame your own statements and affirmations? Results are obtained when we practice these techniques regularly.

But let us understand that the purpose of treatment is to bring about a change in our habitual thoughts, feelings and attitudes—in our consciousness. Sometimes you will experience miraculous results, but more often the changes will come about through slow, steady improvement. Be on the alert for little signs of improvement. Give thanks for them. Be grateful for the miracles, but also for the steps leading up to them. Treatment is now part of your way of life.

Personal Science of Mind Treatment to Understand the World

Consciousness is the only reality. I attune myself to the Inner Reality of the Spirit so that I may properly understand my world.

I am in the world, but not of it. I give thanks for my world. I enjoy it, express through it, and learn from it, but it is in God that I live and move and have my being. To know God aright is life eternal. I seek first the kingdom, and from its inner instruction I come to understand my world. I know God as the First Cause from which all things come. I see my world as the manifestation of as much of the Infinite Intelligence as I understand and express.

The more I understand about myself, the more I understand about the world. The more I understand about my world, the freer I am from it. The world has no power to move me or affect me in any way. I view it with divine indifference, because I know that my kingdom is not of this world. My personal kingdom is my share of the Kingdom of God which is within me. The power of the Kingdom gives me dominion in and over my world.

I claim my divine heritage today. From the vantage point of spiritual understanding, my world comes clearly into focus. I see what needs to be changed, and I know how to change it. There is no power in my world. The Power is within me. I use this Power wisely and creatively. I am sitting on top of my world. I am a just and loving ruler of my domain.

Quietly now, I release all concern for outer things, as I lie down in the quiet consciousness of the green pastures and walk beside the still waters of my soul. I give thanks for the Kingdom of Heaven expressed in my world.

And so it is.

CHAPTER 4 SUMMARY

1. Our consciousness—thoughts, feelings and attitudes—creates our world, and we are responsible for it.
2. The Science of Mind shows us how to raise our consciousness, and express and experience unlimited good.
3. As we develop an understanding of our world and how it is created, it comes into focus and we see it in its proper perspective.
4. Live actively and creatively in your world, but maintain dominion over it without becoming too involved in it.
5. Free yourself from the inferior life of worldliness and materialism in favor of that of Inner Reality.
6. Do not allow yourself to be governed by the world.
7. The secret of living harmoniously is in our ability to tell the real from the unreal.
8. The world is real as fact, but not as Truth.
9. Our individual consciousness is our personal use of the Infinite Consciousness—God.
10. The Science of Mind teaches mental and spiritual techniques to help us rise above the world by conquering ourselves and discovering our true inner nature.

Chapter 5

How to Use the Power That Works Wonders

ALADDIN had a wonderful lamp. Whenever he would rub it, the Genie would appear to do his bidding. Nothing was too much of a challenge for the Genie. He simply obeyed his master's will. He did what he was told to do, no matter what it was. There was nothing he could not or would not do. There was nothing Aladdin asked for that he did not receive.

We think of this as a fairy story, but it is much more than that. It is a symbolic fable revealing one of life's most profound truths, at the same time explaining the technique of using the greatest power ever known—the power of Creative Mind.

Who is Aladdin? You are. Who is the Genie? You are! How is this possible?

Aladdin is the conscious mind, which is our personal use of Universal Intelligence. The Genie is the subconscious mind, which is our individual use of Universal Subjectivity, or Law. The story of "Aladdin and His Wonderful Lamp" is the symbolic explanation of the relationship between the two and how they work together in the Creative Process.

THE BASIC PRINCIPLES

I. There is only One Power in the Universe.
II. Through my mind I have the capacity to recognize and become one with this power.
III. The One Power works through me according to my faith.

Before we discuss these basic principles, let us look first at:

THE ANATOMY OF MIND—INTELLIGENCE

ONE MIND—UNIVERSAL—INFINITE—DIVINE
  A. Objective—Spirit (Universal Intelligence)
  B. Subjective—Law (Universal Creativity)

INDIVIDUAL MIND—PERSONAL—FINITE—HUMAN
  A. Conscious (surface)—Thought, Volition, Choice
  B. Subconscious (deeper)—Feeling, Memory, Power

This is a simple outline setting forth the elements of the mental and creative process. An understanding of these components and processes and how to use them is the science of the mind. The Science of Mind teaches the science of the mind.

It is shown clearly in the above outline that Individual Mind is the *individualization* of the One Mind. It is a part of the whole, just as a cell is a unit of a larger unit, and functions as a part, subject to the nature and law of the whole. As we cover each point, the three basic principles of the Creative Process already set forth will be explained.

ONE MIND

Emerson said, "There is One Mind common to all individual men," which he describes as the Over-Soul. Its attributes are omniscience, omnipotence and omnipresence, i.e., there is nothing it does not know, nothing it cannot do, and nowhere where it is not. This has been discussed fully in Part I, but in this Section, we extend theory to include an understanding of how it works, and how it functions in and through us.

The One Mind is intelligent, knowing only Itself which is All-Intelligence. We are dealing then, with an All-Knowing, Self-Knowing, Self-Existent Oneness which is the One First Cause of all Creation, and by Its Self-Knowing, creates by Itself becoming that which It creates. This is really quite simple, and is the key to everything which we will learn and accomplish through our study of the Science of Mind.

This is the principle: *That which is in potential becomes that which is created, by Itself becoming that which is created.*

A little thought will show us that if this is Law on the Universal level, it is also Law on the individual level, because the individual is part of the whole.

Universal Mind. We have seen that there is a Universal Oneness which contains all things and which is all of the things which it contains. This Universal Beingness is the potential of each atom of energy and intelligence which exists within it. The microcosm is part of the macrocosm and is ever-evolving toward the whole. This then, is the destiny of each of us: *To embody the Universal Being in which we are now embodied, so that our individual nature is identical with its Universal nature.*

Infinite Mind. Infinite means that than which there can be no more nor no less. It is the Ultimate—without beginning or end. "From everlasting unto everlasting, thou art God." (Psalm 90: 2) The Infinite can only be comprehended with that degree of infinitude which we become. Since we are always evolving, we are always growing into a greater awareness and understanding of our true nature which is infinite, but which we do not realize until we become conscious of it. There is nothing beyond the scope of self-consciousness, because the Self of which we are conscious is Infinite.

Divine Mind. This is the Supreme Deity which we worship, and within which we live and move and have our being. We call it God, Brahma, the Absolute, Lord, Allah, and by a score or more of other names by which we try to express the extreme reverence and awe which we feel toward That which is All-in-All. No name suffices, so the Divine Mind can only be properly designated That Which Is. Since That Which Is *is*, Its Self-Conscious awareness is designated as "*I Am.*" The ancient Hebrew name for the Universal Infinite, Divine, One Mind was Yah-veh, *I Am That I Am.* God is Divine Mind—Divine Being.

SPIRIT

Spirit is the knowing or objective function of the One Mind. It is the Power which knows Itself. It is Divine Presence, the activation of Infinite Intelligence, and the embodiment of all that is known and all there is to know.

Spirit, in knowing itself, automatically knows all, since it is the conscious mind of God which is All. Spirit itself is the Infinite Invisible Reality. We cannot see it, but we are aware of its Presence within us, and of the myriad forms which it takes as the manifest body of the Universe. We cannot fully comprehend the whole, but we know we are one with it, and we are comforted and sustained by it. Our security comes from knowing that Spirit is our very being, the Source of all knowledge, all wisdom, and all understanding.

The universal laws, principles, and relationships have their origin in the Mind of God, which is Spirit. The natural laws are perfect in concept and operation because they emanate from that which is perfect. The intricate and meticulous rhythms of the movements of the heavenly bodies are conceived and controlled by Spirit. The mysteries of Time, which is not time, and Space, which is not space—at least by finite concepts—are the province of Spirit.

SUBSTANCE

Since the One Mind, of which Spirit is the conscious function, is omnipresent, Spirit is everywhere present, filling the Universe with Itself. Not only is it the energy and intelligence—the Life Force which permeates everything; It is also the Universal Substance out of which all things are made. The Infinite creates by making things out of Itself. Tangibles appear out of the intangible by the process of Invisible Spirit acting upon Invisible Substance and congealing it into form. This congealed Spirit is called matter, which is not a reality, merely an appearance or a condition into which Substance has been formed. When the nucleus of intelligence which held form together releases itself or is released, the Substance is dispersed into its original state as the Universal Stuff out of which things are made by Spirit.

This Universal Stuff is invisible but not unreal. It is made up of myriad nuclei of energy and intelligence acting upon and reacting to themselves and each other. The nuclei became nebulae, forming a center or body as they combine with one or more nebulae, and spiral into a magnetic orbit which draws other bodies to it until a great body is formed—a planet—a galaxie—or a universe within the Universe.

Spirit, knowing Itself, which is Infinite, thinks infinitely, thereby setting into motion an Infinite Principle which works automatically. This Principle is known as

LAW

Law is the way Spirit works. Spirit is intelligent, objective, self-conscious action. Law is unknowing, subjective, automatic reaction. Law is the mechanical function of the Creative Process. It has been described as "a blind force, not knowing, only doing." Law is the natural response to Spirit knowing Itself, so it is to be thought of not as Spirit *and* Law, but as Spirit *as* Law, and coequal with Spirit as attributes of the One Mind.

The intelligent action of Spirit forms a reservoir of Infinite Power, which is the Immutable Force which moves and creates from the Divine Plan known in the One Mind by the Supreme Intelligence—Spirit. Spirit and Law are counterparts—Spirit objective, and Law subjective, but not inferior to it. Spirit is the knowing part of the Creative Process, and Law the doing part. Both are integral to it. Spirit thinks the Perfect Thought and Law executes it.

Since Law obeys implicitly the dictates of Spirit, it is always bringing into manifestation the outpicturing of Spirit. We discern the thought by observing its creation. We see God by observing what Law creates. In its infinite scope this creation is the Universe. In its finite expression, it is Nature. At the human level it is the world or experience.

SCIENCE

The Law represents Universal Justice, because its workings are always the same—predictable and unvarying, the complete and perfect expression of That which is. The principles of spiritual, mental and material science are based upon our observations and insights of the working of the One Law and the infinite variety of its creativity. We can see then, that human religion and human science, far from being opposites, have a common origin and unity. They are our use of the original Religion—Spirit, and the original Science—Law.

The Science of Mind is dedicated to understanding the Universal, and applying the religion of Spirit and the science of Law to individual human expression and experiences. Understanding the Universal Mind is essential to an understanding of ourselves and our place in the great scheme of things, which is the real purpose of this book and the entire teaching of the Science of Mind.

YOUR INVISIBLE POWER

Jim understood the Law and how to use it. As an inventor, he was often asked how he got his ideas.

"I sit and wait for them. The quieter and the more peaceful I become, the more ideas come to me. Some of them are minor league, but sooner or later I get a good one. It's sort of like fishing. If you're patient, you're bound to catch a whopper."

"Is that all there is to it?" he was asked.

"No, not by a long shot," he laughed. "That's only the beginning. Then you go to work and do what is necessary to bring that idea into form."

"It does take hard work then?"

"Yes, but it also takes something else."

"What?"

"An understanding that there is something working through you—something which is actually doing the work, but needs you to do it with. It's a sort of invisible power. I believe in it completely."

Jim was talking about what we call Law, which is the way God works.

There is much to understand. As our understanding grows, our effectiveness grows. We come to know more when we realize that we already know subconsciously what we seek to know consciously.

This treatment prepares our conscious mind to receive instruction directly from the One Mind. We know, and now we know that we know.

Personal Science of Mind Treatment to Comprehend Universal Mind

There is One Mind, One Life, One Power, One Infinite Good. I am one with the One Mind. What is true of It, is true of me. I worship God as Infinite Intelligence. Universal Intelligence fills my mind. I think as God thinks. God is All. I am an expression of the All. I comprehend the One Mind by letting It know Itself in me.

Spirit flows through me as intelligence and energy. Spirit fills my mind with its Infinite Self-Knowingness. My thoughts are spiritual thoughts. I dwell upon the limitless expanse of the Universe. I see all as evidence of God thinking within Himself upon Himself, and about Himself. I let my mind be swept up into the Infinite working of the One Mind. My thought is God thinking through me.

The Presence of Holy Spirit is everywhere. I am made whole in body, mind and soul, as I surrender myself to Spirit and let It have its way with me. I am guided and directed by Spirit. I rely upon the Infinite Intelligence of Spirit. It is the inspiration and substance of my life.

"O how love I thy law! it is my meditation all the day. Thou through thy commandments hast made me wiser than mine enemies: for they are ever with me. I have more understanding than all my teachers: for thy testimonies are my meditation. I understand more than the ancients, because I keep thy precepts. I have refrained my feet from every evil way, that I might keep thy word. I have not departed from thy judgments: for thou hast taught me. How sweet are thy words unto my taste! yea, sweeter than honey to my mouth! Through thy precepts I get understanding: therefore I hate every false way. Thy word is a lamp unto my feet, and a light unto my path." (Psalm 119: 97–105)

And so it is.

INDIVIDUAL MIND

Your mind is the One Mind functioning in and as you. Our individual mind duplicates the nature and action of the Universal Mind. We are a unit of intelligence and energy within Universal Intelligence. Everything we have explained about the Divine Mind is true of human mind except its scope. But the limit imposed by being individualized disappears when we realize that we have the potential of expanding our consciousness until limitation disappears, and as we think and create with the scope of the One Mind and, without interference, It thinks through us.

SELF-CONSCIOUSNESS

We are "self" conscious beings just as the Infinite is conscious of its Self. When we say "I am," we indicate personal identification, just as the I AM (God) is aware of Itself. The difference is that God is *only* aware of Itself, while we are aware of ourselves *and* something else—many other things.

While God is a Unity, we see ourselves merely as a unit among many other units. We are aware that there is a Whole, but since we see ourselves as only a part, we feel separated from the Whole, and therefore inferior. This, however, is not necessarily so. The full and proper use of our individual mind is to realize that we are one with the One and have within us the potential of being the One. We are part of the One, but not apart. God is all of us; we are that part of God which we can understand.

THE ETERNAL SECRET

By being aware of our true nature, we know God. By knowing God, we become God, extending our personal identity to complete realization of the Universal Beingness. This is the greatest discovery of all time—**that by being himself truly and completely, man is God.**

This is the Eternal Secret, veiled in the allegories, parables and symbolism of the enlightened teachings and writings of the ages, hidden from the unknowing, but always available to those who have eyes to see and ears to hear. Jesus revealed this teaching in the parables, saying, "He that hath ears to hear, let him hear." (Matt. 11:15) And when his disciples understood his teachings, their eyes were opened, and He said, "Blessed are the eyes which see the things that ye see: For I tell you, that many prophets and kings have desired to see those things which ye see, and have not seen them; and hear those things which ye hear, and have not heard them. (Luke 10:23, 24)

THE SECRET DOCTRINE

God asleep is man; man awake is God. This is the Ancient Wisdom, the Secret Doctrine of the Mystery Teachings of all ages. Until comparatively recent times, it was revealed only to the few who by their own dedication, discipline and purification were capable of comprehending it, and once knowing it, were capable of guarding the treasure and using it wisely. These few became the "Way-showers" of the race, and have helped man along the tortuous path of evolution. Jesus is one of them—perhaps the greatest—revealing to the multitude, "The kingdom of God is within you." (Luke 17:20) He then revealed what was necessary to attain this kingdom: "Be ye therefore perfect, even as your Father which is in heaven is perfect." (Matt. 5:48)

THE WAY TO ACHIEVE YOUR TRUE POTENTIAL

Knowing that this potential could only be attained by sincere endeavor on the part of the individual, He taught a Way which included understanding, dedication, devotion, discipline and love. He emphasized that if we make a sincere effort to improve ourselves, God, as Law and Love, will perfect us.

Along with the Great Ones who preceded Him, Jesus taught that there is a spark of the Divine within every man, and that the business of life is to discover this spark, awaken it, and bring it to full flame. This Inner

Reality is called The Christ, the innate Divinity of every man. Paul, the Apostle, recognizing this Truth, taught, "Christ in you, the hope of glory." (Col. 1: 27)

Jesus teaches the power of this Inner Presence, when, speaking as the Presence and as the Power, He says, "I am the way, the truth and the life: no man cometh unto the Father, but by me." (John 14: 6) He is saying that if we are to realize our full potential of knowing God and being God, we must awaken to the Christ of our own being.

INFINITE POTENTIAL

All of Jesus' teachings and the true essence of all of the other original basic systems of spiritual thought (called religions), as well as the basis of idealistic philosophy—all teach us the same thing—that if man awakens to himself-his True Self-he becomes himself in terms of his full potential.

This must be accomplished by conscious thought, effort and endeavor on our part. The individual mind must be utilized for the purpose of consciously cooperating with the Perfect Life within us—by embracing the Presence, recognizing and obeying the Law, and being the sons of God which we really are.

THE CREATIVE PRINCIPLE

Ernest was a writer—at least he said he was. He turned out reams of material every day, but his problem was in getting it published. He regularly dispatched his manuscripts to the publishers, and just as regularly they came back with rejection slips.

Ernest's answer to his failure was to work harder, but it seemed to have no effect whatsoever, except to produce more material for rejection. But Ernest was sincere and persistent in his desire to be a writer. He felt that perhaps the problem was within his own mind. Quite logically, he came to the Science of Mind for assistance. I am no literary critic, but after talking with Ernest and scanning some of his stories, I was quite certain what the trouble was. They were filled with anxiety, frustration and pressure. There was no ease or joy in the author or his output. Quite plainly, Ernest was mistaking effort for accomplishment. He felt that he was doing the whole thing by himself.

After a few talks, Ernest found that he could write a better story if he didn't try so hard. He threw all of his previous years of output into a trunk, and decided to start all over again using a new method. Instead of struggling to get ideas and forcing them onto paper, he adopted a much more casual approach. He started with treatment and meditation, and jotted down the ideas which came to him afterward. While he was working these into form, he interspersed his writing periods with treatment and meditation, occasionally a long walk, and sometimes trips to the mountains, the desert, and the sea.

As we continued our weekly counseling sessions, a great change came over Ernest. And what was even more important to him professionally, this change was reflected in his writing. He still got his share of rejections, but editors became interested in his work, and helpful suggestions from them would often accompany the rejection slips. Finally his work started to sell, and his success increased until he is now firmly established in his profession.

The creative flow continues abundantly through Ernest because he has learned how to cooperate with life instead of resisting it. As a result, his Genie is always there to do his bidding, just as yours is when you learn to use the Creative Principle.

OUR TRUE POTENTIAL

We have gone as far as we can by evolution alone. Wherever we go from here depends upon our conscious decision to cooperate with and bring ourselves into harmony with the Universal Perfection. This is the New Age. Superstition and rigid, narrow orthodoxy are being dissolved on every level as man is awakening to his true potential.

"Be not conformed to this world: but be ye transformed by the renewing of your mind, that ye may prove what is that good, and acceptable, and perfect will of God." (Romans 12:2)

Not only is this advisable, but absolutely essential if man is to survive. The tremendous capacity of man's potential is expressed everywhere. The ingenuity and inventiveness of the human mind are limitless. Our scientific knowledge and technical skills enable us to build, tear down, and rebuild our world at will. It is through the conscious mind that we have also discovered and manufactured the means for our own destruction.

The only thing man hasn't done is to use the magnificent potential of his own mind to discover himself and build—or rebuild—a world fit to live in. This has always been man's challenge. Now, in the New Age, he has no choice other than to meet it. We have always had the Divine gift of individual life entrusted to us. Now we must live up to that trust, or we will lose it.

Through conscious choice, we must release the dynamic potential of our individual mind for the purpose for which it was intended—to re-enact God—to be as God is in the sphere of our own endeavors. When we do this, we will have learned something of how to use the Power that works wonders.

HOW TREATMENT RELEASES POTENTIAL

Ken B. had been hampered all of his life because he couldn't read properly. Teachers and speech pathologists were unable to find the cause of the problem or remove the block in Ken's mind. Hard as he tried, his problem increased as he grew older, until he finally gave up. His reading and writing endeavors included little more than signing his name and following the ball scores.

Ken wasn't stupid; he just couldn't read. He had a fine mind, but his reading problem frustrated and hampered him in his endeavors to get ahead. He resolved to do something about it.

After hearing one of my radio broadcasts on Science of Mind Treatment (he received virtually all of his knowledge and instruction through auditory means), he started to employ this technique to his life in general and to his reading in particular.

He started with simple affirmative statements about himself and his life, and even though he didn't notice any results at first, he felt so much better and had so much more confidence that he continued to practice Treatment daily. He formed the habit of giving thanks for little things of good that came to him, and he was happier than he had ever been, even though he was still bothered by his reading problem.

Suddenly one day he became aware that he was not only reading the headlines and the baseball box-scores in the morning paper, but that he was actually reading the entire accompanying news stories.

"I can read!" he shouted as he waved the paper. "I can read! I can read!"

Once he reached that realization there was no stopping him. He incorporated Treatment into his reading drills by affirming:

"I can read. I know I can read. I am a reader. I am reading. I know I am reading. I read well. I understand what I read. I read anything and everything I want to. There is no limit to my capacity to read. I read."

The results were complete. Even though Ken is still not the world's fastest reader, his rate and comprehension are far above average.

As you treat yourself for mental development now, just relax and make these affirmative statements, realizing that as you do so you are setting causes into operation which will develop your mental capacity just as Treatment developed Ken B.'s ability to read.

We will continue our explanation of the nature and working of individual mind on the conscious and subconscious levels in the next Chapter.

Personal Science of Mind Treatment to Develop My Individual Mind

My mind is one with God's Mind. Every time I think, God thinks in and through me. "I have conscious Divine Intelligence. I individualize omniscience. I have direct knowledge of Truth. I have perfect intuition. I have spiritual perception. I know." (Emmet Fox)

I open my mind to the guidance and instruction of the One Mind of which I am a part. The free full flow of Divine Intelligence envelops and enlightens me. As I become aware of my true Self, the Real Self reveals Itself to me. Truly, I am a son of God. My mind is a point of Light within God's mind. When I think, I set in motion the energy and intelligence of the Infinite Mind.

I re-enact the Nature of God. I know that I am perfect as God is perfect, and I turn every resource of my mind toward achieving this ultimate goal. I cleanse my mind of all negation and worldly thought. I think clearly, positively and constructively at all times. I guard the portals of my mind and heart. I dwell only upon the good, the true and the beautiful. I think what I choose to think. I feel what I choose to feel, and I do what I choose to do. My choice is always that which is true and perfect.

I surrender the personal in favor of the Universal. Universal Mind is my mind now. I surrender the finite in favor of the Infinite. Infinite Mind is my mind now. I surrender the human in favor of the Divine. Divine Mind is my mind now. I surrender man in favor of God. I am one with God. My individuality is an expression of God's Unity. My mind is filled with the All-Good. I am transformed by the renewing of my mind.

I give thanks for my magnificent mind. I give thanks for the ability to think, to understand, and to know. I am grateful that the Supreme Intelligence has given me the responsibility of being and knowing that which It is. God is blessing my mind.

And so it is.

CHAPTER 5 SUMMARY

1. The Science of Mind is the science of understanding and effectively using the mental and creative processes of the mind.
2. Individual mind is the individualization of the One Mind.
3. What is true on the Universal level is true on the personal level, because the individual is part of the whole.
4. Spirit is our very being, the Source of all knowledge, all wisdom and all understanding.
5. The Infinite creates by making things out of Itself by knowing Itself and thereby setting into motion an Infinite Principle which works automatically.
6. Law is the way Spirit works. Spirit is intelligent, objective, self-conscious action. Law is unknowing, subjective, automatic reaction.
7. The Science of Mind applies the religion of Spirit and the science of Law to individual human expression and experiences.
8. God asleep is man; man awake is God.
9. There is a Divine Spark within every man, and the business of life is to discover this spark, awaken it, and bring it to full flame.
10. Our growth depends upon our conscious decision to cooperate with and bring ourselves into harmony with the Universal Perfection.

PRINCIPLES OF THE CREATIVE PROCESS

I. There is only One Power in the Universe.
II. Through my mind I have the capacity to recognize and become one with this power.
III. The One Power works through me according to my faith.

Chapter 6

The Power Works for Us by Working Through Us

> Whatever man has done
> Man can do.
> I am man,
> But also God in man.
> I can do this thing
> And I will!   (Krishnamurti)

"I_T's more than I can take, Dr. Curtis! I just don't think I can go on any longer. I'm at the end of my rope. There is just nowhere to go from here."

There was desperation in Ted A.'s voice as he told me of the problems that were confronting him.

"I will admit that your situation needs some dealing with, Ted, but do you know, it is not as bad as it seems," I counseled him.

"I don't understand it! I'm a sober, hardworking . . ."

"Maybe you work *too* hard."

"I've never heard of that being a vice."

"It can be if you become a workoholic."

Ted laughed in spite of himself—a good sign. "That's a new one!"

"The word, perhaps, but not the problem. From what you've told me, you've been burning the candle on both ends for years. Right?"

"I can never seem to get caught up. There's always more to be done than I can do. But the discouraging part is the harder I work, the farther behind I get."

"That's the pattern."

"How do I get over it?"

The only problem

"You know what I have found out in the past twenty years of Science of Mind counseling, Ted? We only have one problem—ourselves. Solve that one, and all the rest disappear. You see, our problems don't come to us. They come through us. We cause them. Now, here is the principle: *If we have within us the power to cause problems, we also have within us the power to solve them.* It's the same power. The secret is in knowing how to use it. We've made a good start in learning that while we have been talking here. We have reversed your thought by getting you to think about the solution rather than the problem. You are beginning to see that as you make a change within yourself, the outer situation will change."

"I'm willing. What do I do?"

"Two basic things: Number one, get acquainted with the workings of your own mind; and number two, know that the power of the One Mind is working through your mind."

"You know, I like that 'workoholic' approach, Dr. Curtis. Just how does the Science of Mind work?"

"First of all, it works for us by working through us. It helps if we understand how the One Mind works and how your individual mind works. I'll go into that with you next time, after you've had a chance to read some things I want you to take with you. But right now, I want us to share a few moments in prayer. You believe in prayer, don't you?"

"I guess so. I don't know much about it."

"We call our type of prayer, Treatment—affirmative prayer—the prayer that gets results. Now, let's be still for a moment, relax, and let us know these things:

Personal Science of Mind Treatment for Personal Awakening

Quietly now, as we relax completely and release ourselves from all outer concerns, we become conscious of being a part of a great and wonderful Whole. We are in this Something, It is in us, and It flows through us as we are receptive to It. It is flowing through us now, healing, cleansing, renewing, awakening our minds, solving all problems, and making us whole.

There is One Mind. I am one with It. I feel the free full flow of Life as it comes to me from the One Source. I am awakened to greater understanding and awareness as I let the intelligence and power of the One Mind fill my mind. I know who I am, where I am going, and what to do about it.

I am turned on by the One Power. I am tuned in to the Infinite Presence. My mind is clear. My soul is at peace. I am receptive to God, and Good fills my entire being. I am aware of myself as a channel through which Infinite Power flows. I am aware of my potential as a cocreator with God. I am aware of my place in the great scheme of things.

As my awareness expands, my potential expands. I have a new perspective on life and on myself. I am no longer afraid. I am filled with the faith of God which gives me strength. I am calm, confident and contained. I give thanks for myself and for the One Self which expresses Itself in and through me. I get myself out of the way and let the Divine circuits flow through.

I am cleansed of all negative and destructive thoughts and feelings. I am a new person. I am aware of the magnificent wonders of pure Spirit. I am aware that this Spirit is the essence of me. In and with Spirit, I live and move and have my being. I am spiritual. I am whole. I am I.

Quietly and peacefully, I release myself into the transforming action of God—the One Mind—the Infinite Healing Presence. I am awake, I am aware. I am a new person now.

And so it is.

Ted A. was back in my office the next day.

"I don't know what you did, Dr. Don. I feel like a new person. Everything looks different today. I think I'm going to live!" he laughed. "I want to know more about how the Science of Mind works. I know it is working in me and for me. I can see the results. You say that something is working for me by working through me. I stayed up half the night studying those lessons you gave me, but I can't seem to understand it. Will you explain it as you promised?"

BASIC PRINCIPLES OF THE SCIENCE OF MIND

During this session, and many subsequent sessions with Ted A., I went over the basic principles of the Science of Mind and how it works, explaining particularly the relationship between Universal Mind and individual mind which we discussed here in the last chapter. Then I focused upon further understanding of the individual mind and how it works.

From the basis of our counseling sessions together, and his application of Science of Mind principles, Ted A's life changed completely. When he came to see the relationship between his thoughts and attitudes and the situations in his life, and when he understood the workings of his mind as an integral part of the Creative Power of the Universe, he emerged into the full expression of his potential.

He had always been a capable person, but had spent his life bogged down in problems simply because he had not known how to let the Power that works wonders work for him by working through him. Needless to say, he was healed of his "workoholic" problem, and with that, all the lesser ones. Now he is able to handle anything that comes up, no matter how challenging it may be, because he knows he is not alone. The entire power of the Universe is at his command.

THE HUMAN MIND

The One Mind is Universal, Infinite and Divine. The individual mind is personal, finite and human, but we have seen that they are not separate, but unified. It is not God's mind *and* my mind, but God's mind *as* my mind. The personal mind indicates an area or point where the One Mind is functioning. When my mind is clear and receptive, the Infinite Intelligence and Power works perfectly to reproduce Itself, which is perfect. When my mind is contaminated with negativity and closed with ignorance, stupidity and fear, the Law can reproduce only what I have given it to work with. The Law is always working perfectly even when it appears not to be. The results can be commensurate only with the amount of Spirit which is allowed to get through. If Universal Intelligence is blocked by human ignorance, the result is automatic limitation, disorder, conflict, suffering and disease.

This is where the Science of Mind comes in to teach the human mind how to become one with the One Mind, thereby establishing the One First Cause as the one and only permanent cause of our experience.

The function of the human mind is to cooperate with Divine Mind, thereby providing an avenue of expression for health, happiness, abundance, freedom, joy, peace and creativity in our individual and collective lives. Everything that happens to us happens through us, so the first and foremost challenge, lesson and responsibility of life is to learn to use our own mind with conscious effectiveness.

CONSCIOUS MIND

The conscious mind is just what its name indicates. It is the conscious part of our self. It is our personal use of Spirit, the conscious Mind of God. Its counterpart is the subconscious, which is our personal use of the Universal Subjective Mind—Law. The conscious and subconscious functions of our human mind duplicate the relationship between Spirit and Law, which are the two functions of the One Mind. Therefore, it is really *one mind working two ways*. If these two functions work together, and in turn are completely identified with the One Mind, there is no limit to the power that works for us by working through us.

SURFACE MIND

We can think of the conscious level as the surface mind. It is the thinking part of our mental equipment; its primary function is choice or volition, its activity is thought, and its method is reason. This entire process is discussed fully in various parts of this book. For all intents and purposes, the conscious mind is what we mean when we say "my mind." It is not the whole self, but is the part of the self by which we become aware of the Self.

WE LIVE IN MIND

In comprehending exactly what your mind is, do not think of it being in you but of you being in it. The conscious mind is only confined by the limitation of our thought. It is an area of personal identification within the Infinite Mind, and is itself Infinite to the degree that we free our thought and dwell upon the larger scope of things. When we think, we set in operation the entire power of Universal Creativity, which is personalized by our subconscious conditioning and limited by it.

That which appears as manifestation, situation, experience, body, or bodily condition, is the effect of thought dropping from the conscious mind into the subconscious which brings it into form. Hence, "thoughts are things." In order to experience the greatest good, it is necessary for us to free the mind and keep it focused upon thoughts, ideas and objectives which provide the potential of the most abundant and favorable expression.

CHOICE AND SELECTION

"Choose you this day whom ye will serve." (Josh. 24: 15) It is up to each one of us. We have the power of choice and selection. By our choice we initiate action. Our life is determined by the aggregate of all of the choices we make. The objective then is to make those choices which have the greatest potential of good, and to strengthen our thought about them until they appear as solid fact. This takes discipline, training and perseverance, but our conscious mind is the gateway to the kingdom of Infinite fulfillment, whatever we ourselves determine this fulfillment to be. This should be ample incentive and motivation for us to apply ourselves dedicatedly to the discipline and control of our own mind.

DECISION

The conscious mind has the power of decision. What you decide upon must come true, if you believe that it will. "What the mind can conceive and believe, it will achieve." We can think positively and constructively simply by deciding to and by disciplining ourselves to stick by this decision. This is the very first step in using the Science of Mind to bring about health, happiness, prosperity, peace and freedom in our world. We must make up our own mind, or we will follow those who make up theirs.

We can decide to believe the testimony of the senses, accept the picture that the world presents to us and let ourselves be filled with negativity and despair, or we can consciously choose to identify with Spirit, Truth—and live an entirely different kind of life. The choice is always ours. We experience what we think. The Law of Cause and Effect guarantees that.

SUBCONSCIOUS MIND

The subconscious, or deeper mind, is the Law, or Subjective Mind working at the individual level. "Every man is a law unto himself," "As a man thinketh in his heart, so is he." The subconscious, inner, deeper function of our mind actually forms us and the world about us by its creative action, set in motion by our conscious thought.

The conscious mind selects; the subconscious mind is amenable to suggestion. Thought originates in the conscious mind and carries with it a command or suggestion to the subconscious mind to create it into form. The conscious mind acts; the subconscious reacts. The conscious thinks; the subconscious feels.

YOUR CREATIVE MIND

The subconscious is the creative power mechanism of the mind. The scope of its power is limited by our subconscious conditioning or memory. The memory works as Law by reproducing itself in outer form. Whatever goes into the subconscious is stored up as memory and comes out when the creative mechanism has done its work upon it. This is an unfailing, mathematically accurate action.

The subconscious cannot reject what is put into it, nor can it fail to create. Jesus taught the nature of the subconscious and explained its workings when He said, "It is easier for heaven and earth to pass, than one tittle of the law to fail." (Luke 16: 17)

HOW YOUR "PERSONAL COMPUTER" WORKS FOR YOU

The subconscious has been described as the original and perfect digital computer. The comparison is most appropriate. The computer does not think, even though it appears to. Its function is more of a "feedback" operation whereby the information which is programmed into it comes back in definite forms and orderly relationships which add up to a whole picture.

This is exactly what the subconscious does. It receives whatever is fed into it, without any power to reject. It cannot say "no." It says "yes" to everything, even though what is given it may be negative or false. This is why people form such positive convictions about false and negative beliefs. The subconscious can only work with what it is given. If the conscious mind is constantly filled with negative, false, stupid and indiscriminate ideas and conclusions, the subconscious will develop a conglomeration of inner feelings of fear, hostility, inferiority, guilt, resentment, anger, aggressiveness and a thousand and one other destructive feelings and tendencies.

It works for you by working through you

This book is filled with stories of men and women like you who have found the way to richer, fuller living through the practice of the Science of Mind. What they have done you can do if you apply yourself and master the principles.

Sometimes people become discouraged if they don't get startling results immediately. We must not allow this to happen. Keep on, work to free yourself from destructive thoughts, feelings and tendencies, and eventual good is assured. Results are not always achieved easily, but they will come when we do our part. Unfortunately, some abandon the ship just as land is in sight.

Norma V. was a prima donna, even though the status of her life and affairs hardly seemed to warrant the imperious self-centeredness of her manner. Many tried to help her, and even though she sought and even demanded their help, she rejected it and invariably turned upon her benefactors and alienated them. She refused to help herself by putting into practice the principles of love, faith, patience and common sense which are inherent in the Science of Mind and in every approach to constructive living.

Norma could not get along with people simply because she could not get along with herself. She hated herself and took her animosity out on others. Her neurosis followed the classic pattern of blaming others for her misfortunes. She was convinced that the world was against her, and since it was, it was its fault. There was no need for her to change herself, she reasoned. Even though broke, unemployed, friendless and miserable, she preferred to wallow in self-pity rather than change her attitude.

She is convinced that the Science of Mind doesn't work because she tried it one day, and nothing happened. She doesn't realize this, but all the help she could ever need is ready for her when she is ready for it.

CHANGE YOURSELF—CHANGE YOUR LIFE

It didn't take Donna W. as long to find this out. She first came to the Science of Mind because she had heard that it would give you anything you wanted. She wanted a husband and it just wasn't happening. She had no problem attracting men and never lacked attention, but after a date or two, they drifted away.

"What's the matter with men anyway?" she stormed. "Who needs them? They're jerks anyway—jerks, that's all they are!"

But her tirade had a hollow sound. She was really bewildered and hurt, and began to develop deep feelings of insecurity, self-rejection and bitterness. This was her consciousness when she first came to the Science of Mind and started to treat for a husband. She was convinced that the right man would appear as the result of her daily affirmations. When he didn't after a reasonable time, she was ready to abandon the teaching, when it was suggested to her that she might be treating in the wrong way and for the wrong thing.

"What do you mean?" she demanded.

"Perhaps that instead of treating for a husband, you should treat to be a wife," I suggested.

"That doesn't make sense. How can I be a wife without a husband?"

"You want a good husband, don't you?"

"Of course."

"Then suppose we treat for the development in you of those qualities which would make you a good wife."

This angered her, because she felt that she was above reproach and completely desirable in every way, which she seemed to be, except that she lacked love and understanding. She refused to do anything about it, but when complete happiness continued to elude her, she changed her point of view and in so doing, changed herself. She became a good person, and saw and accepted herself as a good wife. Now she is.

CONDITIONING AND HABIT

Since habits are formed in the subconscious, whatever we repeat with frequency, conviction and regularity forms a "track" in the subconscious and becomes permanent, or habitual. Once it is set in the inner mind, it becomes the law of our consciousness and works from the conditions imposed by the belief. This is why "every man is a law unto his own being." Unless we are willing to be held captive by unwholesome thought and reaction, we must watch what we allow to go into the subconscious, because once the creative process is underway it will run its course, and we are enslaved by our own subconscious belief. That is, of course, unless we set about consciously reconditioning the subconscious mind. This is the basis of spiritual mind healing, or the practice of the Science of Mind, which is at the heart of this book, and which we are developing as we go along.

HOW TO BUILD CONSTRUCTIVE PATTERNS

We see, then, how the subconscious works. We have described what happens when the subconscious is filled with negative material. Now, let us see what happens when it is given constructive thought, feelings and pictures. The process does not vary, of course; the results are commensurate with the cause—the thought material—the consciousness that is fed into our subconscious computer.

Thus we can accurately say, **change your thought and the conditions of your life change.** We are working with the Creative Principle—Law. The same thing that made you sick, or gave you problems, now makes you well—when you think constructively.

TREATMENT: CONSCIOUSLY CREATING CIRCUMSTANCES

This is made possible by the very nature of the subconscious itself. Since it cannot reject or discriminate, *it cannot tell the difference between the factually real and the imaginary*. Therefore, whatever we tell it is so, **becomes** so if we think it clearly, strongly and consistently. This gives us the power to consciously create circumstances and control our own lives by consciously using our subconscious mechanism to create good. This is the essence of Science of Mind Treatment which we will explain more fully as we go along.

As you continue your daily practice of Treatment, include this one for personal power. As you recognize the One Power and realize that it is within you and is yours to use, it flows into and through you and accomplishes all good in your life. Repeat these statements with force and conviction, knowing they are true.

Personal Science of Mind Treatment for Personal Power

"For thine is the kingdom, and the power, and the glory forever."
Infinite, immutable power is available to me at all times. There is only One Power. God's Power is my power now. I learn to think constructively and powerfully, thereby turning on the power by a conscious act of my own will. I am a powerful person.

I know it because I know God is my very life, and God is All-Power.

God's Omnipotence is individualized in me. I am aware of my power potential and I use it. I release my mind from all negative and destructive thought. I free it for use as a powerful tool in God's hands. I give thanks for my powerful mind and the powerful way in which it works. I am capable of expressing Infinite Power. I do so now.

My subconscious mind is waiting to receive the impress of my thought and act upon it. I now think only constructive thoughts, feel only constructive emotions, and do only constructive things. I am subject to the immutable power of the Law. By cooperating with it, I make Universal Power my power. My mind is marvelous. Every time I think, I set the entire creative mechanism of the Universe into operation. The powerful machinery of the Law is at my command.

"Still waters run deep." I let the power develop and flow forth from the depths of my being. A great surge of creative power inundates my being and sweeps me along with it. I flow with the invincible tide of God's creative forces. I move when I am moved from within. I eliminate all unnecessary action. I conserve my energy and gather my forces to use in powerful purpose and endeavor.

Quietly now, I lie down in the green pastures which nourish me and give me power. I walk beside the still waters, the Infinite Power Potential with which I am one. My mind is integrated consciously and subconsciously, providing a power tool for God to use. I give thanks for the privilege and responsibility of having great power. I am a powerful person now.

And so it is.

CHAPTER 6 SUMMARY

1. When we take care of our one basic problem—ourselves—the lesser problems take care of themselves.
2. We have within us the power to cause problems; we also have within us the power to solve them.
3. The personal mind is the area or point where the One Mind is functioning.
4. The Science of Mind teaches the human mind how to become one with the One Mind, so that the One First Cause is the one and only permanent cause of our experience.
5. The primary lesson and responsibility of life is to learn to use our own mind with conscious effectiveness.

6. The nature of our life is determined by the aggregate of all of the choices we make.
7. The conscious mind selects; the subconscious mind creates.
8. Change your thought and the conditions of your life change.
9. The same thing that made us sick or gave us problems, now makes us well when we reverse our thought and start to think constructively.
10. Science of Mind treatment is the process by which we bring the conscious and subconscious into agreement with each other and into total agreement with Infinite Intelligence.

Chapter 7

The Creative Principle in You

The individual subconscious is so integral to the entire Creative Process that we can never cease in our efforts to understand it more completely and use it more effectively.

When we think, we create. When we feel, we create. What we think, feel, do, and what we are aware of combine to form our consciousness. Consciousness is what we are in invisible essence. This is planted in the subconscious which produces what we are on the visible level. What your conscious mind places or allows to be placed in the subconscious is either created immediately or is stored in memory as material for progressive creativity.

The process never stops. The subconscious is always working on everything that has ever been placed in it. It can and does work upon an infinite number and variety of projects, all in various stages of development. It may take a long time for the finished product to appear, but it will eventually do so. Whatever is planted in the subconscious must inevitably grow and appear. Whether it is good or bad is of no consequence whatsoever. "The law is no respecter of persons." "The mills of the gods grind slowly, but they grind exceedingly fine."

THE GARDEN OF YOUR MIND

Think of the subconscious as a garden in which a great variety of seeds are planted. Some have been growing for a long time, and others have just been placed there. The majority of the plants are of a pleasant variety, but others are noxious weeds. We may look out upon our garden and its great variety of growing things and marvel at how they got there.

We may arrive at the conclusion that the whole thing just happened, and there is nothing we can do about it.

Such, however, is not the case. We can and must do something about it. This garden is our responsibility. There are four major classifications of plants in our garden: (1) What Nature (Infinite Intelligence) has planted there, (2) What we ourselves have consciously planted there, (3) What we have allowed to be planted there either unconsciously or through conscious negligence, and (4) The subconscious memory of all things since creation began.

I. WHAT NATURE PLANTS

In the subconscious is the master plan for each of us as a creation of God. The pattern of each cell, organ, dimension, and function is there. Our identity as an individual unit of the species is a creation of God and has been placed in the subconscious for development and growth. In the subconscious is the autonomic nervous system, which maintains and sustains the functions of the body, the interrelationships of the various levels of our being, and the relationship of ourselves as a single unit to God, the Infinite All.

The perfect seed

Our personal individuality, the Christ within—God's idea of us as an entity, the son of God, is the master plan which is programmed into our subconscious. This includes everything that is necessary for our maintenance, sustenance, and our evolvement into full God-expression, which is our ultimate Destiny—including the conscious mind which has the powers of reason and choice, and the capacity for self-conscious awareness of Self. Therefore we see that God created us perfect, and placed within us a creative mechanism whose sole function is to work toward the end of self-realization of perfection.

Your freedom to choose

In order to attain this self-realization of Self—to earn it, we must learn how to discipline and use our conscious mind which, having the power of selection, is free to choose evil as well as good.

> Behold, I set before you this day a blessing and a curse:
> A blessing, if ye obey the commandments of the LORD your God, which I command you this day:
> And a curse, if ye will not obey the commandments of the LORD your God, but turn aside out of the way which I command you this day, to go after other gods, which ye have not known. (Deut. 11: 26–28)

How to learn to use our power

If we could choose only good, we would stay in the Garden of Eden and flourish, knowing only the consciousness of God, eating only of the fruit of "the tree of life in the midst of the garden" (Gen. 2: 9), but when we eat of "the tree of the knowledge of good and evil" (Gen. 2: 9, 3: 1–7), we become subject to the law of our own being as well as the Law of God, and must find our way back into the Garden by learning to use our power of choice wisely. This is the province of the Science of Mind—to teach us how to use our thought wisely and thereby bring our creative power into focus with the Will of God, Universal Intelligence.

How to plant personal thoughts for benefits

Clint was an inveterate daydreamer as a child. In his fantasies he conjured up elaborate dramas in which he assigned roles to the actual people in his life. His father was the hero, his teacher was the wicked witch, and his school principal was often the dragon. His other acquaintances were assigned major or minor roles as the situation required.

One day he discovered that his fantasies were extended right into everyday life. People tended to become to him just as he pictured them. It was fine that his father was the hero, but he was beginning to get interested in school, and it was unpleasant to have his teacher a witch. So the boy started to play another game. He began thinking of his teacher as the fairy princess, and lo and behold—that is just what she became! This worked so well that he started doing the same thing with others. He started to see the playground bully as his companion, and he became so. He pictured the principal as his friend, and he was.

One day, however, he got angry at one of his playmates and said mean things to him. The playmate fought back and their relationship was badly strained for days. Whatever Clint thought about his former firiend, the boy seemed to be thinking about him. This was unpleasant so Clint changed his thought, and the boys became friends again.

These experiences were so vivid that as Clint grew to be a man, he continued to recognize the power of his thought to change himself, his his world, and the people in it. Today he doesn't need to escape into daydreams. He likes his world the way it is; he controls his thought and thinks it into existence the way he wants it. We can do the same.

II. CONSCIOUS PLANTING

Next in importance to the tree of life and all of its components which Infinite Mind has planted in the subconscious garden of each of us individually and all of humanity collectively, is what we ourselves consciously place there.

This includes all of our thoughts, plans, ideas, images, goals, aims, desires and needs. The subconscious also receives, correlates and stores up in memory the knowledge and information which we acquire, and the conclusions which we arrive at through reason, experience, learning, comparison, and other activities of the intellectual process. Everything that we think about, consciously or unconsciously, is planted in the garden of the subconscious where it grows and produces its own kind.

Mental discipline

The important thing is not to let anything into the subconscious that you don't want to experience in your life. **Be careful what you think about or pray for, because you'll surely get it.** The conscious mind is an effective gardener when it chooses wisely, thinks clearly, and maintains diligent discipline over itself and what it has planted. The conscious mind is in charge of the subconscious and has control over it when it exercises that control. For effective living these two functions of our mind must be in complete agreement and work together in close harmony at all times. This is the secret of success. This is the major purpose of Science of Mind Treatment which we will explain more fully in the next two chapters.

The secret of success

What are you thinking about right now? Undoubtedly what you are reading, and the points that are brought out here. These concepts go into your subconscious, where they grow in the garden of your mind and produce their harvest. The more clearly you understand them, the stronger the plants will be and the more abundant the harvest.

Start now to be consciously aware of what you are thinking. Focus on that thought, clarify it and modify it so that it is completely acceptable to you. You have this power. Use it. Don't think about anything you don't want to think about.

"You know, Mommy, I feel much better today than I did yesterday," little Susie chortled to her mother.

"Why is that dear?"

"Because yesterday my thoughts pushed me around. Today I'm pushing them around."

THE BUILDER

Your conscious mind is the architect which carefully draws up the plans and specifications. If it is inaccurate or slipshod, the house which is built will be the same way. But if the plans are clear and accurate the house will duplicate them in form. "Except the Lord build the house, they labour in vain that build it." (Psalm 127: 1)

The subconscious is the contractor and building crew, all working together to build exactly what has been given them. They can do no more; they will do no less. When the Proverb instructs, "Keep thy heart with all diligence; for out of it are the issues of life" (Ps. 4:23), it is telling the conscious mind to do its job of planning what it wants to go into the subconscious, and of keeping out what it does not want there.

Give your subconscious builder clear thoughts, goals and plans, and it will build you a magnificent temple in which to dwell. Plant your subconscious with healthy plants of your own choosing, and the garden of your life will be a place of beauty, order, harmony and joy.

Weeding and replanting

Corwin was a man, but he looked more like a question mark. He was almost bent double with crippling arthritis. He endeavored to meet the demands and responsibilities of occupation and daily living, but he was fighting a losing battle. The pain was intense and the frustration of inhibited and limited activity made Corwin ever more bitter and sharp-tongued than he had been before his affliction. But angry and resentful against cruel fate, he continued to fight back.

In an endeavor to get help, Corwin found the Science of Mind. In reading our literature, he came to understand the relationship between his thoughts and feelings and the condition of his body. He accepted the fact that discordant states of consciousness must externalize as distorted expression—problems, disharmony or ill health. Since he had always been a fighter, he accepted the challenge of changing his state of health by changing the thoughts, feelings and attitudes in his mind.

He undertook the task of replanting his mental garden. He was amazed how many weeds of resentment, bitterness, revenge, jealousy and sarcasm he had to get rid of before he could ever begin to plant. But he stuck to it. He had no real assurance that this program of self-change would make him well, but he knew intuitively that it could not make him worse, and would in all probability bring about an improvement. Besides, he knew he could not help but be a better person for the inner changes. He kept on with faith and hope.

When Corwin had made some progress in getting rid of the weeds in his mental garden, he started to plant more desirable seeds. They came up and gave an entirely different character to Corwin's life. He is not yet free from an occasional weed patch, and his body is not yet free from pain and distortion, but he is making progress. He knows he is on the right path. He continues to plant and care for the garden of his life with the regular use of Science of Mind Treatment.

Each statement we make now is a seed which produces healthy plants in our mental garden.

Personal Science of Mind Treatment: Planting My Mental Garden

I survey the vast field of my mind as I prepare to plant it with all that is true, good and beautiful. As I contemplate my powers of choice and creative activity, I see that the fields are white already unto the harvest. I know that what I sow, so shall I also reap. I choose wisely, I sow carefully, and I harvest abundantly. I choose what I want in my life. God produces it through me. I am the field in which the seeds of experience are sown and grown.

First I rid my mental and emotional garden of all unproductive thoughts, ideas and feelings. I rid myself of all debris. The weeds of diffidence, carelessness and purposelessness are cleared away. The rigid rocks and clods of neglect and petty personal blockages and hang-ups are raked off. I am busy preparing the soil of my mind. I prepare a seedbed which is warm, receptive and fertile. I expect abundant harvest.

I dig below the surface. I examine the soil of my mind. The hardened crust of prejudice, biased opinion, and destructive habits is broken up and turned under for reconversion into rich and fertile mental soil. All the elements are reactivated. I employ all facets of my unlimited potential. I use my tools efficiently and effectively. The spade of decision and determination turns my mind over and over and prepares it for its full use. The rake of order and peace smooths the surfaces and removes obstructions.

The rows of my garden are straight and true. Proper length and spacing are given to each one. I plan for the future by clear thought and purposeful right action today. I do not plant too much; neither do I plant too little. I have a balanced garden. I am planting for all eternity. The crop which I plant today reproduces itself into infinity.

I culture, nourish and refresh the thoughts and feelings of love, faith, goodwill, peace, honesty, and joyous expectancy as they grow in my garden. I observe every law of nature as I select carefully, act wisely, bless profusely, release completely, and give thanks constantly for the abundance of the harvest. I am a good steward. I look after my crops. I am a workman in the garden of God. I dwell in the house of the Lord forever—in the garden of my own consciousness.

And so it is.

III. UNCONSCIOUS PLANTING

"The kingdom of heaven is likened unto a man which sowed good seed in his field: but while men slept, his enemy came and sowed tares among the wheat, and went his way." (Matt. 13: 24, 5)

The man is your conscious mind, and the good seed is your careful, disciplined thought. The field is your subconscious. The men who slept are our faculties of judgment, choice and mental discipline. The enemy is our own weakness and lack of self-discipline. The tares are the weeds that grow from careless thought, false ideas, negativity and destructiveness, and threaten to choke out the wheat, or good thought that is growing there. "And went his way" indicates that what is planted in carelessness and weakness grows just as readily as that which we have carefully planted.

Unrelenting guard necessary

Therefore, if we do not want weeds among our wheat we must be on guard every second. We must never relax our mental vigil. Negativity can be an insidious habit. So can uncontrolled and indiscriminate daydreaming. Remember that whatever we consciously think about, or allow our minds to entertain, all grow into experience unless they are removed and replaced with something else. It is much easier to keep thoughts out of the subconscious than it is to remove them once they are growing.

SCIENCE OF MIND FOR THE SICK AND THE WELL

This latter process is not impossible, of course, and it constitutes the bulk of our work in spiritual mind healing as taught and practiced in the Science of Mind.

The Science of Mind works even more effectively as a constructive way of life than it does as corrective therapy, but it is supreme in both. We all have a certain amount of self-correction to do all the time, but it is much easier to polarize the mind positively so that we eliminate negativity before it has the chance to reach the subconscious and become habit.

Science of Mind Healing Treatment has healed thousands of people who have not been helped by other types of therapy, and it has also helped millions find a richer, fuller life where no therapy or healing is needed other than the training and discipline of our own thought.

The Science of Mind is for both classifications of people, and this book presents the effective principles to be used by both.

Just remember that the Science of Mind, the most effective system of thought and of spiritual mind therapy the world has ever known, is not just for the sick and those plagued with problems. It is also the very best philosophy and mental, emotional, and spiritual discipline for those who have overcome these things and are happy, healthy, successful, balanced and mature. Then the Science of Mind really goes into high gear and takes us into orbit, as can be attested to by the many who are living it and the stories of some of these men and women which are told in this book.

He forgot before he remembered

Wally was ragged, hungry and defeated when he came to the door of our church one cold, rainy afternoon. After seeing that he got a warm meal, I invited him into my office for a talk, not as a condition levied for having fed him, but because he asked about the Science of Mind and whether or not it could help him.

"It will help you if you use it," I replied.

"How do I do that?" he asked.

I explained it to him, and Wally became an avid student. He helped around the church, attended all of the classes, learned and practiced Treatment, and made the Science of Mind his way of life. He found a good job, fell in love with a beautiful girl, and faced a bright future.

Then all of a sudden, he wasn't around anymore. After a few weeks I ran into him on the street. When I remarked that we missed him, he dismissed me airily by saying, "Oh, I don't need you any more. The Science of Mind has solved all my problems. So long, Doc! I'll see you around."

And he did, but not in the way he intended. Not long afterward, I was called in the middle of the night to come down to the jail where Wally was being held on a charge of driving while intoxicated. Leaving him there overnight, I returned the next morning to arrange his bail. A subdued and chastened young man accompanied me to my office.

"I just got too big for my breeches," he confessed. "I've had some time to think, and I see now that the Science of Mind helps you only as long as you use it. I forgot all about it as soon as my problems were solved. Doc, will you please help me to use it all the time, and maybe help some other people the way you have helped me?"

Today Wally's rich and abundant life is proof of the efficacy of the principles of the Science of Mind as a sound foundation upon which to build.

How to monitor your planting

In monitoring the planting of our subconscious garden, we must watch not only what we are thinking, but what others are thinking into it.

THE CREATIVE PRINCIPLE IN YOU

Your conscious mind is the door to the house of your subconscious in which you live. You and only you have the power to open or close it.

Suppose a delivery man came to your door with an elephant:

"Here's your elephant sir. Will you sign here please."

"Elephant? What elephant? I didn't order an elephant."

"It has your name on it. Will you sign please."

"No, thank you. I'm not having any, thank you. Goodbye!"

And, if you are wise and on the job, you will slam the door. But if you are not—you can readily see that if you once let the elephant into your house your problems have just started.

Dangers of mass thought and race mind

The elephants of what we call "race mind" or "mass thinking" must be kept out of your house. To believe or accept something just because "they say" it, is to turn your mind and its entire creative mechanism over to someone else to use. Your mind is yours only, and you alone are to determine what you want to do with it. Avoid accepting others' negativity and uninformed and irresponsible ideas. Do not let yourself be hypnotized by the world's "elephants" of opinion and advertising. You are an individual, so be an individualist. Make up your own mind. Marry the thoughts, ideas, opinions, feelings, and concepts which are compatible with the real you. You have to live with them.

Keep open to all that is of good—"If there be any virtue and if there be any praise, think on these things." (Phil. 4: 8)—and close the door to everything else.

IV. SUBCONSCIOUS MEMORY

Not only does your subconscious garden contain what Nature has planted there, what we have consciously planted, and what we have allowed to be planted, but it also contains the memory of Absolute Being and all of its aspects, and of everything that has ever happened since time began.

The portent of this is beyond the scope of our present comprehension and imagination, but it is true. Our subconscious is our individual area in the "collective unconscious" of the race and of the Universe itself. This means that everything that ever happened—that has been thought, felt, done, or experienced, whether on the Universal or the individual level—is stored up in the infinite reservoir of Mind and exists in us as memory, and is part of the law of our being.

Your storehouse of the eternal

We are a product, then, not only of God's thought, and our own thought, but also of evolution as it has unfolded through the thought, instincts, actions and experiences of everything and everybody that has ever existed. The memory of the first living cell is imprinted in our subconscious and is produced in infinite number in our bodies. All instincts of all living things are either active or vestigial within us. The most noble thoughts, feelings and deeds of the human race have been added to the Universal storehouse and are active within us. The lives of all individuals, nations, civilizations, races, worlds, planets, universes—the Life of God Itself lives within our subconscious memory. This would, of course, include all of our individual previous lives as we have travelled the path of evolution and eternal life. Since there is no time or space in the Infinite, all that ever was, is. "Before Abraham was, I am." (John 8: 58)

What the will of god means

If all that is good is stored up to be identified with and used, are the evil thoughts, deeds and painful experiences of the race also within us? Some, yes, but not all. There was never any evil until man with his conscious choice was both evolved and created. Man was created as a spiritual entity, and has evolved physically and mentally until he has recognition of himself and his power of choice and self-initiated thought. Until that point, there was no evil because all was God—Good, of God, and in God. God which is perfect could not create anything imperfect, because He made all things from Himself. So perfect did He make man that he instilled within us His own perfect spiritual, mental and creative equipment, including will or self-determination.

As long as the personal will maintains its identification with Divine Will, only good, harmony, order and perfection exist. When we depart from "that good and acceptable, and perfect will of God" (Romans 12: 2), the trouble starts and evil appears. Evil is actually nothing of itself. It is the absence of good and appears to be something, but really is not. We believe the appearance, however, and give it power. The spiritual message of the Science of Mind teaches the non-reality of evil and the Reality of Good–God.

The science of constructivity

What about our subconscious memory of the evil which the human race has committed and experienced? Much of it has been dissolved by the principle of overcoming evil with good. Constructive consciousness cancels negative consciousness. Constructive action cancels destructive action. Good deeds cancel bad deeds. Since man, through both his conscious and subconsious awareness of his true nature as a son of God has always endeavored to do good rather than evil, we have done a fairly good job of keeping pace. We are evolving out of death into life, out of darkness into light, and out of ignorance into enlightenment.

BUILDING GOOD KARMA

The negative karma, therefore, of the race is minimal, while the good karma is continually expanding. As we identify ourselves with the good of the past and of the present, we help to dissolve whatever residue of bad karma may still exist. Karma is not to be thought of as fate or as something to be afraid of or worshiped. Karma is the working of the Law of Cause and Effect in the consciousness of the race and of the individual. Everyone has the consciousness of the race and of himself within his own consciousness. The Science of Mind is the science of building constructive karma through right thought and awareness.

We have nothing to be afraid of. We free ourselves from the past and live abundantly in the present by the intelligent use of our own mind. The individual mind—conscious and subconscious—is the key to everything. If each of us takes care of his own, everything else will take care of itself. Realizing this should take a tremendous load off our shoulders, and at the same time free us for the joyous adventure of abundant living. That's what the Science of Mind is all about.

How to know the real power in yourself

The great area of our subconscious memory, and therefore the only Real Power in ourselves, is the One First Cause—God. The experiences of the race and our own experiences are stored up within us as we have seen, but these are of nothing compared to what is really there. God indwells every particle of Creation with Itself. All we have to do is to consciously remember that, and the subconscious then works as Law to make our lives a replica of God's perfection. We are open to God through our consciousness, which consists of conscious thought and subconscious memory. These together determine the level of our self, or spiritual awareness-our real consciousness.

In the Science of Mind we teach that God is everywhere, and that when we see good in everything, we are seeing and knowing God. We develop this capacity to see and know God through the understanding of the principles which we are discussing, and through Science of Mind Treatment, the technique of scientific prayer which we are sharing in each chapter of this book, and which we will explain in detail in the next two chapters.

How conscious and subconscious reciprocity work

The importance of the detailed presentation here of our personal individual mind with its conscious and subconscious functions, can readily be discerned when we realize that their relationship and action is reciprocal. That is the whole point. The conscious mind seeds the garden of the subconscious with thoughts, and the subconscious nurtures and matures them and sends them back as a harvest of experience.

In addition to this, the subconscious, a vast storehouse of knowledge, wisdom and insights, is constantly instructing and guiding the conscious mind in its growth, decisions, and nature of its thought. When we make friends with our subconscious, we are making friends with God himself. There can be no better friend, but this friendship can only be shown in terms of that which we give and receive.

We give in thought, word and deed. We receive by inner knowing, by becoming aware of the Presence of God as the only reality. We learn to listen as well as to speak. We learn to be still. We develop the Silence. We let God walk with us, talk with us, and tell us that we are his own. We listen to the "still, small voice" which is the Voice of God using our own subconscious as His instrument of communication. We become quiet and invite our soul, because we know that "all things proceed from the quiet mind."

This is what we do in the following Treatment. As we make constructive statements and intersperse them with periods of silence, we attain a consciousness of inner peace and unity from which all good flows forth.

Personal Science of Mind Treatment: Conscious and Subconscious Agreement

Peace abides in my house today. The inhabitants are one with each other. Vital health is in my body today. My mind and heart are in perfect accord. Happiness is within and all around me today. My thoughts and feelings agree with each other. Prosperity and success come to me today. My will and my imagination work together perfectly. My conscious impressions and my subconscious expressions are a balanced team in the creative process.

My thought marries my feeling, and I have the power of strong conviction. I know that I cannot go in two directions at the same time. I work together with myself. In unity there is strength. According to my faith it is done unto me. There is no point in thinking one thing and believing another. I bring thought and knowing into perfect accord.

Selection becomes creation. My conscious mind chooses and my subconscious creates. My conscious mind plans and my subconscious produces. My conscious mind selects and my subconscious brings the increase. My conscious mind initiates and my subconscious completes. My conscious mind gives orders and my subconscious obeys them. My conscious mind is intelligent. My subconscious is powerful. As they work together they produce great good. My conscious and my subconscious are a perfect team.

My conscious and subconscious partners love each other. They are man and wife. They form an eternal union. "Male and female created he them." My conscious mind is the father of all things in my life, and my subconscious is the mother. They are perfectly mated. Their love is pure and enduring. They are the parents of many beautiful and perfect children. They are the progenitors of all things to come.

There is no discord in my family. Perfect love casts out all things other than itself. The bridegroom of my consciousness and the bride of my subconsciousness live happily ever after. They have been brought together by the great laws of polarity and attraction, and they fulfill their destiny by the laws of their own nature.

My conscious and my subconscious blend together and work

together to express God. I am whole in the Wholeness of God now.

And so it is.

CHAPTER 7 SUMMARY

1. Consciousness is the sum total of what we think, feel, do, and what we are aware of.
2. We are created perfect, and within us is a creative mechanism which moves us toward self-realization of our perfection.
3. The Science of Mind teaches us how to use our thought wisely and bring our creative power into focus with Universal Intelligence.
4. The secret of successful living is to keep the conscious and subconscious mind in complete agreement and working together in complete harmony at all times.
5. Our personal subconscious is our individual area in the "collective consciousness" of the race and of the Universe itself.
6. Man was created as a spiritual entity, and has evolved physically and mentally until he has recognition of himself and his power of choice and self-initiated thought.
7. As long as the personal will maintains its identification with Divine Will, only good, harmony, order and perfection exist.
8. The Science of Mind teaches the non-reality of evil and the Reality of Good.
9. Constructive consciousness cancels negative consciousness. Constructive action cancels destructive action.
10. The conscious mind seeds the garden of the subconscious with thoughts; the subconscious nurtures and matures them and sends them back as a harvest of experience.

Chapter 8

How Individual Mind Expresses Universal Mind

Since the individual consciousness has the potential to comprehend and express universal consciousness, the major endeavor of each one of us inevitably must be to work toward that potential. The part eternally seeks to be one with the whole of which it is a part.

In nature, the law of centripetal action which draws all things to the center, and the law of attraction which unites all things which belong together, are confirmation of this truth. Its operation in human consciousness is eloquently expressed by St. Augustine when he prayed, "Thou hast created us for thyself, and our hearts are ever restless until they return to thee."

YOUR DIVINE SPARK

There is within each of us that divine spark which subconsciously remembers its origin and reality as part of the one fire of Infinite Intelligence, and seeks to burst into full flame, completely expressing its individual identity as one with the whole. The frustrations of life come from being able to glimpse this promised land of full personal expression, but in not being able to achieve or express it. This is why Emerson admonished, "Get your bloated nothingness out of the way and let the divine circuits come through."

HOW TO REMOVE YOUR PERSONAL INTERFERENCE

There is no doubt but that we stand in our own light and that we block the channels through which good seeks to flow to us on every level. All we really need to do is to keep our thoughts clear, our emotions balanced, and our awareness sensitive to higher influence and guidance, and let Nature take its course.

However, through ignorance, error, and negative experience, the individual subconscious builds up memory patterns which not only block the flow of good, but also feed back to the conscious mind spurious material which is believed and reacted to, and forms a syndrome of false belief and negative creative activity from which we seem unable to escape. As Freud stated, "Our neurotic thought patterns repeat themselves over and over again with monotonous regularity."

HOW TO REVERSE NEGATIVE THOUGHT

We actually create the prison in which we dwell. It is not real, but we remain in it because we believe it is. We become conditioned by our thoughts and feelings, and our conditioning affects our thought and feelings. It is obvious that this process can only lead to, and prolong a vicious circle. Something has to break it. This is what the Science of Mind does. By training the conscious mind to assume its rightful authority in the creative process and through the exercise of this authority, we are able to reverse the direction of our thought and start a new chain of causation. We learn that things aren't so just because someone has told us they are or because we have happened to think so.

The story is often told of the prisoner during the French revolution who was confined for many years in a solitary cell. His food and water were passed to him through a slot in the door. Otherwise he had no contact with the outer world. For years he languished in this state, often dwelling upon possible escape, but finding no way to so. One day, after many years, he tried the door and discovered that it was not only not locked, but it had never been; the door had no lock on it.

HOW TO UNLOCK YOUR PRISON

Likewise, there is no lock on the door which connects the individual consciousness with the larger sphere of consciousness that surrounds us and into which we have the potential of moving. However, we ourselves must open the door. We ourselves must take the steps toward our own freedom. We must dissolve the illusions of the locks that block and the blocks that lock.

How Jim found himself

Jim was afraid of his own shadow. While there were many things that he would have liked to do and be, he made no progress toward any of them. He was always afraid of something—what people would say or think, how difficult it might be, that he might fail, or even that he might succeed.

In addition to the limitations of fear, Jim was further hampered by an acute case of inferiority and low esteem. The feedback from his meager life limited him even further, locking him into the narrow confines of hopelessness and despair. However, hope springs eternal, and the spark within us may flicker but it never dies out. The thrust of life through Jim was not to be denied.

He was able to unlock himself by reading and practicing the Science of Mind. He came to realize that when we change our self-concepts, ideas and habits, our lives will change. Jim started by saying nice things about himself—and believing them. This process dissolved the negation and condemnation which had started in his childhood. He moved out of self-rejection into self-acceptance. He found a new self-image in which he saw himself in new situations and circumstances. Each day he did something which he had never done before, until he had no fear of doing anything that came up.

Through Science of Mind Treatment, Jim unlocked himself and emerged from the cell of his own cramped consciousness. The way has not been easy and the progress slow, but he keeps on, and Jim is definitely making progress as he climbs his own particular mountain.

HOW TO BREAK HYPNOTIC SUGGESTION

We are all hypnotized by what we see, hear, taste, touch and smell, and by what we experience. The testimony of the five senses tells us a story which we believe, and then we act accordingly, just as did the man in the cell. Even after walking out of the cell a free man, he was still restricted by the subconscious pattern which it had formed in his memory. For the rest of his life he paced the pattern of the cell, four steps by two, still imprisoned by a habit which remained unbroken. His body was free, but his mind was not.

THE SCIENCE OF MIND FREES US

Each one of us carries within him the reality of his own freedom and the means for achieving it. Science of Mind techniques enlighten the conscious mind and recondition the subconscious mind. It is estimated that we use less than ten percent of our mental and creative potential.

Isn't it time that we awaken to the dynamics of our own potential? Does it make any sense that we are content to languish in circumstances that are meager and unsatisfactory? Is there any reason for accepting less than the best? Is there any basis in natural law for limitation, pain, suffering and disease? Is there anything that says we can't be healthy, happy, successful, prosperous and free if we choose to be and if we believe we can? Doesn't the hostile world disappear when we approach it with love and positive expectancy? Do not all difficulties melt away when we build confidence in ourselves and faith in that Infinite Power that works through us in terms of our faith in it? Since we are created free and equal, why aren't we? Since we are conceived in love, why do we live in hate, expressed as war and unrest? Since we are made whole, why do we fall apart? Since we have the gift of eternal life, why do we die? Since we have been given dominion, why are we slaves?

How problems blind solutions

A hungry rat crawled through the narrow neck of a large bottle in which there was some corn. Voraciously he devoured the food until he was filled. His hunger sated, he started to crawl back out of the bottle, but now his swollen body was too large to get through the narrow opening. The harder he pushed the tighter wedged in he became. This frightened him, and he struggled and fought desperately, blindly threshing about in an endeavor to get free.

Finally he dislodged himself and fell back into the bottle, exhausted and painstricken. He ran wildly about the inside periphery of the bottle, able to see out but not to get out. His exertions made him hungry so he stopped to eat, again stuffing himself with the corn. Regaining his strength, he again tried to escape, but to no avail. He repeated the sequence endlessly, caught in his own problem, and blocked by himself. The solution was there, but the rat shut himself off from it.

We are not rats in bottles, and we are not suggesting that our situation is as desperate, but an honest appraisal of ourselves, our society, our country and our world is bound to show us that even though we may not be confined in bottles, there is a lot of running around in cirlces. This is because we either don't know what to do or how to do it, or because we are under the compulsion of our own limitations and experience.

The best time to start beating problems

Where do we start? This book is written for the purpose of providing a starting point and some follow-through techniques for awakening the conscious mind and reconditioning the subconscious. As you read it carefully and put its principles into practice, you will find your life changing and expanding in ways which you have not thought possible. The true stories in these pages of the many men and women who have found new lives through the Science of Mind provide eloquent testimony of its effectiveness.

WAKE UP AND LIVE—NOW

Don't delay any longer. Start right now to free yourself from the prison of false belief and destructive conditioning. Wake up, look around you, and get with it. Put yourself in the driver's seat and assume command. When you do, the entire resources of the Universe are at your command. Let go of the old; embrace the new. Be bold, be original, be yourself. Clear out the debris, and refurnish the house of your consciousness.

Be strong by using the power that is there waiting to be used. You can do it. Know that you can. Others can help you, but the real job is yours alone. No one can think for you, no one can grow for you, no one can live for you. Don't let them try. Think for yourself, grow for yourself, chart the course of your own life and live it for the benefit of all.

An example of how science of mind showed the way

George had no place to go. Yesterday he had been a busy executive, his calendar of activities full and pressing, and his responsibilities great. Then before he knew it, he was 65. A banquet was held honoring him for his many years of faithful service, and he took his gold watch and went home, seemingly a free man, but actually a victim of compulsory retirement.

It was pleasant to sleep late, to have no responsibilities, and to be able to play golf every day, but within a week George was sick of the whole thing and longed for something to do. But he didn't know which way to turn. He certainly couldn't go back to his old job, and when he suggested to former associates that he come to work for them they laughed him off, and later ignored him. Puzzled and hurt, George withdrew into himself and spent whole days sulking in sullen bitterness. All efforts to cheer him up failed, until he accompanied his wife to a Church of Religious Science one day.

Intrigued by its teaching of science, philosophy and religion, George began to take our classes and to apply the constructive mental and spiritual techniques of Treatment to his own problems of adjusting to retirement. As soon as he started to do this, he found that he wasn't retired anymore. He found so many things to do that he said, "I'm so busy I don't see how I ever had time to hold a job." George is truly "about his Father's business," and is having a whale of a good time doing it.

HOW TO TREAT FOR TRUTH

We can all be more and do more than we realize. There is no need to be bored, frustrated, unhappy, or to settle for second-best in life. The following Treatment plants concepts deep within our subconscious and moves us along the road to greater achievement. Repeat these statements until they become an integral part of your consciousness. They are the truth about you.

Personal Science of Mind Treatment for Creative Achievement

My self-image is clear and bright today. I see myself as I really am, not as I thought I was, or as others have said I was. I am a strong and capable person. There is nothing I cannot do, nothing I cannot be. Whatever my mind can conceive and believe, I can achieve. I assume the responsibility and courage to be myself.

I look out at my world today and I see that it is good—very good. That which I see and accept becomes true for me. If I don't like the world the way it is, I make a new and more acceptable one. I remake the world by remaking myself. As I clear my thought, I recondition my subconscious mind. I re-examine everything I believe. If what I believe is consistent with my new self-image of unlimited potential and expression, I keep it; if not, I free myself from all negative conditioning. I refuse to be a prisoner in a prison of my own making. I am the ruler in the kingdom of my own choosing.

I free myself from all subconscious memory of the foibles and failings of the human race. I align myself with all that is noble and true, and dissolve all the rest. I let the dead past bury its dead. My only interest in the past is the good that has evolved to form my consciousness today. My consciousness is a clear transparency through which the Infinite Healing Presence shines. The enlightened wisdom of the ages joins with the infinite power of Life itself within my own being and moves me up the spiral of creative achievement.

There is nothing to stop me, nothing to block me. There is nothing to frighten me, nothing to shock me. I will never meet anything worse than myself, and I am now free from everything but good.

I know only good, so I do only good and experience only good. Old habits, traditions, and superstitions are dissolved as I move forward into new and glorious experience. I believe. I achieve. My life is the constant expression of constructive, creative achievement. I achieve creatively now.

And so it is.

HOW TO USE YOUR FULL MENTAL CAPACITIES

The reason why it is so important to develop the capacities of the conscious mind and free the powers of the subconscious mind is so that they may always work together efficiently and harmoniously. The more clearly we understand our mental equipment, the more effectively we can use it. A clear understanding of the way the mind works is most important and is set out for organizing your power in the following:

The mental process

To understand fully the creative process, it is necessary to first understand the steps in the mental process which sets it into operation. We will consider six functions within the mental process and their interlocking relationships: Thought, Will, Concentration, Attention, Imagination, Visualization.

Thought

First comes thought.
> In the beginning was the Word and the Word was with God; and the Word was God.
> The same was in the beginning with God.
> All things were made By Him; and without Him was made not anything that was made. (John 1: 1–3)

The Word is the thought or consciousness of God. My word is my thought or consciousness which sets the creative process into operation. The thought or idea is the cause behind all manifestation. There is nothing for the creative process to work upon until the thought is planted in the subconscious.

Our thought is the invisible form of that which is to come. It may be invisible, but it is nonetheless real. The clear and well-defined thought, idea or plan will obviously provide a better basis from which to start than a confused one. As we have seen, thoughts are things. They are seeds from which grow the harvest. The better quality the seed, the better is the plant. The more carefully the thought seed is planted and cared for, the better is the harvest.

We must choose our thoughts wisely, form them, believe in them and direct them. We should never accept an unproductive, negative or destructive idea; we should never fail to embrace and have faith in the productive, constructive and promising ones.

> So shall my word be that goeth forth out of my mouth; it shall not return unto me void, but it shall accomplish that which I please, and it shall prosper in the thing whereto I sent it.
> (Isa. 55: 11)

Will

"Not by might, nor by power, but by my Spirit, saith the Lord of hosts." (Zech. 4: 6)

Accomplishment is not brought about through effort or by will power, but by the nature and power of our thought and our understanding, and use of the mental process as our part in activating and sustaining the creative process.

The personal will is not for the purpose of coercing action, but for keeping the attention focused upon the thought or idea until it is brought into form. The will is to be used in selecting and choosing the idea, and initiating action, not for forcing the action. Once the creative process is under way, the will is the guardian, keeping the consciousness free from negativity or neglect by keeping the attention strong with faith and expectancy.

When the personal will is one with the will of God, its faith will be strong, because it will maintain a strong mental, emotional and spiritual conviction that cannot conceive of its opposite.

Concentration

Power flows to the focus of attention. "To concentrate" means "to bring to the center."

> The light of the body is the eye: if therefore thine eye be single, thy whole body shall be full of light. (Matt. 6: 22)

What we concentrate on becomes real to us because we bring our powers of knowing to bear upon it, but without effort. Concentration is the most important step in self-contemplation, which in turn is the most important step in the creative process, which produces the "body," the form, from the "eye," the identification. Do not let your attention wander from the center of your desired goal, objective or thought, and it will manifest in your experience.

We become that which we concentrate on by taking on the characteristics of that which we contemplate. Concentrate upon beauty, and your soul is nourished. Concentrate upon excellence, and you become a person of great worth. Concentrate upon love, and you become kind. Concentrate upon service, and you find God. Concentrate on God, and you become God.

Attention

Attention is that which we concentrate. It is our conscious awareness of the reality of the desired good. Attention recognizes and holds in consciousness our anticipation and expectation. When we give our attention, we give our entire thought and feeling.

"Paying attention" is doing whatever is necessary to assist the creative process in bringing the thought, idea or plan to completion. Attention is taking care of that which it is our responsibility to look after—our thoughts, feelings and actions. Attention turns on the power and keeps it flowing. There is no accomplishment without attention.

Mental attention keeps the thought clear and direct. When coupled with spiritual awareness, it is called prayer. Emotional attention engenders empathic identification by which we infuse our plan or project with the creative force of our own life. It is called love. Physical attention is the focus of all of our sense impressions and our bodily energy, strength and action in doing what needs to be done. It is called work.

Pay attention!

Imagination

Our imaging faculty is our most powerful mental tool. Creative imagination is the most vital factor in giving form to invisible thoughts and ephemeral ideas. When people say to you, "It's all in your imagination," take it as a compliment because it indicates that you are assisting the creative process in the most effective way possible. In imagination, we give life to thought by making it real. We can live an experience so vividly in our imagination that when later it actually happens, it is an anti-climax.

Imagination is actually the subjective realm of thought. Nothing can come into form as experience without passing through the creative power of the imagination. Imagination is your creative power, and knowing how to use it effectively is your greatest asset. Everything—whether it be a toothpick, a city, or an empire—is born out of thought coming alive through the gestating impetus of imagination.

Have faith in your imagination. Paul taught this when he said, "Now faith is the substance of things hoped for, the evidence of things not seen: ...things which are seen were not made of things which do appear." (Heb. 11: 1, 3)

What are they made of then? If not out of things that appear, the things must be made out of things which do not appear, such as the imagination and the creative forces within. Objects are not made out of nothing, but out of faith that things do not have to be visible in order to be real.

The importance of imagination is emphasized by the psychological discovery that **the subconscious does not know the difference between that which is actual and that which is imagined vividly and in detail.**

We do not escape into an imaginary world, but we purposefully use the creative power of the imagination to create a tangible world of greater significance and meaning. The world of the imagination is infinite, limited only by our capacity to imagine. Our outer circumstances place no restriction upon the imagination.

> O God! I could be bounded in a nutshell, and count myself
> a king of infinite space, were it not that I have bad dreams.
> (*Hamlet*, Act II, scene 2)

An example of creative imagination

Myrna was bored with housework. She had a good husband and three lovely children with whom she lived in a beautiful home. They loved each other dearly and had a wonderful life together. Myrna often gave thanks for her many blessings, but she also chafed under the necessity of housework. However, being realistic and emotionally well-balanced, she made the most of it.

To make the endless daily chores of housekeeping less onerous, she used to make up stories while she went about her daily tasks. She turned on her imagination while she was doing her housework, and was often amazed to discover that she had accomplished great amounts of work while on her flights of fancy. Some of her stories were so vivid that she began telling them to her husband and children at dinner. It became a daily ritual.

"You know, you ought to publish some of those wild tales of yours," her husband joked one evening.

That was enough. Immediately Myrna's fertile imagination went into high gear. She could see herself as a famous author, turning out novel after novel, all best sellers. She started to write down her stories, and after a time several were accepted by publishers. Myrna is far from being a best-selling author, but with her imagination—who knows?

THE POWER OF UNLIMITED IMAGINATION

Imagination is unlimited thinking. Free yourself from the limiting restrictions of tangibility and practice moving out into a larger realm where you imagine the ideal. The more you free your mind for unlimited experience, the more unlimited expression will appear in your world. Imagine yourself the kind of person you want to be. Imagine your life the way it would be when life is at its highest and best. That's the way it will be if you practice the constructive and creative use of your imagination.

The secret is in bringing the will and the imagination into complete agreement. William James said, "When there is a conflict between the will and the imagination, the imagination always wins." The will is a conscious faculty, the imagination subconscious. The subconscious must always be controlled by the conscious, but the imagination can be consciously used to expand our potential on every level. Truly, "It's *all* in your imagination."

Visualization

Visualization is the faculty of imagination which can actually see inwardly as well as outwardly. This faculty is more active in some than in others, but like anything else, it can be developed. While imagination includes the entire scope of inner experiencing on every level—material, physical, emotional, mental, personal, spiritual and universal—visualization is limited to actually seeing the desired good, and ourselves in relationship to it. Imagination is the entire creative area of the mind; visualization is its most important part.

THE FILM IN YOUR MENTAL CAMERA

The subconscious reproduces the pictures that are given it. The subconscious can be likened to the film in the camera. The picture which the camera—you—sees, is impressed upon the film—the subconscious—when the shutter—will—is snapped. The film is developed and an exact reproduction of the picture appears. This is exactly what happens when you impress pictures on the subconscious. We always believe what the eye sees outwardly, don't we? If we also believe what we see inwardly, we have discovered the secret of controlled experience. If we can vividly visualize inwardly what we want to see, there will be a proportionate diminishing of what we don't want to see outwardly.

Two types of visualization

There are two major types of visualization: (1) Inwardly seeing a picture that you consciously place in your mind, and (2) Becoming still and letting a picture form in your mind. If either of these are vividly perceived and believed, a strong image will be impressed upon the subconscious where it will be developed, and what you saw as a picture will appear as object and experience.

You may use this technique in any area of your life—yourself, your family, your home, your business, your experience—anything. Get the picture, believe in its reality, sustain it, and it will appear. This is the creative law.

TREATMENT IS USING YOUR MIND CONSTRUCTIVELY

Having become acquainted with our own mind and how it works, let us continue to learn how to use it through Science of Mind Treatment.

There are any number of ways to use the Science of Mind Treatments such as this next one. Read them, think about their statements, repeat them out loud, say them with someone, learn them, or write them out. The important thing is to spend sufficient time with the Treatment so that it becomes impressed deeply upon your mind. Make each Treatment your very own.

Personal Science of Mind Treatment for Intelligent Action

I give thanks for my magnificient mind today. I give thanks for Intelligence and the capacity to use it intelligently with my mind. My mind is a gift from God, given to me to use. I learn what it is, how it works, and how to use it intelligently, wisely and well. I learn to think clearly and with purpose. When I think, the whole world moves.

I am a thinker. I am a knower. Through my mind I become one with the One Mind, and become a co-thinker and co-creator with It. I think with God's mind. God thinks through my mind. The gift of thought is a challenge, a responsibility, and an opportunity. I accept the challenge. I meet the responsibility, and I embrace the opportunity. I am a good steward. I take care of my mental kingdom.

My thought is clear and constructive. I align every thought with the perfection and purpose of the Infinite. I have nothing to do with unworthy, trivial, inferior or limited thought. I think on purpose and with purpose. I am my thought made visible. My life is the expression of my thought. My actions spring from my thought. I determine to engage only in intelligent right action.

I discipline my thought with my will. I decide what I am going to think about, when, and for how long. I choose my thoughts, and concentrate my attention upon them until they are fully implanted in my subconscious. My attention is complete, my concentration is sustained and strong. I activate the creative process with self-contemplation. My mind provides the perfect plan for perfect action and creation.

I see vividly the pattern of all good things. As I visualize the wonder and beauty of the unlimited world of imagination, I see that I can decree what I will and nothing shall be impossible to me. The pictures which I see are all masterpieces. I do not allow myself to look upon anything unseemly. I see only the good, the true and the beautiful. I visualize wholeness at all times.

I give thanks for my creative imagination which enables me to know who I am, what I am to do and what I am to be. I give thanks for the shape of things to come which my imagination presents to me. I give thanks for the world of imagination which makes my actual world more real. I know that God creates through me with my imagination.

Quietly and confidently I go forward into my world, expressing intelligent right action at all times.

And so it is.

CHAPTER 8 SUMMARY

1. By training the conscious mind to assume and use its rightful authority in the creative process, we dissolve negative conditioning and start a new chain of causation.
2. Each one of us carries within him the reality of his own freedom and the means for achieving it.
3. The more clearly we understand our mental equipment, the more effectively we can use it.
4. Inductive reasoning is a step-by-step process leading up to an unknown answer.
5. The more evidence that is logically presented, the more the conscious mind will be convinced that something is so.
6. In deductive reasoning, we accept a certain premise unequivocally, and base all subsequent thought, belief and conclusions upon that basic premise.
7. The conscious mind can reason either inductively or deductively; the subconscious can reason only deductively.
8. Our thought is the invisible form of that which is to come.
9. We become that which we concentrate on by taking on the characteristics of that which we contemplate.
10. Imagination is unlimited thinking.

Chapter 9

How the Science of Mind Makes You Happy

"You know, I don't have a problem in the world, Dr. Curtis," the prosperous looking businessman began as he sat across my desk from me.

"I'm glad to hear that," I laughed. "And I might add, it's most refreshing. Most people who come to see me are loaded with problems."

"I know that," he replied, "That's why I'm here."

"But you just said...." As I took a long, steady look at my patient, though I did not complete the sentence. There was no point. His opening remark was simply a lead-in to tell me what his real problem was. It would come, so I waited. He continued.

"As I said, I have no problems. I have a going business, I'm solid financially, I have a good marriage, I have plenty of time to do what I want, but still...." He paused and laughed nervously as if ashamed to go on.

"Yes?" I encouraged him.

"Still I'm not happy. Dr. Curtis, what in the world is the matter with me? Can you help me?"

"Let's work together on it, and we'll see. I'm sure we'll work something out. Go ahead, fill me in on the deatails, Bill."

THE DILEMMA OF SUCCESS

Bill's story was similar to many I have heard during twenty years of counseling with troubled people from all walks of life. He was suffering from what I call the success syndrome, which can be pretty well summed up by a question which the greatest of counselors asked 2,000 years ago: "What shall it profit a man, if he shall gain the whole world, and lose his own soul?" (Mark 8: 36)

Of course Bill had not lost his soul in the theological sense, but he had certainly lost himself. In his headlong drive for success and material achievement, he had lost track of some basic values. He could have been the model for a satirical cartoon which appeared in a popular magazine recently:

An obviously affluent and worldly, successful middle-aged man was sitting staring glumly into space, oblivious of everything else except his misery.

"Look at him!" his wife exclaimed to a friend. "Just look at him! For years he did nothing but work. He struggled, he fought, he stepped on anyone who got in his way, he wouldn't let anyone or anything stop him. He clawed his way to the top! And now . . . he doesn't like it at the top!"

LAWS OF LIFE

If we would be happy, we must obey the rules that bring happiness. Of primary importance is the Golden Rule: "All things whatsoever ye would that men should do to you, do ye even so to them; for this is the law and the prophets." (Matt. 7: 12) Our happiness can never be achieved at the expense of others, nor can we expect to be happy unless we obey the two basic commandments:

> Thou shalt love the Lord thy God with all thy heart and with all thy soul and with all thy mind. This is the first and great commandment. And the second is like unto it. Thou shalt love thy neighbor as thyself. (Matt. 22: 37–39)

WHAT IS MEANT BY THE LOVING HEART

"Love your enemies, bless them that curse you, do good to them that hate you, and pray for them which despitefully use you, and persecute you." (Matt. 5: 44)

Explicit directions? Yes. Difficult to practice? Of course. Impossible? Definitely not. It can be done. The choice is ours. We can do these things if we want to, and if we think we can. Some choose the other way: "An eye for an eye, and a tooth for a tooth." (Matt. 5: 38)

How hate produced ulcers

"I love to hate!" was the startling snarl which came from the writhing sufferer on the hospital bed. "I hate that miserable person with every part of me. I'll kill him! I'll kill him!"

There was little doubt that the sick man meant what he said. Larry had called me to come to his bedside prior to major surgery—his third in two years—this time to remove most of what was left of his stomach as the result of a spreading ulcer. From the venomous utterances that came from him, it was obvious that he was consumed by hate. His mind and heart were obsessed with it; his body was eaten up with it. This he readily understood and admitted.

"Is it worth it?" I asked.

"Yes, it is!" he rasped. "I'm living just to get even with him. I'll kill him if it's the last thing I do!"

"Come now," I remonstrated.

"I mean it!"

Larry's deep feelings were understandable. I knew the story. He and a buddy had come to California a few years before to seek their fortune. They pooled their funds and started a business together on a small scale. It prospered from the beginning. The two partners were close friends and trusted each other implicitly—perhaps too much so as it turned out. Eventually Larry's partner not only squeezed him out in a tricky legal maneuver, but also absconded with $35,000 of Larry's money.

That had been nearly four years before, and since that time Larry had lived for revenge. He had recouped his modest fortune in a new business venture, but his hatred for his former friend continued.

The hatred soon produced the ulcer, and the several surgeries followed. But Larry did not change—ever. He knew the lesson, but he refused to learn it. He could have, but he preferred to hate rather than love and live. He survived his surgery and was given his chance, but he died less than a year later after the fourth operation. His hatred killed a man, but not the one he intended.

THE PRACTICAL SCIENCE OF LOVE

"I don't see what that has to do with me," Bill protested when I told him about Larry. "I just came to see you because I thought you could help me find happiness. I don't hate anybody."

"Of course not," I admitted. "I was just making a point."

"You mean that what a man thinks or feels can actually do that to him?"

"You've just heard one example. I could give you others."

"Never mind. I'll buy it. I can't promise to love everybody but I'm surely not going to hate anyone either. Can the Science of Mind actually help me love people—all people?"

"If you want to, and if you are willing to work at it."

"What do I do?"

"Start by getting interested in people. Look for the good in them. Think about what you can do to help them. Put yourself in their place. Try to understand them. You'll get so interested in them that you'll forget all about yourself. You want to be happy. This is one of the best ways to achieve it. It is called the yoga of love."

Then I told him an ancient apocryphal story illustrating the steps necessary in developing true love and compassion as follows.

Evolution toward love

A man was sitting in his garden reading in the cool of the evening when an intruder attacked him, knocked the book aside and struck him over the head. Outraged, the man pursued his assailant, overtook him, and the two engaged in a fierce fight in which both were severely injured. As he nursed his wounds and broken bones, the man decided there must be a better way to deal with such situations. He seriously considered the instruction:

"Whosoever shall smite thee on thy right cheek, turn to him the other also." (Matt. 5: 39)

"Nonsense!" he exploded. "If anybody strikes me, they are going to get it right back!" He groaned with pain as his exertions agitated his wounded body. "But still. . . ." He decided to at least handle the situation differently if he were ever attacked again. He would control himself.

As time went by, he practiced self-control and cultivated feelings of interest and goodwill toward all people, even those whom he had previously disliked. His life was filled with peace and well-being.

Many years later he was again sitting in his garden reading a book in the cool of the evening, when he was again attacked. He instinctively reacted with shocked rage and started to pursue the intruder. As he was about to attack, however, he regained control of himself and stopped. He was angry, puzzled and hurt, but he decided not to compound the error as he did before. He returned thoughtfully to his garden.

HOW THE SCIENCE OF MIND MAKES YOU HAPPY

"Why do these things happen to me?" he pondered. "Why should I be attacked? What can I do about it? I know it says, 'Love your enemies, bless them that curse you, do good to them that hate you,' but why should I have enemies, and why should others curse me or hate me or treat me badly? I haven't done anything to deserve such treatment. Or have I?" He became still and meditated long into the night.

Attaining grace

The years passed, and the man devoted his life to cultivating the virtues, doing good deeds, and helping his fellow man. He "waxed strong in spirit, filled with wisdom: and the grace of God was upon him." (Luke 2: 40) He was kind and compassionate, revered and loved by all. He was a thoroughly good man.

Again, he sat in his garden reading a book in the cool of the evening. This time, however, as the assailant struck the book from his hand and lifted his hand to strike his victim, the man turned and looked directly into his eyes, openly and unafraid. The attacker's striking blow was arrested in mid-air. A puzzled look came over his face. He stood transfixed for a long moment, held by the compassion and love of his intended victim. Finally he turned and started to run, but the man caught him, put his arm around his shoulders, sat him down, talked with him, served him food, and ministered to his needs. He loved the man, and the two former antagonists enjoyed the cool of the evening together in complete peace.

DARE TO LIVE BY LOVE

"That's quite a story," Bill remarked as I finished.

"Yes," I agreed. "It's pure Science of Mind, teaching the relationship between what we think and feel and what happens to us."

"I still don't see what kept the attacker from hitting him the third time."

"That's the whole point of the story. Cause and effect. When the man became filled with love and goodness—when his heart was completely free from hostility—it was impossible for the negative and destructive action to touch him. Just like the holy man who is not attacked by the savage beasts. Most destructive actions come from fear. 'Perfect love casteth out fear.'" (I John 4: 18)

Personal Science of Mind Treatment for Love

Love is God in action. Love is the sum total of all constructive thoughts and feelings. Love is the most important thing in the world. I learn to love.

My heart is cleansed of all destructive feelings and attitudes. I love. I am free from all hostility. I love. There is no resentment or anger in me. I love. I forgive freely. I love.

I see God shining from every person. I love my neighbor as myself. I am filled with love. Love flows forth from me and blesses my world and all who are in it. I am a loving person now.

And so it is.

HOW TO RECONDITION FOR HAPPINESS

Bill repeated this treatment after I had written it down for him, and had explained that by repeating affirmative statements, the mind becomes reconditioned.

"Is that all," he asked, "Isn't there more to it than that?"

"A great deal more. But this is where we start."

"I'll do whatever you say."

"Good. You started with a desire to be happy. You see that this happiness will come as the result of what is within you—your consciousness. You also see that your consciousness is developed along constructive lines by your personal attention to what you think, feel, say and do. You must discipline your mind to think and feel along constructive lines—and with love. This is going to entail some change, but you are willing to change, aren't you—especially since this is the way to achieve your objective of happiness?"

"You know I am."

The importance of accepting treatment as workable

"Good. Repeat this short treatment several times each day until it gets deeply ingrained in your mind. Believe it. Accept it. Then work out similar affirmative statements of your own. Write them down. Also in your prayer and treatment periods, let the thoughts and feelings flow spontaneously from your heart into words."

"Dr. Curtis, I'm a practical man. I also have to *do* something. What can I *do*?"

"Be yourself. Do what comes naturally. You will naturally express what you are. If you are filled with love, you will express love. A consciousness of love will be your control and your guidance. As St. Augustine said, 'Love God, and do as you please.'"

We had talked through most of the afternoon. We shook hands as Bill started to leave.

"Dr. Curtis, you've opened my eyes to things I've never even considered. What you say makes sense. When can I see you again? I'm going to need you to guide me through this."

We set up a series of appointments over the next few weeks. Bill was already a changed man.

THE KINGDOM OF HAPPINESS IS ALWAYS WITHIN YOU

Bill could well be each one of us. His quest for happiness is the same as yours and mine. The blockages are always the same, but so is the solution. "The kingdom of Heaven (happiness) is within you . . . as a man thinks, so he is. . . ." Find the kingdom of personal dominion and you will be as happy as you make up your mind to be.

Our individual and group happiness is the direct result of the inner life which each of us must develop for himself. We are intended to be happy. The Science of Mind has been developed for the purpose of helping everyone strengthen those inner attitudes which will bring us into focus with God's Infinite Plan—the Kingdom of Heaven expressed in this world as happiness within and among its inhabitants.

TREATMENT INSTRUCTION

Use the following longer Treatment just as you have the others in each chapter. Treatment conditions the mind to accept good. The Treatment in itself doesn't make us happy, but it conditions the consciousness to accept happiness. A happy mind makes a happy person.

You may wish to share some of these treatments with someone close to you. Read them over together or to each other. Sharing Treatment is a beautiful way for two or more people to draw closer together. Also, our individual consciousness is amplified, and greater results are achieved when we pray with others.

"Again I say unto you. That if two of you shall agree on earth as touching any thing that they shall ask, it shall be done for them of my Father which is in heaven.

"For where two or three are gathered together in my name, there am I in the midst of them." (Matt. 18: 19, 20)

Personal Science of Mind Treatment for Happiness

Knowing that my happiness comes from within, I seek first the inner wholeness, and I know that all things necessary to produce happiness are added unto me. I know that I am just as happy as I make up my mind to be.

My happiness is not dependent upon person, place, nor thing. Happy people, places and things come into my life because of the kingdom of happiness within me. All things other than the nature of God are dissolved from my consciousness. I am free from all hostility. I am filled with love. Love causes happiness for me and for all people in my world. I am in love with life, and I live it fully. I express love at all times.

My heart and mind are untroubled and unafraid. My entire being is a reflection of Infinite Being. I get out of the way of my own happiness and let the light of Spirit flow through me. God is peace. I am peaceful. God is joy. I am joyful. God is good. I am a good person. God is love. I am loving, compassionate and kind. My consciousness is filled with virtuous qualities because my mind and heart are filled with God.

Today "I will lift up mine eyes unto the hills, from whence cometh my help." (Ps. 121: 1) My guidance comes from within. "He leadeth me in the paths of righteousness for his name's sake. Surely goodness and mercy shall follow me all the days of my life; and I will dwell in the house of the Lord forever." (Ps. 23: 3, 6)

I give thanks for my complete and perfect happiness. I give thanks for the privilege of making others happy. I give thanks for the kingdom of happiness which is available to all. I give thanks for this happy world. I live my happiness now and always.

And so it is.

CHAPTER 9 SUMMARY

1. If we would be happy, we must obey the rules. Our happiness can never be achieved at the expense of others.

2. The two basic requirements for happiness are a heart free from hate and a mind free from worry.
3. If you want to be happy, forget yourself and get interested in people. Look for the good in them, think what you can do to help them, and try to understand them.
4. For every effect there must be a cause; for every cause there must be an effect.
5. The Science of Mind teaches the relationship between what we think and feel and what happens to us.
6. Destructive actions come from fear. Eliminate fear with love and faith.
7. When we repeat affirmative statements, the mind becomes reconditioned.
8. Discipline your mind to think and feel along constructive lines, and with love.
9. Our individual and group happiness is the direct result of the inner life which each of us must develop for himself.
10. The Science of Mind strengthens those inner attitudes which bring us into focus with God's Infinite Plan for man.

Chapter 10

How the Science of Mind Makes You Healthy

THE name was the same, but I didn't know that the man was *the* famous George J. until he walked into my office.

There was no doubt about it. The eyes were haunted and tortured, but they were set in the same handsome face which had shown from thousands of silver screens in thousands of theatres since the time of my youth. It was now withered and lined, the mouth and chin were weak and flabby, the hair was straggly and gray, the shoulders were slumped and defeated, the body inert, but there he was—George J., former matinee idol, heart-throb and all-around hero, now a spectacular ruin.

How had it happened, and why? In my profession I am accustomed to dealing with all manner of human problems and tragedies without letting them affect me, but I felt real shock and hurt as I looked at George. No one likes to see his idols tumble. This one had fallen, or was unmistakably tottering. I recovered my composure quickly and welcomed my patient.

"Mr. J., how good of you to come to see me," I greeted him. "I've wanted to meet you for years!"

"Why?" he grunted hostilely. "Why would you want to meet me?"

Instantly I knew the problem. George J. was a hurt man—mentally wounded and wanting to die.

He looked at me sullenly for a good minute, then, great wracking sobs shook his body as he cried uncontrollably. I put my hand on his shoulder, but otherwise left him alone. I was otherwise occupied. I was praying—giving an affirmative spiritual treatment for my patient. I was knowing the truth about him—seeing the wholeness within him—integrating the whole man in my own consciousness—doing the kind of work developed by the Science of Mind and which has healed and helped so many. This time of silent inner knowing—true prayer—is the essence of our therapy. Spiritual Mind Treatment is the practice of the Science of Mind. It is the method by which healing and demonstration are accomplished. The response from my patient was immediate, as it usually is.

"Sorry to lash out at you like that." The voice was still mellow and rich, even though somewhat weakened. "Please forgive me. Things haven't been going too well for me."

The path of a falling star

Part of George's story was the familiar one of the Hollywood fallen star. Inevitably the day came when the popularity began to wane. Then came the series of bad pictures to complete the cycle. Up one day and down the next. Very few are prepared to ride the toboggan. George was not. He refused to believe that his fans had deserted him. He pursued them by producing his own pictures, and lost a fortune as well as his fans.

Still in his early forties, he broke under the strain. His battered ego led to morbid states of mind, to alchohol, and to escapade. His body reflected the sickness in his soul, and he had been in and out of sanitariums and hospitals for years. He was never seriously ill, but he had never been really well since his fall from the heights.

However, now in his late fifties, the spark of former greatness was still flickering and striving to come to life.

How new life took place

And it did, through the release of the natural life force within him through our counseling and the regular use of Science of Mind Treatment. Like the Prodigal Son, George "came to himself." He returned from the wasted years and became a man again as he recovered from the regrets, hurts and bitterness which had nearly destroyed him.

"There's life in the old boy yet," he exulted as he walked into my office several weeks later under his own power. "Thanks to you, I've come back from the dead. It is so good to have my health back!"

"Thanks to God and to yourself. You two did the work. I just enjoyed the show, and I still am."

"I would never have seen the light if you hadn't turned it on. I'll never be able to thank you enough."

"You might give me some tickets to your new picture," I suggested.

"Movies? What are they?" he laughed. "I wouldn't go near a studio for a million dollars. I've found something a lot better."

"What's that?"

"All right, fellows! Bring it in!" My office door opened, and a beautiful bookcase was brought in.

"I'm sick of seeing your books scattered all over the office," George laughed. "Thought you could use this. So long—see you tomorrow!"

George had made the beautiful piece of furniture with his own hands. Yes, he was well. He had become re-integrated—head, heart and hand. The Science of Mind had helped another person become a whole man.

HOW THE HEALING POWER OF MIND WORKS

There is no limit to the healing power of your mind. Our health comes from the One Mind which is whole. Our individual minds and bodies are our use of the Universal Spirit and Substance which are perfect. Health means wholeness. Wholeness results when we are spiritually, mentally, emotionally and physically integrated. When Jesus healed, he invariably admonished, "Thou art made whole!" (John 5: 14) There is no health or healing without inner and outer balance.

The Greeks taught, "A sound mind in a sound body." This is the basic principle behind health and healing today. The physician, the psychologist, the teacher, and the priest all deal with their specific and necessary areas within the individual, but there is no health unless these areas are all properly related. The Science of Mind is the great modern teaching which brings them all together. Again, remember Dr. Ernest Holmes' definition of Religious Science (The Science of Mind): "It is a correlation of the laws of science, the opinions of philosophy, and the revelations of religion, applied to human needs and the aspirations of man."

HEALTH MEANS WHOLENESS

George J. had lost his physical health in the first place because of the breakdown in his consciousness. He lacked the inner strength and integration to support him when the outer structure of his life came apart. His mental and emotional reaction to catastrophe undermined his physical health. He was unable to "meet with triumph and disaster, and treat those two imposters just the same." (Rudyard Kipling, "If.") The body is tough and resilient, but it cannot stand up indefinitely under the buffeting of discordant mental and emotional states. Something has to give, and it always does. Accompanying carelessness, dissipation and neglect of the laws of diet, exercise and rest also add to the destructive processes of deterioration and degeneration.

HEALING THE WHOLE PERSON

Healing starts when a constructive step is taken on any of the various levels, but complete health cannot be attained and sustained without strengthening and integrating all the levels. Our work with George was accomplished on all levels. The physician continued his attention to the physical body, but the rest of the therapy was through the Science of Mind. Spirit, mind and emotion are all intermingled within the individual consciousness, so it is inaccurate and impossible to separate the therapy for soul, mind and feeling. It is a matter of emphasis at any given point. Eventually they are all brought together to form the whole person.

The healing consciousness

Nature is constantly healing our bodies, repairing and strengthening them without us knowing anything about it. Now, as we treat for healing, we consciously cooperate with the natural subjective process. Treatment is for the purpose of attaining a healing consciousness. This not only heals us, but also heals others with whom we come in contact. Repeat these statements out loud about yourself. After doing this, substitute the name or names of others and repeat the Treatment again. In this way you will be giving *them* a Healing Treatment.

Personal Science of Mind Treatment for Healing

> My faith makes me whole. According to my faith it is done unto me. I know that I am a whole person. I am balanced and strong on every level, spiritually, mentally, emotionally and physically. The life force flows through me and heals me.

My health is evidence of my wholeness. I keep ever before me the image of myself the way I really am—healthy, strong and whole. God is infinite wholeness. I am made in the image and likeness of God. I am perfect, even as my father in heaven is perfect.

I become still and know that the power within me is God. The life-giving power of Spirit flows through me, healing and strengthening me on every level of my being. I am attuned to the perfect pattern that resides at the center of my being. I am in harmony with the eternal laws. The rhythms of Nature regulate my entire system. Divine love, in and through me, heals my soul, my mind, my heart, and my body.

The processes of restoration and regeneration are at work within and through me. I am cleansed and purified in my consciousness and in my body. I am aware of the creative forces and energies of life. Creative Mind works through my mind. Right action is taking place. I keep my heart with all diligence, for out of it come the issues of my life. My subconscious is cleansed of all negative feeling, false belief, and destructive memory. My consciousness is filled with faith, with love, and with truth.

I give thanks for my wholeness today. I am filled with the vital energy of life. I realize and express my dynamic potential. The free, full flow of life is surging through my being. I am healed by the action of God's wholeness in my life and in my being.

I am whole. I am healed. I am.

And so it is.

SCIENCE OF MIND FOR HEALTHY PEOPLE

William James called the Science of Mind type of teaching "the religion of healthy-mindedness." Religious morbidity, fear, guilt and superstition have no place in our approach. The Science of Mind is a way of life—a healthy way—a whole way. We are supposed to be healthy. Let's know it, and let's stay that way.

Dr. Harry Gaze, for many years a vigorous crusader for vital health, youthfulness and longevity, used to tell his audiences, "Of course you have to die, but you don't have to die sick." Eventually we will come to realize that we don't have to die, either. Let's make that eventuality possible by doing, feeling, thinking and being those things which establish, maintain and sustain health.

Health is the natural result of balance or ease. Disease is absence of ease. Sickness is absence of health. Correct the cause and healing results. Maintain balance and integration by unification with the original First Cause—God—and health is maintained.

REAL PHYSICAL HEALTH

We have seen that life is made up of laws that must be obeyed if we are to be happy and healthy. These include laws which govern the body—laws of diet, rest and exercise. Break the laws and the laws break us. A body that is improperly fed, used and maintained, and not rested, eventually breaks down.

What we call "race mind" accepts the false belief that the body must weaken and deteriorate with the advance of years. For most, it does, but for some—an increasing number—it does not. Why? Luck—fate—chance? Don't you believe it. The body is under the law of cause and effect just like everything else.

Since our field is the Science of Mind, we are dealing primarily with emotional, mental and spiritual causes. How we think and feel directly affects the body. As for your attention to the body itself, we admonish you to care for it carefully and scientifically. Find out about food, hygiene, scientific exercise and relaxation, and practice the regimens and do the things which are necessary to assist the overall condition of health in expressing itself on the physical level.

Do not pamper your body by paying too much attention to it. It doesn't need artificial care, stimulants, soothings and coddlings if all of the natural matters are observed. Do that which you know is sensible and right, and stop worrying. Stop interfering with your body. Feed it, cleanse it, exercise it, rest it when necessary—then leave it alone!

So much for some of the more technical aspects of health. Let's go on to the areas of consciousness and the health of the whole person.

EMOTIONAL HEALTH

"How are you feeling?"
"I feel bad."
"I don't feel good."
"I'm feeling better."

"I feel great!"

Feeling seems to have more to do with health than we realize. Good feelings tend to produce good health—bad feelings, ill health. There can be no question but that our prevailing mental and emotional attitudes *are* our health. Emotion, expressed or repressed, reflects *directly* into the body. The conscious mind thinks, the subsconscious (feelings and emotions) acts, and the body is acted upon. Undoubtedly this relationship is of vital importance in both regaining or maintaining health.

The key is in learning how to control your emotions. The Science of Mind helps you do this.

A mental healing for physical health

Virginia suffered from heart palpitations, chronic constipation and a skin condition. After receiving no relief from physical remedies, she decided to try the Science of Mind.

During our counseling she told me of the deep feelings of guilt which had plagued her for many years. During the early years of her marriage, she had had an affair with another man. It was not found out, and she had never confessed to her husband, but her life since that time had been filled with fear, guilt and self-condemnation.

She sobbed as she told me the story. "How could I have done such a thing. My husband is the most wonderful man in the world, and he idolizes me. That's what hurts so."

"Hurts, yes—hurts. You have hurt for a long time. Don't you think you've suffered enough?"

"But I have to be punished!"

"Haven't you been? We are punished by our sins, not for them."

"But what should I tell my husband—or should I?"

"The important thing is for you to be a good wife to him."

"Oh, I have been, except for being ill most of the time."

"Then why don't you show him how much you love him by being well."

"Oh, wouldn't I like to! But how?"

"Why not start by forgiving yourself?"

She did, through the Science of Mind techniques of reconditioning the subconscious mind by dissolving the destructive feelings and replacing them with healthy ones. Virginia is now a vibrant, happy, healthy woman, and her ideal marriage is completely happy as a result.

THESE WERE HEALED

Many others have regained their health by cleansing their consciousness of destructive feelings:

Elsie T. was healed of reported cancer as the result of conquering her consuming jealousy.

Jim S. was healed of a painful back condition when he got out from under some of the load of responsibility in his business by learning to delegate authority.

Margaret E. recovered from tuberculosis when she once again took an interest in life after five years of grieving over her dead husband.

Ken B. fully recovered from a near-fatal heart attack and predicted life-long invalidism when he got over his resentment of authority. He now works *with* and *for* his employers rather than against them, and he is constantly promoted to positions of greater authority.

YOUR KEY TO HEALINGS

Reversing the flow of energy at the emotional level is the key to this approach to healing. The thing that makes us sick when used wrongly is the same thing that makes us well when used rightly. The power within creates what it is given to create. The emotions can be controlled and transformed through constructive use of the mind. The mind is cleared and developed through spiritual awareness and attunement.

THE QUALITY OF RADIANT WHOLENESS

Discipline, dedication and devotion help us develop a consciousness of the Presence of God as the source of our health. Discipline the body *and* the mind. Dedicate your desire and thoughts to noble and worthy objectives, and devote yourself to the good, the true and the beautiful, and your world, your body and your entire being will reflect as health the radiant wholeness within you.

As you repeat the following Treatment, you will be forming a mental equivalent of wholeness, which is the source of your health. Treatment defines and strengthens our belief. What we believe determines what we experience. A healthy consciousness insures health—wholeness.

Personal Science of Mind Treatment for Health

I am naturally healthy. I know it and accept it. The kingdom of health is within me. Everything I am and everything I do is an expression of complete and perfect health.

The universe surrounds me with balance, order and harmony. The song of the spheres releases its celestial melody into my soul. I love the Great Law of Unity and the principles by which it expresses in my life. I see wholeness everywhere in Nature. I express and experience health in my self and in my world.

My soul drinks deeply from the great well-springs of Spirit. I am nourished and refreshed as I assimilate the elixir of life which flows forth from the One Source. I am spiritually healthy.

I think logically and clearly. My thoughts are my use of the Infinite Intelligence. My ideas come directly from the One Mind. Reason and logic lead me into the wisdom and understanding which insure healthy-mindedness. I think constructively at all times. I am mentally healthy.

Love fills my heart. Faith strengthens me. Peace envelops me. Confidence steadies me. Joy bubbles forth from me. Enthusiasm expresses my outlook. I am forgiving, kind and compassionate. Considerate of others, I endeavor to be mature in all feelings and reactions. My prevailing emotional attitudes are cheerful and balanced. I am emotionally healthy.

Perfect circulation, perfect assimilation, and perfect elimination express through my body. I am functionally and organically sound. My body reflects the harmony of my soul, the discipline of my mind and the balance of my emotions. Physically pure and strong, I give thanks for my healthy body. I am physically healthy.

Integrated spiritually, mentally, emotionally and physically, I am unified with the currents of the One Life. I am a healthy person now and always.

And so it is.

CHAPTER 10 SUMMARY

1. Health is the result of the uninhibited flow of the natural life force within us.
2. There is no limit to the healing power of the mind.
3. Health comes from the One Mind which is whole.

4. Health is spiritual, mental, emotional and physical integration.
5. Health and healing are evidence of inner and outer balance.
6. Correct inner causes and you will experience outer health.
7. Think, feel and do those things which establish, maintain, and sustain health.
8. Regain your health by cleansing your consciousness of destructive feelings.
9. That which makes us sick when used wrongly is the same thing that makes us well when used rightly.
10. A consciousness of the Presence of God is the source of our health.

Chapter 11

How the Science of Mind Makes You Wealthy

How much are you worth? Suppose someone wanted to buy you, and if you sold, you couldn't have yourself anymore. How much would you ask? What would be your price?

Perhaps you would like a moment to think it over as Jack Benny did in one of his famous radio skits.

"Your money or your life!" threatened the holdup man as he pointed a gun at the famous comedian.

A long silence.

"Well—which is it—your money or your life?"

"I'm thinking it over," retorted Jack in tortured indecision.

You are much more likely to reach the conclusion that your worth cannot be measured in terms of money, and that you wouldn't sell at any price. There is no way to adequately measure the worth of a human being. Life cannot be bought or sold, because it is the gift of God, therefore of infinite worth.

WHAT REAL VALUES ARE

There are always those, however, who overlook the greater for the lesser, and by setting a price upon themselves which is too low, they pay a price which is too dear.

Such is the theme of Goethe's *Faust*, which tells the tragedy of a man who sells his soul to the devil in exchange for wordly gain. The same story is told in more modern times in Stephen Vincent Benet's *The Devil and Daniel Webster.* It has also been the theme of many of the world's great works of literature.

Many of Shakespeare's mighty dramas depict the struggles and difficulties of men and women who lose their way in the labyrinth of worldly involvement because they chose outer values rather than inner. They pursued the false and lost the true.

Real worth is not measured in outer values but by something else. What is this "something else?" Jesus said, "My kingdom is not of this world," (John. 18: 36) and then tells us something of what this kingdom is when he instructs, "Seek ye first the kingdom of God and his righteousness, and all these things shall be added unto you." (Matt. 6: 33)

Insight as to how to find this kingdom comes when we believe Jesus' revelation that "The kingdom of God is within you." (Luke 17: 21) The inescapable need for finding this kingdom as the prime requisite for the worthwhile life is pointed up when Jesus asks, "What shall it profit a man, if he shall gain the whole world, and lose his own soul?" (Mk. 8: 36) and when he declares, "A man's life consisteth not in the abundance of the things which he possesseth." (Luke 12: 15)

INNER REALITY

The inestimable value of the inner reality to the individual life is illustrated when Jesus says:

> Again, the kingdom of heaven is like unto treasure hid in a field; the which when a man hath found, he hideth, and for joy thereof goeth and selleth all that he hath, and buyeth that field. Again, the kingdom of heaven is like unto a merchant man, seeking goodly pearls: Who, when he had found one pearl of great price, went and sold all that he had, and bought it. Again, the kingdom of heaven is like unto a net, that was cast into the sea, and gathered of every kind: Which, when it was full, they drew to shore and sat down, and gathered the good into vessels, but cast the bad away. (Matt. 13: 44–48)

The great need in the individual life seems to be to find this kingdom. Since it has been established that the kingdom is within us, there is little doubt where we should look and what will result.

"When thou prayest, enter into thy closet, and when thou hast shut thy door, pray to thy Father which is in secret; and thy Father which seeth in secret shall reward thee openly." (Matt. 6: 6)

WHAT TRUE PRAYER DOES

True prayer, as we have come to understand throughout this book, is the process by which we become filled with the consciousness of the kingdom—the infinite inner space of our own being—the largely undiscovered realm which is our true abode. To the degree that we penetrate into this kingdom of the spirit, we are wealthy on all levels of expression, because we are releasing a greater potential on every level. We are all potentially wealthy. Knowing it and then experiencing abundance inwardly, is the first step in demonstrating it outwardly. Science of Mind Treatment, properly practiced, coincides with Jesus' instruction about prayer just given.

Treatment is prayer, and all instruction applying to prayer applies to Treatment. Your Treatment is an inner experience. Get quiet inside and out, and enter into the awareness of your own being. In this secret inner experience you develop a conviction of your own worth. Repeat the following statements slowly and with confidence. They are true.

Personal Science of Mind Treatment for Abundance

The Infinite Law of Abundance flows through me. I am the channel of love and blessing through which all good things are expressed.

Quietly now, as I become peaceful and still, I go to that great region within which is the area of great wealth. The Kingdom of God is within me. Not only is God the source of my supply, God is my supply.

The pearl of great price is awaiting my grasp. Great wealth is my possession. I experience greater good than I have ever known. I am filled with life. The free full flow of life emanates from Spirit and enlivens my entire being. I am filled with light. My soul is filled with God and my whole being is filled with light. The energy of abundant life is mine to use and I use it.

I am filled with love. I live to love. I love to live. I live to give. I love to give. I give thanks for my good. I accept it, I use it and I share it—passing my good along to my world and all of the people in it. I hold nothing back for myself alone. All that the father has is mine, therefore all that I have I give to all. I am a good steward of all good. I am a good and faithful servant. I use the riches of life for the benefit of all.

I am filled with power. All power is given unto me in heaven and in earth. God gives me the power to do good. I am king in my kingdom. I have been entrusted with great power. I use it wisely and well.

I am filled with peace. All things proceed from the quiet mind within me. My peaceful thoughts and feelings are my inner recognition of the great continent of peace within me. I experience the peace that passes all understanding.

The beauty of eternal abundant life lies stretched before me in all directions—inward, outward, upward and downward. I see the glory and abundance of the cosmos expressing throughout the entire universe.

Joyously, I give thanks for the abundance of the full life. My heart sings out the glad tidings that the kingdom of abundance is at hand. I experience infinite abundance *now*.

And so it is.

THE LAW OF THE INNER AWARENESS

This is the Master Law of which the Law of Mental Equivalents is one expression. Inner awareness constitutes the entire consciousness. It is the richness of our inner being which determines the fullness of our lives.

We have been talking about the concept of our individual worth, asking the question, "How much am I worth?" We have seen that a true answer depends upon a sense of values that goes far beyond monetary values—far beyond mere human values. To properly evaluate ourselves or any man, we must get into the realm of infinite invisible values. These are intangible, but the evidence of their expression is very tangible. You can't see the Law of Inner Awareness, but you can't miss seeing what it does and what it produces. It is constantly giving form to itself in our lives.

We determine our own worth in direct relationship to the sense of values by which we determine worth. No one can tell us what we are worth, but the world rewards us in terms of the worth we recognize within ourselves. *The Science of Mind makes you wealthy!* **Our wealth is determined not by what we have but by what we are**. No one can ever take from us that which we really are.

This inner awareness is constantly flowing out into manifestation. The reality takes many forms, circumstances and conditions, sometimes even expressing as problem, difficulty and lack. Whether we have or have not is of no importance whatsoever in determining the state of our true worth. This is constantly increasing if we cooperate with the Law of Inner Awareness. Jesus said, "Heaven and earth shall pass away, but my words shall not pass away." (Matt. 24: 35)

HOW TO PROFIT FROM PROBLEMS

Trial, trouble, tribulation, suffering, tragedy, illness, loss and hurt can all be of value in building our inner awareness and worth—our true wealth of consciousness.

I once asked Dr. David Fink, the eminent psychiatrist, what was the most valuable attitude a person could take toward life. Without hesitation he replied, "To be able to say **and mean**, no matter what the outer circumstance of life may be, 'Father, I do give thee thanks for this evidence of thy love for me. It is by this means that I grow. Thank you, Father.'"

This affirmation can turn seeming misfortune into fortune. We transform losses into gain. Disadvantages become advantages. Handicaps become strength. This attitude sustains a constant flow of wealth through our lives. Every experience, good or apparently bad, can present us with another pearl of great price. Every failure is a rung on the ladder leading to eventual success and its attendant rewards.

Learning from our mistakes is one of the most effective ways of increasing our inner awareness, which often leads to outer wealth. Life insures us the privilege of making our own mistakes. We have freedom of choice—probably the most valuable gift God has bestowed upon us with the exception of life itself.

Mental alchemy effective

Alchemy is the process of turning base metal into gold. The folk lore of all nations is rich in tales, legends, and mystic and symbolic allegories and parables relating how elements of lower nature and value can be transmuted into objects of great value. All of these expressions, of course, are veiled teachings of the Law of Inner Awareness.

All of the Scriptures of the various religions of the world are storehouses of this secret wisdom. Jesus taught it freely by calling this inner awareness the Kingdom of Heaven. "The kingdom of heaven is like unto leaven, which a woman took, and hid in three measures of meal, till the whole was leavened." (Matt. 13: 33)

SELF-CONCEPT

He also taught the inestimable value of the self-concept when He said,

> Ye are the salt of the earth: but if the salt have lost his savour, wherewith shall it be salted? It is thenceforth good for nothing but to be cast out, and to be trodden under foot of men. Ye are the light of the world. A city that is set on an hill cannot be hid. Neither do men light a candle, and put it under a bushel, but on a candlestick: and it giveth light unto all that are in the house. Let your light so shine before men that they may see your good works, and glorify your Father which is in heaven. (Matt. 5: 13–16)

HOW CONSCIOUSNESS OF WORTH WORKS FOR YOU

The individual who develops his inner awareness not only becomes of greater worth, but is able to set the creative law into operation and do and procure things of great value. This story is told over and over again in the accounts of the miracles of Jesus. These are all symbolic of the power that flows forth from the individual who develops a consciousness of his true worth.

> And there were set there six waterpots of stone, after the manner of the purifying of the Jews containing two or three firkins apiece. Jesus saith unto them, "Fill the waterpots with water." And they filled them up to the brim. And he saith unto them, "Draw out now, and bear unto the governor of the feast." And they bare it. When the ruler of the feast had tasted the water that was made wine, and knew not whence it was: (but the servants which drew the water knew;) the governor of the feast called the bridegroom, And saith unto him, "Every man at the beginning doth set forth good wine; and when men have well drunk, then that which is worse: but thou hast kept the good wine until now." (John 2: 6–10)

This account indicates that the water, or potential of life, is elevated to valuable expression when it is quickened by an individual who recognizes his true worth. Down through the ages, those who have recognized this power within them have performed miracles and accomplished mighty works.

LET THE POWER USE YOU

The history of the worthy accomplishments of the human race is the record of those who have cooperated with the inner power by letting it flow through them into abundant expression.

We are all familiar with Moses, Buddha, Jesus and other great spiritual leaders who did not use the power so much as they *let it use them by providing a channel through which it could work.* We also are aware of the great humanitarian accomplishments of Lincoln, Ghandi, Schweitzer and others who let the power use them.

Leonardo da Vinci, Michelangelo, and scores of other great artists painted and sculpted that which they saw and interpreted with the inner eye. Wagner, Dante and Shakespeare tapped this inner source when they wrote, just as Bach, Beethoven and Mozart did when they composed their immortal melodies. Emerson became one with the same philosophical stream that nourished Pythagoras, Plato and Plotinus.

HOW TO DRAW ON YOUR INNER RESOURCES

Anyone who has ever done anything worthwhile has drawn upon the inner resources of his own being where the One Power resides.

What others have done, you can do. There are infinite riches within you. As Paul said, "the fruit of the Spirit is love, joy, peace, longsuffering, gentleness, goodness, faith, meekness, temperance..." (Gal. 5: 22, 3)—all aspects of the inner awareness, the source and cause of true wealth.

Note that "longsuffering"—patience and forbearance in the face of obstacles, discouragements and setbacks—is one of our most valuable assets. Life's greatest rewards are reserved for those who earn them, who do not weaken in the face of adversity, and whose patience is not worn out by waiting.

HOW THE PLUS FACTOR BRINGS RESULTS

"It seems that I've never done anything right," Tom told me one day. Everything I do goes wrong. I've tried, Dr. Curtis. Oh, how I've tried...."

"I'm sure you have," I comforted him. "Now let's add something to your effort. Let's work to a plus factor."

"What's that?"

"Your self-concept and the power of your thought."

"My self-concept is pretty low right now."

"That's just the point. So is the level of your thought. Listen to the orders you give your subconscious: 'Everything I do goes wrong.'"

"Yes, but...."

"You said that's the truth. No it isn't! That may be a temporary fact, but it's not the truth. Now all we have to do is to know the truth and get the facts to coincide with it. The truth about you is that you are a capable, successful, prosperous person. This will become a fact when you reverse your thoughts and feelings, your concept of yourself, and your attitudes and expectancies. We'll start with a simple affirmation. 'I am a capable and prosperous person, successful in all that I do.'"

"I am a capable and successful person, successful in all that I do."

"That's it! Now, say it as if you really believe it."

"I don't know if I can believe that, Dr. Curtis."

"You can, and you will. Start thinking about it. Believe it. Act as though it were true. Repeat the affirmation frequently. Keep putting it into the computer of your subconscious mind."

"Computer?"

"The original and best one that was ever invented—the creative mind within you—your subconscious."

"Is that the way it really works—like a computer?"

"Whatever you put into it, is worked upon in detail instantly and comes out in terms of tested experience. The computer only comes up with answers. Your inner mind produces complete results.

HOW TO GET SUBCONSCIOUS AGREEMENT

"Your subconscious knows what your conscious or thinking mind knows. It cannot think by itself. Your subconscious mind does not know the difference between the factually real and the imaginary. It believes whatever you tell it to believe. If through discouragement, you negatively tell it, 'Everything I do goes wrong,' your subconscious creative mechanism will make this come true! If, however, you constructively and convincingly tell it, 'I am a capable and prosperous person, successful in all that I do,' it produces for you results that match your belief."

"It sounds almost too good to be true."

"Well, it isn't. It works. Do it, believe it, and it works for you."

How to turn liabilities into assets

"But how about all of my goof-ups? I've made so many mistakes. How do I forget them?"

"By learning from them and by turning them into assets. Don't be ashamed of your mistakes, just stop repeating them. "They will stop as your thought is reversed from negative to positive. Stop regretting your mistakes now, they are valuable components in the structure of your life."

"You mean my mistakes are really assets?"

"They are. From a remote village in Persia come some of the most beautiful and valuable rugs, noted for the intricacy and the originality of their designs. The unusual effects are brought about because the rug-makers there do not try to undo their mistakes; they simply make them the starting point for a new design, weaving around them and making them an integral part of the pattern. You can do the same thing. Forget about the past and don't worry about the future. Do what you have to do now and all will be well. Remember, 'You are a capable and prosperous person, successful in all that you do.'"

Tom reversed the entire pattern of his life from that moment on. The years of heartache and frustration were forgotten as his recognition of his inner worth coupled with his understanding of the laws of mind and of life led him to fortune and fulfillment.

Tom is another of the increasing number of men and women who find that not only is the Science of Mind the science of spiritual finance, but it is the complete science of successful living in whatever degree you want it to be.

LOVE: THE COIN OF THE UNIVERSAL SPIRIT

The experience of Elsa W. is eloquent testimony to the resiliency and indestructibility of the human spirit. Not particularly blessed by nature to start with, she was weak and sickly as a child. Orphaned when little more than a baby, she was unloved and unwanted throughout her bleak childhood.

School was difficult for her, and because she was forced to work to make her own way, she dropped out before she finished high school and settled into a drab existence of a succession of unskilled jobs. However, there was one thing which brought light and joy into Elsa's life: *She loved people.* She found them interesting and she did all she could to help everyone, on the job and off. Her love and generosity were not always returned, but the more she did for people, the happier she was, whether they returned it in kind to her or not.

Eventually, Elsa found her way into social work, where today she heads a large staff in one of the large metropolitan agencies which has but one purpose—to help people.

However, Elsa found herself only by identifying with that Inner Reality which is in all people. She found herself not so much in others as in That which she had in common with others. Once she was sure of her own identity as a spiritual being of infinite worth, the more she gave to others, the more was returned to her and the more she had to give.

The following Treatment will reveal to you what Elsa found through experience. Treatment is the upward path to spiritual realization. Repeat, ponder, and think about each statement. Your affirmation and inner conviction will reveal to you the true worth of your real self.

Personal Science of Mind Treatment for True Wealth

Father, I do give thee thanks for this evidence of thy love for me. It is through this that I grow.

No matter what comes to me, I know I can and do profit by it. I have learned how to turn base metal into gold. The mystical alchemy of spiritual energy is dynamically active in my life. I profit from everything as I gain from all experience. Failure turns to success, limitation is the first step toward expansion, and every problem is a device for providing glorious solutions.

I am wealthy because I know my true worth. Infinite riches are within. I have the capacity for unlimited expression of good. Good lives in my heart. Nothing exists except thinking makes it so. My thought is attuned to the unlimited abundance of God's kingdom. This kingdom is within me. I am aware of the great riches of the kingdom: love, faith, hope, gratitude, common sense, and a never-wavering constructive approach to life—these are my wealth.

I understand the basis of spiritual finance. I do not need money to be rich, but when I know I am rich with or without money, then I always will have all the money I need. Money is God in action. The action of God as Creative Law is the substance of my life. All that the father has is mine. There is no limit to the riches of the kingdom. All are mine to use and to share. I stake my claim, I expand my consciousness, I receive gratefully, I use wisely, and I share abundantly.

I am a capable and prosperous person, successful in all that I do. I find my greatest success in being a good steward, in taking good care of the great gifts that God has given me:

> O Lord our Lord, how excellent is thy name in all the earth! who hast set thy glory above the heavens.
>
> When I consider thy heavens, the work of thy fingers, the moon and the stars, which thou hast ordained;
>
> What is man, that thou art mindful of him? and the son of man, that thou visitest him?
>
> For thou hast made him a little lower than the angels, and hast crowned him with glory and honour.
>
> Thou madest him to have dominion over the works of thy hands: Thou hast put all things under his feet:
>
> O Lord, our Lord, how excellent is thy name in all the earth! (Psalm 8: 1, 3, 6, 9)

I am a wealthy person now and always.

And so it is.

CHAPTER 11 SUMMARY

1. The value of life cannot be measured because it is of infinite worth.
2. If you set a price upon yourself which is too low, you may have to pay a price which is too dear.
3. The great need in the individual life is to find the inner kingdom of the real self.
4. True prayer is the process by which we become filled with the consciousness of the inner space of our own being, the largely undiscovered realm which is our true abode.
5. It is the richness of our inner being which determines the fullness of our lives.
6. Our true worth is measured in terms that go far beyond monetary and human values.
7. The world rewards us in terms of the worth we recognize within ourselves.
8. Our wealth is determined not by what we have but by what we are.
9. The potential of life is elevated to valuable expression when it is quickened by an individual who recognizes his true worth.
10. The Science of Mind is the science of spiritual finance, the complete science of successful living.

Chapter 12

How the Science of Mind Makes You Wise

"Wisdom is the principal thing: therefore get wisdom: and with all thy getting, get understanding." (Pr. 4: 7)

The purpose of living is to grow out of darkness into light, out of death into life and out of ignorance into knowing. Before we can reach these ultimate objectives we must evolve or consciously move through the various stages through which intelligence expresses. The tool which we are given to do this is the mind. Its mode of expression is intelligence.

UNIVERSAL MIND: SOURCE OF ALL KNOWLEDGE

All things proceed from the One Mind which is Infinite Intelligence. Our individual minds are cells within the One Mind—each cell capable of unlimited expansion until it becomes one with the One. Evolution moves us in this direction, but evolution must be assisted by our conscious cooperation if we are to attain our full potential in consciousness—wisdom and understanding and beyond. The destiny of each of us is to experience our personal mind as one with Universal Mind. As Paul admonishes, "Let this mind be in you, which was also in Christ Jesus" (Phil. 2: 5), indicating that the attainments of the Master were attributable to the wisdom and enlightenment that came to him from the One Mind.

THE ANATOMY OF MIND

As we have seen, intelligence is available to us. Consciousness is what we do with it. The business of life is to cooperate consciously with Infinite Intelligence in attaining higher and higher levels of consciousness. This movement is progressive. We will call this structure "The Anatomy of Mental Action," listing its levels and then discussing each one in turn:

INTELLI-GENCE
(*Potential*)

1. Thought
2. Knowledge
3. Information
4. Ideas
5. Concepts
6. Opinions
7. Convictions
8. Attitudes
9. Wisdom
10. Understanding
11. Vision
12. Imagination
13. Intuition
14. Inspiration
15. Meditation
16. Contemplation
17. Attunement
18. Awareness
19. Enlightenment
20. Illumination

CONSCIOUS-NESS
(*Attainment*)

THOUGHT

Thought deals with the entire process of cerebration or brain action: thinking, reasoning, selecting, comparing, measuring, mulling, musing, observing, summarizing, concluding, correlating, synthesizing. Logic is essential to the intellect. Whether the thinking mind is reasoning inductively or deductively, what it deals with must be acceptable to it. It must make sense to us or we will reject it.

If we are to attain wisdom and understanding, we must free our thought from the bondage of the "foolish consistency" which Emerson says is "the hobgoblin of little minds." We are what we think, therefore our thoughts must be kept on a constructive level if we are to move toward our goal of wisdom and understanding.

True thought is much more than just thinking. It is the original stuff out of which consciousness is built.

KNOWLEDGE

"Knowledge is power."

"Knowledge is the beginning of wisdom."

The proverbs of all civilizations attest to the importance of knowledge as the first step in attaining anything. We are not likely to achieve power or dominion without having knowledge. "To know a thing is to own it," says the popular expression.

Since we must put forth effort to acquire knowledge, we are likely to negate its importance and try to take shortcuts. We often try to do things without prior knowledge and then rail against "outrageous fortune" because we fail. "You don't get something for nothing," could well be changed to, "You don't get anything without knowledge."

It might be well to remember the Chinese definition of Luck:

    L—ABOR
    U—NDER
    C—ORRECT
    K—NOWLEDGE

INFORMATION

Facts, figures, details and statistics all come under the heading of information. We should have all necessary information at our fingertips either by knowing it or by knowing where we can find it. The gathering and dispensing of information constitutes one of mankind's largest occupations.

So vast is the information available and necessary that, capacious and unlimited though man's memory is, it has been found necessary to invent memory and information-giving machines called computers. As interesting and valuable as these are, they will never replace the human brain and its senses in acquiring information.

We think of these senses as touch, taste, smell, sight and hearing, which give us vast amounts of information. However, beyond these is the "sixth sense" and other powers which we are covering in this chapter—all vital areas of study in the Science of Mind.

We gather information through observation, study, instruction, experience, exchange, experimentation and reasoning, but there are still other ways—the ways which develop insight—such as penetration directly into the Mind of God and receiving the true information known there. More about these other ways as we go along.

IDEAS

"What an idea!"

"Where did you get that idea?"

"Wait a minute! I have an idea."

Where do ideas come from? They come and go, usually, without any direct effort on our part. Sometimes these ideas are completely original on our part, unrelated to anything we ever heard of or thought about before. At other times they are a new arrangement or conclusion based upon prior ideas as thoughts.

So important are ideas that creative people sometimes go for days looking for *an* idea. Some companies employ "idea men" whose only function is to think up new ideas. Groups sometimes hold "brain-storming" sessions for the purpose of coming up with ideas.

One explanation of the origin of ideas is that "they come from God." True, but so does everything else, so we need to know how. They come in three ways: (1) From the conscious or thinking mind which correlates previous thoughts and ideas; (2) From the subconscious, which feeds ideas computer-like to the conscious mind; and (3) From the higher, or "superconscious" mind, which is the area of the individual mind which is a direct expression of Spirit, Infinite Intelligence—Universal Intelligence.

From whatever level they emanate, ideas are most important. They come most readily when we are receptive to them. A state of expectant relaxation is the proper attitude. As an Oriental proverb states, "All things proceed from the quiet mind."

CONCEPTS

A concept can be that which leads up to the idea, or it may be that which results from an idea or series of ideas. A concept is an idea, but all ideas are not concepts. Just as an idea is a sort of "super-thought," concepts are "super-ideas."

For example, someone long ago had the idea that there was a relationship between the thoughts and feelings of an individual and the state of his physical health. From this idea, the "sound mind in a sound body" concept was born, and continues to this day as the basic concept of psychosomatic medicine and of spiritual mind healing as practiced in the Science of Mind.

Concepts are most important because they actually form our philosophy and our approach to life. For instance, from the idea that all people are hostile because of one or a series of seemingly confirming experiences, a man forms the concept of a hostile world and even a hostile universe and responds accordingly with fear and a sense of rejection. This, of course, is a false concept, but it affects and forms the entire life of this person. Fortunately, the reverse concept can be formed to coincide with Truth. What we believe becomes true for us.

As a concept is an organized unity of thoughts, ideas, and conclusions formed from experience, the relationship of concepts to consciousness is obvious. Our concepts form our lives.

OPINIONS

An opinion is what we think about a particular thing. Sometimes they are arrived at through logic, but more often they are the result of emotions engendered by experience and previous conditioning. Our opinions are our beliefs and may or may not be true, just as with our concepts. For instance, an individual's opinion and/or the public opinion may be overwhelmingly in favor or against a certain issue, but this has nothing to do with whether the issue is good or bad. It simply indicates what is thought about it.

We usually follow the dictates of our thought, so it behooves us to form our opinions wisely. "Keep thy heart with all diligence; for out of it are the issues of life." (Pr. 4:23) We must guard our opinions, because they can be swayed by outside persuasion or by giving way to our weaknesses and lower nature.

For maximum effectiveness, our opinions should be formed wisely from a combination of logic, reason, inner guidance, and conclusions reached from the highest and best feelings within us. Insofar as possible, opinions should be formed without prejudice.

CONVICTIONS

Thought + Feeling = Conviction. We reach a conviction when our thoughts and feelings agree. Strong conviction is the expression of faith. When we completely feel what we had previously thought, we have conviction. Conviction is power; it integrates our entire being and moves it forward toward accomplishment. Conviction results when there is complete agreement between the conscious mind and the subconscious.

The power of conviction within

Arnold seemed to have all the right ideas, say all the right words, and do all the right things, but he was never able to get anywhere.

Personable and likable, he seemed to have all the ingredients necessary for success. He had no trouble getting jobs, but he had difficulty in holding onto them. He would come on strong in every situation, and appeared to be filled with confidence and enthusiasm. But then things would start to go wrong. Arnold would start to express his dissatisfaction with everyone and everything around him, and constantly complained and made excuses. Finally, when the situation got bad enough, he would either quit or be fired. This pattern repeated itself over and over again.

Finally, Arnold sought help through the Science of Mind. We found that he lacked conviction concerning himself. He had never been able to get his thought and feeling to agree on the same time. He understood this when it was pointed out, and through affirmative treatment we were able to bring about consistent agreement between his conscious and subconscious mind. The result was consistent improvement and accomplishment. When Arnold found agreement within himself, he found it in his world of experience.

ATTITUDES

The nature of our life is determined by our prevailing mental and emotional attitudes. An attitude is the way we look at things. This, of course, is determined by what we think and feel about that particular thing. Our attitudes are also determined by what we think and feel about ourselves. A person with inferiority feelings is likely to have a defensive attitude. A person with spiritual understanding and inner peace will have an attitude of love. Attitudes are the mental and emotional expression of our total consciousness.

Change your attitude; change your world

Maude was one of the most negative people I have ever known. She looked at everything through smudged glasses. Nothing was ever right; nothing could ever be done. A pall of defeat hung over her like a great, black cloud. She walked through life surrounded by smog. People shunned her, and she lived her life in brooding sullenness, and seemingly devoted herself to making others as unhappy as she was.

When she came for Science of Mind counseling, we uncovered a deep hurt within her which caused her to want to get even with others by subconsciously trying to make them unhappy. She was able to understand the reason for her hostile and destructive attitudes and what they were doing to her life.

She embarked upon a definite program of Treatment to reverse her thought and build new attitudes. The going was slow at first, and Maude constantly slipped back into her old attitudes and habits, but gradually she started to change. When she realized that she couldn't continue to blame the whole world for something that had once happened to her, her attitudes changed, and the world's reaction toward her likewise changed.

WISDOM

Human wisdom can be thought of as the culmination or sum total of all of the mental processes which we have covered so far. If we understand the marvelous intricacies of the human mind, monitor them, work to perfect them, and keep eternally at it, we will arrive at wisdom.

We have seen how we are shaped by our thought, knowledge, information, ideas, concepts, opinions, convictions and attitudes. As we discipline these and apply them toward good, we become wise. If they are uncontrolled and unattended we are certain to end up foolish—without wisdom. In the school of life, experience is the great teacher. If we learn the lessons presented to us, we "get wisdom."

"How do I become wise?" asked the student.

"Keep eternally at it," replied the master.

"Oh, Wise One, how may I, too, become wise?" asked another student of another master.

The sage ignored him.

"How do I become wise?" persisted the student.

The teacher walked away toward a river nearby.

"How do I become wise?" shouted the aspirant, as he pursued him.

The wise man reached the edge of the water.

"Give me wisdom!" demanded the young man.

The old man grasped the young one's head and held it under the water. The youth struggled to come up, but to no avail; the teacher held him fast. As his efforts to free himself became feebler and feebler, the wise one brought him to the surface.

"What did you want more than anything else when you were under the water?" he demanded.

"Air! Air!" gasped the student.

"Exactly," confirmed the wise man. "When you want wisdom as much as you just wanted air, you will attain it."

Since the teachings of experience play such a large part in developing wisdom, we usually associate wisdom with age. This is not necessarily so. There are some wise younger people, just as there are many foolish older ones. However, wisdom certainly demands maturity.

"Wisdom is the principal thing: therefore get wisdom." (Pr. 4: 7)

The following Treatment is to develop wisdom. Of course, we don't become wise just by giving a Treatment about it, but through these affirmations we plant the idea of wisdom and open our consciousness to the potential and the development of it. Besides, we are wiser than we know. Treatment opens the way for our natural wisdom to unfold.

Personal Science of Mind Treatment for Wisdom

I open my mind and heart to the instruction of the One Mind. Divine Intelligence flows into my consciousness. I am instructed and guided by Infinite Wisdom as it reveals itself to me. I am receptive to Wisdom, I desire Wisdom, I seek Wisdom, I develop Wisdom.

I cleanse my thoughts and feelings so that my mind is clear and pure and my heart warm. I correlate my storehouse of knowledge and information so that my ideas may be formed with wisdom. I am ever receptive and grateful for the flow of ideas from God's mind into mine. My concepts and opinions are based upon Truth. I am free from bias and prejudice. I am free from the tyranny of the small mind as I open myself to the influx of the Great Mind. My convictions are based upon my inner certainty that God is all in all, and that to know God aright is life eternal. My attitudes toward life are pure and whole. I am prepared for wisdom.

To the best of my ability, I act wisely at all times. I dwell upon wisdom-making thought. I speak words of wisdom, and I act wisely at all times, guided by the inner wisdom which comes from my real self. I am a wise person now.

And so it is.

UNDERSTANDING

". . . And with all thy getting, get understanding." (Pr. 4: 7)

Understanding is how we use our wisdom. Understanding makes wisdom a living reality. Wisdom + Love = Understanding. An understanding person expresses both wisdom and love. These two together give us balance. Balance and maturity are essential if one is to be truly wise.

The Science of Mind is the science of understanding. It teaches us how to use the laws of life. The wise man knows what these laws are. The understanding one knows how to use them. The greater part of wisdom is in using it wisely. Understanding is knowing how to do this. Understanding could be described as knowing what to do, when to do it, how and where.

Importance of discrimination

Discrimination is one aspect of understanding. It is an inner knowing. Krishnamurti says, "There are two kinds of people in the world, those who know and those who don't." But just as we can become wise if we want to, we can become understanding also. The purpose of the Science of Mind is to develop understanding and how to use it.

Understanding of ourselves, of God, of the universe, the world, and the relationship between them, all of which we dealt with in Part I of this book, help us to be more understanding of our fellow human beings who are on this journey with us.

Empathy

"Never judge a man until you have walked a mile in his moccasins," says an American Indian proverb.

"Judge not, that ye be not judged," (Matt 7: 1) admonishes the Master.

Both of these statements instruct us to develop that understanding known as empathy—the expression of love by identifying ourselves with another person and knowing him from the inside out. Empathy is becoming one with a person. When we can do that we will understand him. It is wise to try. There is no substitute for the understanding heart.

YOUR INFINITE POTENTIAL

We have shown how wisdom and understanding can be developed through proper development and use of our mental and emotional capacities. This brings us to the starting point of exploring the further potentials of consciousness by developing and using the second ten areas in the Anatomy of Mental Action: Vision, Imagination, Intuition, Inspiration, Meditation, Contemplation, Attunement, Awareness, Enlightenment and Illumination. These will be dealt with at the very end of the book in Chapter 16, of Part IV.

But let us not wait. Let us begin right now to develop our potential for wisdom and understanding by devoting ourselves to mastering the principles of the Science of Mind. It is largely common sense applied to every level of being, knowing and doing. We all know more than we think we know. Let us dissolve the cloud of unknowing and develop true wisdom and understanding:

> Whether there be prophecies, they shall fail; whether there be tongues, they shall cease; whether there be knowledge, it shall vanish away. For we know in part, and we prophesy in part. But when that which is perfect is come, then that which is in part shall be done away. When I was a child, I spake as a child, I understood as a child, I thought as a child: but when I became a man, I put away childish things. For now we see through a glass, darkly; but then face to face: now I know in part; but then shall I know even as also I am known. (I Cor. 13: 8–12)

TREATMENT DEVELOPS UNDERSTANDING

Some understanding comes through experience and natural unfoldment, but most of it must be developed by conscious discipline and application. We become an understanding person by developing understanding.

In this Treatment, declare that you **are** understanding. Know that you are an understanding person. Be understanding.

Personal Science of Mind Treatment for Understanding

My wisdom blossoms forth into understanding. I learn to use my wisdom wisely and well. I open my heart to love as I have opened my mind to wisdom. As wisdom and love grow in my consciousness I develop true understanding. Balance and maturity unfold in my mind and in my soul.

The great laws of life reveal themselves to me. I know that all is Law, but all is Love. I perceive the workings of the Infinite through all creation. Through experience, self-discipline and personal application, I school myself to learn and apply the principles of Truth. Life is my school. God is my teacher. Experience is my course of study. I know not only "what," but "how." This is my understanding.

I understand what there is to know and how to know it. I ask, I seek, and I find. I study, I observe, I think and I reason. I probe deeply into the mysteries of life. Nothing escapes my probing mind. I absorb the wisdom of the universe, and I express it with understanding and love. That which I need to know, I learn. I am guided to do that which I am to do, and I am instructed in how to do it.

I understand that God dwells at the center of all things. God lives in the heart of all people. My heart beats in rhythm with the heart of the Universe. Love is the bond which unites me with all mankind. This enables me to understand others and to relate myself to them with empathy and compassion. I understand how to help others and how to cooperate with the Laws of Spirit for the good of all.

I thank God for common sense—for knowing what to do and how to do it. I give thanks for a consciousness filled with love, wisdom and understanding. I live, I love, I learn, I grow, I know, I understand. I am an understanding person now.

And so it is.

CHAPTER 12 SUMMARY

1. Our thoughts must be kept on a constructive level if we are to move toward our goal of wisdom and understanding.

2. Knowledge is the first step toward attainment.
3. Ideas come most readily when we maintain a relaxed attitude of expectant receptivity.
4. What we believe comes true. Our concepts form our lives.
5. Opinions should be formed wisely from a combination of logic, reason, inner guidance and conclusions reached from the highest and best feelings within us.
6. Conviction is the result of complete agreement between the conscious and subconscious mind.
7. The nature of our life is determined by our prevailing mental and emotional attitudes.
8. Experience is the great teacher. If we learn the lessons presented to us, we become wise.
9. Wisdom + Love = Understanding.
10. The Science of Mind is the science of understanding.

Chapter 13

How to Use the Science of Mind in Business

"This is a funny business."
"I'm tired of this monkey business."
"What kind of business is this?"
"Mind your own business!"
"Business is terrible."
"Business is good."
"Business! Business! Business!"

We are all in business of one kind or another. We get up and go forward each day, confronted with the infinite possibilities of that day—its challenges and its opportunities—its victories and its defeats—its joys and its sorrows—its profits and its losses. There is no limit to the potential of any given day in this business of living. That is our business—living!

What business are you in—living or loafing—learning or leaning? There is no standing still in any kind of business. Your business must constantly be growing, expanding and making a profit. This is true of our common business—daily living—and is also true of our specific business whatever it may be. The business of the butcher, the baker and the candlestick maker are subject to the same infinite laws to which the universe itself is subject.

PRINCIPLES OF SUCCESSFUL LIVING

There are definite techniques and procedures that we can follow which will keep us in tune with these invisible but active principles—

procedures which will turn failure into success, and put us in line for our full share of life's profits. This book as a whole is dedicated to explaining the principles of successful living. This chapter in particular develops the techniques for sound business success.

Where do we start? Are you a success? If so—good! If not—why not? There are reasons either way. Success or failure are the result of your prevailing mental and emotional attitudes. What we think about all day long is the major factor in the level of our success.

THE ATTITUDE OF SUCCESS

"What are you going to be when you grow up, Sonny?"

"I'm going to be a doctor."

"Wonderful! What kind of doctor?"

"I'm going to go to medical school and get my degree. Then I'm going to specialize in neuro-surgery, and I'm going to be the greatest brain surgeon in the world."

"That sounds very ambitious. Do you think you can do it?"

"Of course I can do it!"

"The competition is likely to be pretty tough isn't it? There are a lot of doctors in that field."

"Those other fellows are going to have to look out for themselves. I'm going to specialize and become the greatest brain surgeon in the world."

There you have it. This young man had the key. He became a success because of the clarity and worthiness of his objective and the positiveness of his attitude. He had to succeed. No other idea ever entered his mind. The clarity of his goal and the intensity of his desire to achieve it were so clear and strong that his prevailing mental and emotional attitudes were completely positive at all times.

Among all the other helpful things it does, the Bible gives sound instruction for business success. In Proverbs it instructs, "Keep thy heart with all diligence; for out of it are the issues of life." (Pr. 4: 23) "As he thinketh in his heart, so is he." (Pr. 23: 7) The principle is unshakable: *Our success in living and our success in business are one and the same, and are both dependent upon our attitudes toward ourselves and toward our business.* Success does not come to us. It comes **through** us.

YOUR ATTITUDE TOWARD YOURSELF

It all starts within your own consciousness. What do you think about yourself? How do you feel about yourself? How do you see yourself? What are you doing about yourself?

If you would use the Science of Mind in business, start right now polishing up your self-image. Your idea about you is the most important factor in your success. See yourself as capable, intelligent, personable, attractive, energetic, enthusiastic and good. Goodness must always go with it. Be sure you see yourself as the kind of person you can like and who likes others and is interested in doing good for them.

Examine your inner feelings. What is really going on inside of you? Look at yourself closely. Get your conflicts and complexes out in the open. Admit your fears and failings, but then start to do something about them. "Be ye transformed by the renewing of your mind." (Romans 12:2) Don't hang on to old thoughts, feelings and attitudes that have been a pain to you and everybody else. Change them. You can decide right now that you are what you want to be as a person and in relationship to your particular sphere of activity. There is no way to keep success from you if you think and feel successful inside. You can if you think you can. Or as has been stated, quoted and requoted so many times, "Whatever you can conceive and believe, you can achieve."

DON'T LOOK WHERE YOU ARE; LOOK WHERE YOU ARE GOING

The business world is full of successes who at one time were looking up to touch bottom. What happened to reverse the tide and move them out of despair and defeat into joy and victory? The answer is always the same: *A change of attitude.*

"I don't know what I am going to do, Dr. Curtis; I'm at the end of my rope. I have absolutely nowhere to turn. I hate to admit it, but I am beaten—whipped, finished. I've had it."

The gray-haired man who sat across from me gripped the edge of my desk, and a shudder shook his slender body as he sobbed out his story.

"Easy now—easy. Let's relax a minute and take a look at the situation. Maybe things aren't as bad as they look."

"They're worse!"

"I know they look that way, but let's give it a try anyway. Let's just sit quietly for a minute and see what happens."

My visitor sat back and relaxed, and we just sat there for a few minutes in the peace of my study and let the healing waves of silence have their way with us. After a time, I spoke a few words of calm and positive assurance as preparation for further discussion. My patient continued.

I had heard it all before—hundreds of times. Only the details differed. It was the familiar story of the businessman who let himself be lulled into the false security of believing that he "had it made."

Without realizing it, he lost the interest, enthusiasm and dedication which had put his business at the top of the heap twenty years before. Since that time he had been coasting, taking everything from the business and putting nothing back into it. He was content to run today's business by yesterday's methods, while in the meantime the rest of the world had orbited into the Space Age with its new methods and advanced techniques.

Since the Science of Mind is a science of practical common sense, we started with an analysis of my patient's personal life. The man came first. It was obvious that a complete overhaul of his mental and emotional attitudes was necessary. Our objective was to reverse the creative process so that it was working constructively instead of destructively. This is what we did. This is what you can do in setting things right in your world and in your business.

A TECHNIQUE TO SOLVE YOUR PROBLEMS

The process is really quite simple. It has to be. The large number of people who seek my counsel in using the Science of Mind in solving business and personal problems requires techniques which get to the core of the problem in the shortest possible time and produce the necessary results. Here are the steps to follow:

1. Make a list of all of the things you have to be thankful for. Take time with this. Think about it. Nothing is too insignificant to be grateful for. Don't forget to list problems and difficulties, too. They are often blessings in disguise. Learn to look at every situation which confronts you—

favorable or unfavorable—and say, "Father, I do give thee thanks for the abundance which is mine."

2. Begin a personal inventory. Make a list of all of your good points. Be thorough about this. Look for those qualities which make you the wonderful person you really are. Avoid false modesty. Be realistic. Enumerate as many favorable characteristics as you can.

3. Now—continue your inventory by taking a good, long, honest look at yourself. See what is going on inside of you. Examine thoughts, feelings, attitudes, actions and habits. Be ruthless in your self-examination. Look for everything that needs changing in order for you to be the wonderful person you really are.

4. Be willing to change. Relax your defense mechanisms. There is no use kidding yourself. Eliminate false pride. Admit your faults, shortcomings and weaknesses, but at the same time start dissolving them and affirming their opposite. Build your self-image according to specifications that are acceptable to your higher self.

5. Sustain this program of examination, action and affirmation until you start to feel joyous, enthusiastic and happy. Keep your attention upon the good, the true and the beautiful. See yourself the way you want to be. The greatest personal and business counselor of all time said, "Be ye therefore perfect, even as your Father which is in heaven is perfect." (Matt. 5:48)

The change which comes about in you as you follow this program of personal reconstruction is usually more than enough to correct all personal and business problems. *When we change inside, the outside has to change.* What you are inside determines how you look at things. "What you are looking for, you are looking with, and you are looking at." (Ernest Holmes) *What we put our attention to always seems real, it always increases, and we always get what we are looking for.*

How a change of attitude saved a business

Nathan proved to be an apt pupil. He came for help and he found it. The change was immediate as soon as he reversed his thought. He saw immediately that the real cause of his personal and business problems was within himself. Shakespeare said, "The fault, dear Brutus, is not in our stars but in ourselves, that we are underlings." (Julius Caesar, Act I, scene 2) But we can always change ourselves. Paul said, "Be ye transformed by the renewing of your mind." (Romans 12:2) As soon as our personal transformation is accomplished, the world around us is transformed.

This is what happened with Nathan. His "new" mind created a new business. Everything that seemed wrong before was actually a stage in the development of his business along different lines. The entire picture revealed itself as soon as his eyes were opened through his new understanding brought about through the techniques of the Science of Mind. The same thing will happen to you. Put this process into operation right now. Your business will reflect the change within you. The sick business will get well. The profitable business will become more so.

HOW TO BLESS YOUR BUSINESS

After we get ourselves in order by a careful monitoring and control of our attitudes toward ourselves and everything in general, it is most important that we examine our attitudes toward our business and our customers. Remember, *rich attitudes produce abundant profits*. We are all in business to make profits. If we are not interested in making a profit, we'd better close up shop and do something else. Remember, there is no standing still in business. There is no such thing as "just getting by." If we are not making profits, we are taking losses. Our business is as profitable as our attitudes are constructive. Some of these attitudes are obvious; others are subtle. My job is to show you how, through the Science of Mind, we can tell the difference and what to do about it.

The Science of Mind is in the "people business," and is concerned with "people" problems and how to solve them. The specific details of conducting your business are left up to you. You will know what to do about them when your mind is clear of the conflicts caused by negative attitudes. The Science of Mind rebuilds your attitudes.

What do you think about your business? How do you feel about it? Remember, these two areas determine attitudes and govern your actions and procedures. These in turn determine your profits or losses. It is all a matter of chain reaction.

WHY YOU SHOULD LOVE YOUR BUSINESS

Your business will return profits to you in direct proportion to your interest in it and your affection for it. Can you imagine a business returning a profit to anyone who ignored it or condemned it? Of course not! So, be sure that you *feel* right about the business you are engaged in. Find reasons to like what you are doing. If you simply cannot, it is obvious that you are in the wrong work. Be courageous! If a change is necessary, make it, so that the creative forces of life are free to produce profits on every level.

What does work profit you?

It is not sufficient just to work to make money. Profits are automatic if we understand the two major reasons for working:
1. Self-Expression
2. Service to Others

Any business which is based upon a proper balance of these two factors always succeeds.

Self-Expression. Find out what you can do best, and do it in the best possible way. Lose yourself in creative action. Love what you are doing. Pour your entire heart, mind and soul into your work. Whatever we do is the image of ourselves translated into form and action. Let every aspect of your business be a flowing forth from the Higher Self. Let the goodness within you take form in your product and in the way you do things. Give of yourself—and Life, through your business, will return this giving a thousandfold.

Service to Others. "The customer is always right" is the smart businessman's recognition that unless he pleases his customers he is not going to succeed. The customer does not want to be coerced, bullied, persuaded, instructed or "sold." The customer is looking for help in terms of the services or the products which you have to offer, otherwise he would not have come to you. Help him. He deserves everything you can give him and do for him. Make your customer king and he will do business with you from now on.

WHAT THE SCIENCE OF SERVICE MEANS

The Science of Mind teaches the science of service. True service is based upon love and giving. Your customer must feel that you care about him. In order for him to feel this, you must *really* care about him. Customers always go where they are loved. Don't you? Love is good business, and besides, it is good for you.

Mr. Albert Gordon, proprietor of Hollywood's "Room at the Top," one of the world's most successful restaurateurs, serves the largest portions that I have ever seen. I have tried for years to do justice to the sumptuous helpings that he sets before me.

"Al, I simply cannot eat all of this food!" I remonstrated one day. "Why do you serve such large portions?"

He laughed, "Did you ever hear of a customer coming back to a restaurant where he didn't get enough to eat?"

I got the point, and after looking at the restaurant full of people and the long line of those waiting for reservations, I was convinced of it. Mr. Gordon and his fine staff have mastered the science and the art of service. They are having a good time doing it and are growing rich in the process.

THE TRUE MEANING OF SALESMANSHIP

Salesmanship is at the heart of all successful business endeavor, just as it is the essence of all successful living. We are all salesmen. We are constantly challenged by the necessity of selling ourselves.

Successful salesmanship, of course, is not really concerned with buying or selling. The science of salesmanship must be based upon the science of being yourself at your highest and best at all times. It is not so much what a successful salesman does or says, as what he is. This in turn is dependent upon what he thinks and feels all day long—what his prevailing mental and emotional attitudes are. *Consciousness is the only reality.* This is the basic teaching of the Science of Mind.

The successful salesman remembers that God is on both sides of the desk. He is the third party in every transaction, and He never works against Himself. *Remember, right where you are, the action of Life—the action of God—is taking place.*

HOW TO PARTICIPATE IN LIFE'S PROFITS

There is no limit to the profits that accrue to those who are sincerely and joyously interested in the business of living, and who give themselves wholeheartedly to it. If we would fully participate in Life's profits, we will

Do more
Make more
Get more
Have more
Give more

We will remember that "All things that the Father hath are mine." (John 16: 15) "It is your Father's good pleasure to give you the kingdom." (Luke 12: 32) "Ask, and it shall be given you; seek, and ye shall find; knock, and it shall be opened unto you." (Matt. 7: 7)

So let's get out and get going! Follow the Science of Mind techniques outlined in this book. Practice them regularly and faithfully, then go forth into your world to do your job. The riches of the kingdom will be your reward.

HOW TO TREAT FOR SUCCESS

Develop your success potential and your business acumen through regular use of these two Science of Mind Treatments:

As we treat first for personal success, we are establishing the cause and laying the foundation for success on every level. We must start by becoming a successful person. As we develop inner attitudes of self-acceptance and recognition of our true worth, we establish a consciousness of wholeness, strength and faith which are the essentials for success. Success is built from within outward. Success is not something that happens to you. You *are* success. Your business *is* successful. The repetition of these two treatments establish this conviction. When we reach inner conviction, outer demonstration is assured.

Personal Science of Mind Treatment for Personal Success

There is an invisible, invincible tide of creative productiveness which flows through all life, creating, maintaining, and sustaining all things in order, harmony and balance. I am one with this productive action of nature. I am one with all good. The Infinite Law of Abundance flows through me. I am the channel of constructive action through which all good things are expressed.

I contemplate the wonders of Nature; I see Infinite Abundance everywhere. The Infinite Intelligence is infinitely productive. The universe is successful on every level. That which is—is —completely—in abundance and wholeness. There is plenty of everything. The air, the skies, the seas, the earth are all teaming expressions of Nature's fertile creativity. The sun rays out its light, energy and life into all creation, and all is well.

I am established in the midst of all of this beauty, activity and expression of Infinite Abundance. I am rich in thought and feeling. I see good around me everywhere. I am strengthened by the vital forces of Spirit that flow through all things. I evaluate myself in terms of all that is good, strong, beautiful and true. I am an expression of the bountiful life which surrounds and indwells me. I am a complete success.

I move ever forward into my Infinite Potential. I am forever free from limitation and restriction. The free, full flow of life makes me a successful person. I am a success inside, therefore I am a success outside. My entire life is a projection of the kingdom of success within me. I am a success in the business of living. My successful life is the source of my successful business.

And so it is.

Personal Science of Mind Treatment for the Success of My Business

My business expresses me. I express the business of life. I am here to live, to love, to learn, to work, to do, to build, to give. "I must be about my Father's business." God's business is my business. My business is God's business. Both prosper, because prosperity is the result of the working of the law of right action.

I have chosen my activity wisely and well. I do what I like to do, and that which I am good at. I love my business. I love to work. I love to build. I love to serve. I am in business to express myself, to do good for others, and to make a just harvest and abundant profit. I give abundantly and I receive abundantly. My business is the channel through which the riches of the universe flow into my experience. My business provides me with a lavish and dependable income, consistent with integrity and mutual benefits. My business is a channel through which the profits of life flow into my life, and into the lives of others.

I am a good businessman. I pay attention to business. I tend the store. I mind the shop. I am always ready to serve. I look for ways to give. I am interested in my work. I love my customers. I believe in my product. I take pride in what I do. I pay attention to details. I use creative imagination in the conduct of my business. I am a good and faithful servant. I am a good steward. I am a successful businessman.

The light and blessings of the Infinite surround my business, increasing and expanding it. All who contact my business are prospered and blessed. My business is a channel of good for all. I give thanks for my wonderful business now.

And so it is.

CHAPTER 13 SUMMARY

1. Success or failure are the result of our prevailing mental and emotional attitudes.
2. Success does not come to us; is comes through us.
3. Your idea about you is the most important factor in your success.
4. The Science of Mind is the science of practical common sense.
5. When we change inside, the outside has to change.
6. What we put our attention to always seems real, it always increases, and we always get what we are looking for.
7. Transform yourself and the world is transformed.
8. Rich attitudes produce abundant profits.
9. Your business returns profits to you in direct proportion to your interest in it and affection for it.
10. Give of yourself and you will prosper.

Chapter 14

How to Use the Science of Mind in Personal Relationships

"I just can't face it again—I can't!" The attractive young woman in her mid-thirties shouted desperately as she sat across my desk sobbing out her story, "I've had twelve jobs in four years. I can't stand another job turnover."

She had been fired; this was really what she couldn't stand. Each time it happened she was hurt and angry. She could never understand why she was asked to leave. She appeared to have all of the qualifications for a good secretary. She was attractive, intelligent, well-trained and highly skilled, but she could never hold a job. She didn't know why, but as she talked with me, she took great pains to explain why the fight with one of the other secretaries had not been her fault, and why she couldn't help it that the assistant manager had never liked her.

Of course not. It is never our fault that other people can't get along with us, is it? What is the matter with people anyway? Why are they the way they are?

HOW TO CHANGE OTHER PEOPLE'S OPINIONS OF YOU

I knew the young woman's problem, of course. She had told me in word and attitude, but how was I to tell **her**? The direct approach would only set her on the defensive. She knew she was right and everyone else was always wrong. I suggested that there was a possibility that the reverse might sometimes be true, but she was adamant. I used the very simple device of calling her two most recent employers for references. Both confirmed what I had discerned. She was a statistic in a conclusion reached by a recent study which revealed that 70 percent of job turnovers are caused by an inability to get along with people.

"I can't believe it's true," she reacted when confronted with the references. "That's just not fair. The other people always cause all the trouble."

"Yes, I know," I consoled her. "But something has to be done about it. Let's see if we can change them."

"Change them?"

"Of course."

"How can we do that?"

This was the only opening I needed. The technique of changing other people is very simple: *We change other people by changing our attitudes toward them.* And as we have seen in previous chapters, when we change our attitudes, we change. And this is the whole point, isn't it? When we change for the better, everything else changes likewise. Try it, for it never fails. It works like magic. This is one of the most practical principles of the Science of Mind.

HOW TO GET ALONG WITH OTHERS

Jesus was the best teacher of human relations who ever lived. Let's look at some of the instructions he gave for getting along with other people and with ourselves. Study these guides carefully and you will see that they all tell us either directly or by inference something to change about ourselves, what we should be, and what we should do if we want to live in peace and harmony with others.

> Therefore if thou bring thy gift to the altar, and there rememberest that thy brother hath ought against thee; Leave there thy gift before the altar, and go thy way; first be reconciled to thy brother, and then come and offer thy gift. Agree with thine adversary quickly, whiles thou art in the way with him; lest at any time the adversary deliver thee to the judge, and the judge deliver thee to the officer, and thou be cast into prison. Verily I I say unto thee. Thou shalt by no means come out thence, till thou hast paid the uttermost farthing. (Matt. 5: 23–26)

HOW TO GET ALONG WITH YOURSELF

When Jesus says that we "shall be cast into prison," he is telling us that we are the ones who must suffer and be held in bondage by our feelings.

Why make ourselves vulnerable to such unpleasant consequences? Why not stop doing the things which cause problems, and start doing the things which help us get along with ourselves and others?

> Judge not, that ye be not judged. For with what judgment ye judge, ye shall be judged; and with what measure ye mete, it shall be measured to you again. And why beholdest thou the mote that is in thy brother's eye, but considerest not the beam that is in thine own eye? Or how wilt thou say to thy brother, Let me pull out the mote out of thine eye; and, behold, a beam is in thine own eye? Thou hyprocrite, first cast out the beam out of thine own eye; and then shalt thou see clearly to cast out the mote out of thy brother's eye. (Matt. 7: 1–5)

Not much doubt about the instruction here, is there? It is simply the law of cause and effect—of reciprocal action. What we give out, we get back. What we think about others is what they think about us, because it is really what we think about ourselves. The law of reflection is explained here by telling us that we see ourselves in others. We try to explain away or avoid facing our faults by assigning them to others. But it never works. It is pointed out very clearly that we can't change others without first changing ourselves. When we get rid of those things which are "hanging us up," blocking our consciousness and generally making us miserable, we will be able to see clearly, and know the truth about ourselves and each other by seeing God in both places and everywhere.

In order to do this, the commandments are the same as for many of the other matters which we have discussed—the very heart of the teaching: "Thou shalt love the Lord thy God with all thy heart, and with all thy soul, and with all thy strength, and with all thy mind; and thy neighbor as thyself." (Luke 10: 27)

WHERE YOUR GREATEST LOVE SHOULD REST

We can't love others without loving ourselves, and we can't do either without loving God completely—that is, loving and desiring good for all of our being—becoming filled with good—love. That is the key, isn't it? Love—that much misused and misunderstood word. Of course, it is more than a word, or even a concept. It is a way of life. It is more than that. Love is God, because God is love.

We are all familiar with the magnificent treatise on love which concludes, "And now abideth faith, hope, love, these three; but the greatest of these is love" (I Cor. 13:13), but we may not be as familiar with this passage in which we learn more about love as the basis of human relationships:

> Beloved, let us love one another: for love is of God; and every one that loveth is born of God, and knoweth God. He that loveth not knoweth not God; for God is love. In this was manifested the love of God toward us.... Herein is love, not that we loved God, but that he loved us.... Beloved, if God so loved us, we ought also to love one another. No man hath seen God at any time. If we love one another, God dwelleth in us, and his love is perfected in us. Hereby know we that we dwell in him, and he in us, because he hath given us of his Spirit. And we have known and believed the love that God hath to us. God is love; and he that dwelleth in love dwelleth in God, and God in him. There is no fear in love; but perfect love casteth out fear; because fear hath torment. He that feareth is not made perfect in love. We love him, because he first loved us. If a man say, I love God, and hateth his brother, he is a liar: for he that loveth not his brother whom he hath seen, how can he love God whom he hath not seen? And this commandment have we from him, That he who loveth God love his brother also. (I. John 4: 7–21)

HOW TO APPROACH YOUR NEIGHBOR

This, of course, is based upon the basic concepts of love and Jesus' code of human behavior based on love:

> Ye have heard that it hath been said, An eye for an eye, and a tooth for a tooth: But I say unto you: That ye resist not evil: but whosoever shall smite thee on thy right cheek, turn to him the other also. And if any man will sue thee at the law, and take away thy coat, let him have thy cloke also. And whosoever shall compel thee to go a mile, go with him twain. Give to him that asketh thee, and from him that would borrow of thee turn not thou away. Ye have heard that it hath been said, Thou shalt love thy neighbour, and hate thine enemy. But I say unto you, Love your enemies, bless them that curse you, do good to them that hate you, and pray for them which despitefully use you, and persecute you; That ye may be the children of your Father which is in heaven: for he maketh His sun to rise on the evil and on the

good, and sendeth rain on the just and on the unjust. For if ye love them which love you, what reward have ye? do not even the publicans the same? And if ye salute your brethren only, what do ye more than others? do not even the publicans so? Be ye therefore perfect, even as your Father which is in heaven is perfect. (Matt. 5: 38–48)

THE SINGLE STANDARD

Quite an order, isn't it? If we are to be happy with others, if we are to get along with them, we are adjured to be perfect. That's all, but no less. Do not worry about what the other person says, does, thinks or feels. That is not our concern. Our job is to be about the "Father's business" of attaining that perfection with which we were created. Nobody ever said that it was easy, but that it was necessary. We must live by the single standard of love. This will take care of everything.

> A new commandment I give unto you, That ye love one another; as I have loved you, that ye also love one another. By this shall all men know that ye are my disciples, if ye have love one to another. (John 13: 34, 5)
> Greater love hath no man than this, that a man lay down his life for his friends. (John 15: 13)

If we engage in double dealing and break the law of love, we then become subject to correction. "Love is the fulfilling of the law." (Rom. 13: 10)

TRUE FORGIVENESS

In the Lord's Prayer we implore, "Forgive us our debts as we forgive our debtors." (Matt. 6: 12) We can only be forgiven as we forgive. We cannot receive anything without first having it in our hearts. We all want love, consideration, respect, and attention. We can't have them without giving them. We frequently find ourselves in a position of begging compassion, understanding and forgiveness from others. Whether we get it or not depends upon our willingness and ability to forgive ourselves and others. "To forgive" means "to give for"—to give new attitudes for old—to dissolve destructive and negative feelings and tendencies with love.

LOVE IS ACTIVE DOING

Love is completely ennobling. It causes us always to act and behave toward others as we would like them to act and behave toward us if the situation were reversed.

We can't just talk about love or even just feel it. Love is an active principle. We must do something about it. Deeds speak louder than words. "By their works you shall know them." When we are unable to help ourselves, we depend upon the love and compassion of others to help us out. Love is the only true religion—the religion of meaning and practical action.

We must have love in our hearts and express it toward others even if it entails inconvenience and expense. This willingness to place another's good above our own is the very essence of love, and the key to harmonious relationships with others.

The great mystery is that when we are willing to give all, we are seldom called upon to do so, simply because this willingness is true love, the elixir which transforms and heals the person who has it, and all to whom it is given. If we have it and give it to all, the transformation is complete. We must love, however—not just try to be loving. Love is the "whole armour of God." If there is any chink or flaw in it, it is worthless.

There can be no reservations or conditions to love. It must be complete or it is nothing.

"Daddy, do you love me?"

"I'll love you if you will be good."

"Daddy, I love you anyway."

Out of the mouths of babes—Love is total commitment.

THE GOLDEN RULE

The Master Key to human relationships is the ultimate expression of love which we know as the Golden Rule: "Therefore all things whatsoever ye would that men should do to you, do ye even so to them: for this is the law and the prophets." (Matt. 7: 12)

This principle is stated in all of the world's religions,* and is the absolute

---

*Donald Curtis, *Daily Power for Joyful Living* (Englewood Cliffs, N.J.: Prentice-Hall, Inc., 1963), p. 23.

standard for getting along with other people. We don't have to do anything about getting along with people, except to get along with ourselves and treat others the way we would like to be treated. Reasonable enough, isn't it? Simple? Let's do it.

As you use the following Treatment, let these statements impress themselves upon your subconscious. Become acquainted with yourself. Like yourself. Know the truth about yourself. Build a consciousness of love.

Personal Science of Mind Treatment to Get Along with Myself

"Thou wilt keep him in perfect peace, whose mind is stayed on thee." (Isa. 26:3)

I am at peace today. There is peace in all the earth, and I know it begins with me. There is one perfect Life. This Life is my life now. My mind is filled with God, therefore, there is peace in my heart. My heart is filled with love, therefore, there is peace in my world. There is peace within, around and through me. I am a peaceful person.

All conflict is dissolved from my heart, mind and soul. That which is within me is greater than that which is in the world. I am an integrated individual. There are no enemies in my household. My thoughts and feelings are friends. My mind and my heart agree. I dwell in unified consciousness. My soul is ordered and cleansed by the free, full flow of Spirit. I am filled with beauty and joy. I look within myself and find goodness there. I look out upon my world and see order and harmony everywhere. I lift up my eyes to the hills and across the deserts and seas, and peace is everywhere.

I love God, I love myself, I love my neighbor. I seek always to do that which is kind and helpful. I am grateful for the gift of life and for the abundance which flows to me from God. I help others in their need. I give to them, I encourage them, I instruct them, I help them find strength within themselves. I can only get along with myself when I get along with others. I can only get along with others when I get along with myself.

I take personal inventory and eliminate all troublesome traits. I will not allow myself to dwell upon anything other than the noble, encouraging and inspiring. My self-image is clear, vital and strong. I love the Self within me—the Christ Self—the Son of God—the Infinite Invisible Reality which is my Father. I seek ever to be perfect as this Father is perfect.

I dwell in the heaven of quiet consciousness. I am one with the Infinite which lies stretched in smiling repose. I turn my mind toward the cheerful, the optimistic and constructive aspects of life. I think only good and do only good. I live to love, and I love to live.

"Surely goodness and mercy shall follow me all the days of my life: and I will dwell in the house of the Lord for ever." (Psalm 23:6)

And so it is.

LOVE HEALS ALL

When we are peaceful and secure within ourselves, we will demonstrate peace and harmony with others, troublesome though they sometimes seem to be. No matter what they say or do, endeavor to see and bring forth the good in them. It is there, but has become obscured by false belief and false conditioning. We cannot afford to react to the unpleasantness in others or to send any animosity back to them. The seeming evil in them is not real; it only seems real. The Reality—the Truth—is that everyone is a son of God, and when he is expressing his true Self he will act like one.

If a person is not doing this by himself, it is our responsibility to help him by forgiving him and correcting him by keeping our thought about him clear and true. Do this by seeing only the good in him. Dwell upon this, and everything but good will disappear. Even if this seems implausible to you, try it. It works. Even though this method may seem impractical and unrealistic at the outset, it is really the only practical way of getting along with other people.

Harmonious relationships with our fellow human beings are the prime requisites of happy, productive living. One of the great spiritual lessons is to live by the law of love, unequivocally, in every situation. There can never be any deviation. Be strong, be practical, be realistic—take action, correct and discipline where necessary, but do all with love. There is no permissible deviation from this principle.

As we have come to know ourselves better and how to get along with ourselves, we automatically develop more love, compassion and empathy for others, thereby getting along with all people. This Treatment helps us do this.

Personal Science of Mind Treatment to Get Along with Other People

We are all children of God. God loves us all. God loves me, and I love all that God loves. I am my brother's keeper. I owe him my love. I give him my love. I see the good in all people and help them see it in themselves. Love is the guiding influence of my life.

People are wonderful. I give thanks for my place in the great human family. I love to see people, I love to talk with them, work with them, live with them, learn with them and from them. I love people. I seek always to understand my neighbor. I know that what he does is the result of the conditioning of thought and experience. When I understand this, I understand him. In understanding him, I can forgive him when necessary. I know that if I were to think and feel as my neighbor does, I would do just as he does. I act always toward him as I would like him to act toward me. This is good for both of us.

I have empathy for everyone. I know that we are all confronted with the same challenges, problems and needs. Our urges, desires and appetites are similar. We have the same basic equipment with which to build our lives. We are created equal, even if not born equal, so it is the duty and responsibility of the strong to help the weak. It is my privilege to give of the riches which God has given me. I share knowledge, wisdom, love and understanding.

I am genuinely interested in people. I forgive them their trespasses as I seek also to be forgiven. I am no better than anyone else, and no one is any better than I. I have compassion for the whole human race. I do all that I can to help it learn and live graciously and abundantly. I love the human family.

I give credit where credit is due. I always have something good to say to everyone. I compliment them, I praise them, I make them laugh. I let the love and goodness within me flow out and make them feel good. Life is a joyous game. I know this is so, and I help others to know it also.

Thank you, Father, for my life and the joy of living it with others. Thank you for the Fatherhood of God and the brotherhood of man. Thank you for the love which unites us all. Thank you, Father.

And so it is.

CHAPTER 14 SUMMARY

1. We change other people by changing our attitudes toward them.
2. Negative attitudes make it impossible for us to get along with ourselves or with others.
3. What we think about others is what they think about us.
4. We try to explain away or avoid facing our faults by assigning them to others.
5. We can't change others without first changing ourselves.
6. We can only be forgiven as we forgive.
7. Love causes us always to act and behave toward others as we would like them to act and behave toward us.
8. Love is the only true religion—the religion of meaning and practical action.
9. The willingness to place another's good above our own is the very essence of love and the key to harmonious relationships with others.
10. We don't have to do anything about getting along with people except to get along with ourselves and treat others the way we would like to be treated.

Chapter 15

The Practical Techniques of Science of Mind Treatment

Ponder deeply and often the following principles:
I. There is only one power in the universe.
II. Through my mind I have the capacity to recognize and become one with this power.
III. The one power works through me according to my faith.

These three principles, first stated in Part II, Chapter 5, provide the fundamental basis of Treatment—the Practice of the Science of Mind. We now have a grasp of the Science of Mind—What It Is and How It Works—the activity of Intelligence and Law throughout the Universe, and therefore in the individual.

INDIVIDUAL PERSONAL APPLICATION

It is possible to understand how something works without knowing how to work it. Therefore, our emphasis from this point on will be upon your personal application of these principles to your daily life through Science of Mind Treatment. You have already been working with Treatment in the previous chapters, since two or more are given in each chapter of this book, and you have already noticed the benefits, but now we are going to explain in greater detail just what Treatment is and how you can use it.

In addition to the instruction on Treatment throughout this volume, the student is directed to my three previous books on Treatment in which hundreds of case histories and techniques are given, as well as other valuable background material on the Science of Mind and related subjects.*

During the past twenty years, my time has been devoted to teaching, ministering, counseling and healing with the Science of Mind and in reporting on this work and my experience and discoveries in it through my writings. In my three previous books, I have reported on the miracles which the Science of Mind has brought about in my own life and in the lives of others. I wouldn't be alive today were it not for the efficacy of these principles and techniques and their application. I know the same is true of countless other men and women in all walks of life. I sincerely present this book along with my others so that you, too, may use the Science of Mind to structure your life. Following are actual cases of healings secured from Treatments given in this book.

Healings of health from treatment

Doris was completely incapacitated by a stroke. Partially blinded, she could neither speak nor walk for many months. She worked with a Religious Science Practitioner and regained her sight. As she was able to read and study, she learned how to use Science of Mind Treatment, and her speech and full physical mobility and health returned. Her entire life was changed by the experience. Today she is a busy, dedicated practitioner and teacher of the Science of Mind.

Samuel H. was told he had terminal cancer. Surgery and cobalt treatments followed, but he was told that it was just a matter of time. Frightened and in constant pain, he turned to the Science of Mind. The pain subsided, and he regained full health. Today he lives an active and healthy life. He tells everyone that he attributes his recovery to Science of Mind Treatment.

His case is typical of many others. There are many businessmen who have recovered from heart attacks through Science of Mind Treatment. Healings of tuberculosis, ulcers, blindness and deafness are known to all practitioners of the Science of Mind. Healings have been recorded for

---

*Donald Curtis, *Your Thoughts Can Change Your Life* (Englewood Cliffs, N.J.: Prentice-Hall, Inc., 1961).

*Donald Curtis, *Human Problems and How to Solve Them* (Englewood Cliffs, N.J.: Prentice-Hall, Inc., 1962).

*Donald Curtis, *Daily Power for Joyful Living* (Englewood Cliffs, N.J.: Prentice-Hall, Inc., 1963).

nearly every physical condition and ailment through the use of Science of Mind Treatment.

Personal problems respond to treatment

Bob W. was down on himself and on life. A homosexual and an alcoholic, he was in the receiving hospital after attempted suicide when I first saw him. Emergency therapy saved his life; Science of Mind Treatment helped him live. His alcoholism under control and his homosexuality completely reversed to normalcy, he is happy for the first time and leads a productive life. He continues to use and help others through Science of Mind Treatment.

Treatment solves financial matters

Dan W. had been in financial trouble all of his life. From a background of poverty and lack, he had a low estimate of his own worth and was never able to earn even a respectable salary. Discouraged and defeated, he enrolled in my Science of Mind Prosperity Class. His consciousness expanded through Treatment, and his income tripled within one year.

Jack L., on the contrary, had always had money, but was never able to keep it or get any enjoyment from it. He squandered a small fortune which he had inherited, and even though he was able to earn large amounts, this money too, trickled through his fingers. While studying the Science of Mind, he discovered the reason. Through Treatment, he developed respect for himself, for others, and for money, and today is a wealthy man. He uses his money wisely, and with it gives happiness to himself and others.

Treatment effective for achievememt

Myra W. had a beautiful voice, a lovely face and body, but an unattractive personality. She had been pursuing a singing career for ten years and had gotten nowhere. She couldn't understand why, but during the course of our Science of Mind counseling, she came to realize that her inner feelings of inferiority and fear produced defense mechanisms which reflected into her personality as coldness and harshness, all of which grated on others. Through Treatment, she dissolved her inner tensions and with

THE PRACTICAL TECHNIQUES OF SCIENCE OF MIND TREATMENT 177

the inner energies released, developed a warm, outgoing personality to go with her talented voice. Today she is on her way to the top of the musical world.

Jonathan B. thought the world was against him. He thought everything was difficult to do. Even though well-trained and educated for a career in business, he could never seem to make the right "connection." He always thought "pull" was necessary to succeed, and since he didn't have any, he became bitter and resigned to defeat. Someone brought him to one of my lectures on the principles of success, and he came to me for Science of Mind Treatment and counseling. He was able to formulate some well-defined aims and goals, and through Treatment leading to intelligently directed action, was able to direct and develop them to successful achievements.

HOW TREATMENT CHANGES CONSCIOUSNESS

From these case histories above, which are typical of thousands with whom I have counseled and treated personally, it can readily be seen that Science of Mind Treatment helps to bring about a change in the consciousness of the individual that results in a change in his life so that he experiences health, happiness, prosperity and success, and creative achievement. What these people have done, you can do. I make no personal claims for my part in the healings and demonstrations, but I do make sound claims for the method of Science of Mind Treatment. You can learn to do it and use it yourself.

I wish to make it clear that Treatment is not something that is done *to* you or directed *at* you. It is done *for* you or *with* you.

If you are treating for yourself, it is the process by which you bring about a change in yourself and your life by changing your consciousness.

When engaged in for the purpose of healing, it may be in cooperation with other methods of therapy or, if the individual develops a high enough level of faith, it can be sufficient in itself. The Science of Mind is so complete in itself that it is not rigid nor dogmatic. We take no stand against any other approach. We cooperate with physicians, psychiatrists, psychologists, sociologists, lawyers, other counselors, practitioners and ministers, and all who minister to human needs. And more and more of the people in these fields are using the Science of Mind in their own lives and for their patients, and are cooperating with those of us who practice it professionally.

The Science of Mind is a way of life, a religion, a philosophy, and a healing approach for the New Age. Take your choice; it is up to you how you want to use it—but—use it daily.

TREATMENT INTEGRATES THE MIND

Treatment is the process of integrating the mind mentally, emotionally and spiritually so that its full potential may be utilized in maintaining and sustaining health in the body, the achievement of worthwhile goals, the harmonious adjustment of personal affairs and relationships with others, and the guidance and direction of our energies and endeavors for maximum effectiveness. Science of Mind Treatment is aimed toward getting results by accepting ourselves as a whole being and living as one. Treatment always results in getting or experiencing something, but not just because we try to get, but because we seek to be. The whole approach is geared toward bringing about a change within the person.

FUNCTIONS OF TREATMENT

There are four major functions of Science of Mind Treatment: (1) To correct what is wrong in consciousness, (2) To construct what is whole and balanced in consciousness, (3) To direct this consciousness into outlets for worthwhile accomplishment, and (4) To maintain and sustain inner balance in consciousness as the basis of the normal life.

This fourth area is perhaps the most important of all, because it indicates that Treatment and the constant practice of the Science of Mind in daily living is a way of life that keeps people healthy, happy, prosperous, and with everything running smoothly. As we have said before, the Science of Mind with its treatment techniques is not only for sick or problem people, although it is probably the greatest healing approach in the world today. It is without question the most effective method by which normal people may live their lives constructively, and by which those who have found recovery may sustain it.

The Science of Mind is an idealistic, constructive, practical approach to religion, philosophy, psychology and general living based upon an understanding of universal principles and how to cooperate with them and use them in the individual life. Treatment is the process of bringing this about.

Since example and demonstration are the best methods of instruction, here are four treatments below; one for each of the four purposes just enumerated. Study them carefully; together they form one complete Science of Mind Treatment for your personal use.

PERSONAL SCIENCE OF MIND TREATMENT

To Correct:

Everything unlike the nature of God is dissolved from my consciousness as I place myself in the hands of the Infinite. I release my mind from all concern with outer matters, as I turn it inward and upward toward that which cleanses and heals. I am purified by that which is pure. I am healed by that which is whole.

All negative and destructive thoughts, feelings, and attitudes disappear from my mind and heart as I become self-emptied and God-filled. The false and inferior have no place in my thought; I dwell only upon the good, the true and the beautiful. The violent and the depressive have no place in my feelings; my heart is filled with love and joy. I keep my mind and soul with all diligence, for out of them come the issues of life. My conscious and subconscious work together in perfect accord.

All fear is dissolved; I am filled with faith. I believe. I know. All hostility is dissolved; I am filled with love. I am warm and friendly. I am kind. All inferiority is dissolved; I am filled with confidence. I am capable and strong. I believe in myself. All guilt is dissolved; I forgive myself and others. There is no condemnation, only understanding and dedicated resolve to keep my mind awake and my heart pure. I give thanks for my corrected consciousness now.

And so it is.

To Construct:

I am a builder. I work with the Master Builder in constructing my own soul. My immediate assignment is to construct a clear mind, a willing heart, and a strong body. I accomplish this efficiently and permanently as I use the perfect materials and tools which are provided for me.

I decide what I want to build, how to go about it, and what to use in doing it. I am building the house of consciousness in which my soul lives and flourishes. I start right now by disciplining my thought and controlling my feelings. My tools are my mind and heart—my conscious and my subconscious. My materials come from Spirit, the Infinite Intelligence from which flow my thoughts and ideas.

Integrity, honesty, purity, peace, love, joy, truth, strength, beauty and reverence form the foundation which supports the structure of my life. I construct the foundation for strength and endurance, and my house stands forever. I use only those materials which measure up to the highest standards. I insist upon whole stock and balanced beams, and I put them together with impeccable workmanship.

"I am the master of my fate; I am the captain of my soul." I am the builder of my life. I am grateful for being the instrument through which the Master Builder constructs in and through me. I am well constructed now.

And so it is.

To Direct:

God provides. I use. He leads me "beside the still waters and into paths of righteousness," but it is up to me to follow His lead by learning how to lead myself by directing my thoughts and feelings into outlets for worthwhile accomplishment. Just as the Infinite Mind is God unto me, so my personal mind is god unto my thoughts and feelings. I lead them wisely and well.

My consciousness is formed from my thoughts, feelings and spiritual awareness. My consciousness is what I am. I am a son of God, and I act like one. My consciousness is high and whole. I go forward into glorious experience. I am aware of life's infinite potential and I make the very most of it. My life is a living monument of worthy deeds and significant accomplishment.

I hitch my wagon to a star. I choose worthy goals and move forward toward accomplishing them. My objectives are clear and definite. I know that my job is to do God's work on earth, and I waste no time being about it. I establish the flow and keep it going. I have no time to waste. There is much to be done. I am under assignment. I get my bloated nothingness out of the way and let the divine circuits come through.

My consciousness, which is the creative intelligence and energy of my being, flows into outlets for worthwhile accomplishment now and always.

And so it is.

To Maintain and Sustain:

Divine Law and Order within me sustain and maintain me in healthy, happy and abundant life. I am ever in tune with the Infinite. I align myself with all that is normal, natural and good, and all that is normal, natural and good is expressed in my life. The harmony and peace of the Infinite are expressing through me at all times.

I maintain balance and order in my outer world by establishing them in my heart. Inner harmony produces outer order. I am at peace with God and myself; therefore I am at peace with the world and mankind. I cannot be disturbed or upset, because I am deeply anchored in Truth and the lasting values that flow from it. God—Infinite Good—is the substance and essence of my life. I am one with all that is real.

I never allow outer occurrences or appearances to throw me off base. I live from within outward. I never react to; I always act from my awareness of my spiritual identity. Spirit, the very life of all life, sustains and maintains me forever. Throughout each day of my eternal life I express the order and harmony of Universal peace, order, harmony and right action.

God maintains and sustains me in perfect life.

And so it is.

TREATMENT CONDITIONS YOU BY CHANGING YOUR CONSCIOUSNESS

After studying the foregoing treatments and repeating them as statements of truth about yourself, it can readily be understood that Treatment is not for the sole purpose of getting something or making something happen. These are secondary to the overall purpose of Treatment, which is to change the consciousness of the individual. This is illustrated in the foregoing treatments.

When we treat ourselves or are treated by someone else, *an inner change takes place.* Part of it consists of reconditioning the subconscious through the corrective step of dissolving and removing obstructions, blocks, and negative and destructive memory patterns. Neuroses, complexes, fixations, and even psychoses can be removed through treatment, when the individual or the practitioner understands what he is doing and how to do it.

Treatment is done with and in the conscious mind, which is completely in charge of the process. Treatment utilizes the power of choice and selection. The key to effective treatment is to decide what you want to think about, and then concentrate on it in an orderly and disciplined manner. The mind must be kept focused upon Truth and Perfection until is accepts them as the natural order of things.

When the conscious mind accepts higher levels of Truth and understanding than it did before, these are impressed upon the subconscious, which then creates from the *new premise*. This is what we mean by reconditioning the subconscious and by raising the consciousness. As long as we maintain and sustain the acceptance and faith in ideas and statements of Truth, they will manifest in our experience.

Whatever the individual mind believes, both consciously and subconsciously, is the law of our experience. So, you see, we have it within our own power to determine what happens to us. How could it be any other way?

TREATMENT IS TRUE PRAYER

Treatment can best be designated as scientific prayer—positive prayer—the prayer that gets results. It is true prayer, talking with and listening to God—recognizing, unifying with, and realizing our oneness with the One. People often pray *to* God. Not so with Treatment—the new kind of prayer—the true prayer. In Treatment we pray *as* God knowing Himself. When God knows Himself in and through us, then we know ourselves as we really are—One with Him. So that this inner knowing may take place, we must turn our thoughts and words toward statements of Truth. As we accept Truth, error disappears. As we accept good, evil disappears. We can only experience what we have in our minds. Treatment is the process by which we condition and control our minds to dwell on the highest possible level.

In order to do this, we must establish conscious control of our thought. We must become "self-emptied and God-filled." Treatment is the complete experience for the consciousness of the individual. It brings mental, emotional, psychological and spiritual integration and balance. It reaches the spiritual level of being, without which no permanent change of consciousness can be accomplished.

WHAT TREATMENT IS NOT

From this explanation and instruction, it can readily be seen that Science of Mind Treatment is a much higher technique than either auto-suggestion or self-hypnotism. These two methods can bring about a momentary change and may have some value for purposes of relaxation and concentration, but at the best, they are merely steps on the way to the higher experience. There can be no permanent beneficial change in experience until the consciousness is raised. The consciousness cannot be raised until it is in contact with that which is higher than the mind alone—that is, Spirit. The mind cannot rise above the level of the mind by itself, but when it is used for the purpose of contacting Spirit, and as an instrument of Spirit, it performs its true function, and healing demonstration and sustained good take place.

Science of Mind Treatment is worship in its true sense, meaning "to make worthy." This is what we do in Treatment—we make ourselves worthy by consciously recognizing and affirming our worthiness. Treatment—scientific spiritual conditioning—is the most significant advance that has ever been made in the mind of man. Through Treatment we can change and control the whole world by changing and conditioning ourselves to become one with the Perfection within.

YOUR PERSONAL TREATMENT

Treatment, then, is the mental, emotional and spiritual process of bringing about a particular desired good and for sustaining overall good in every part of our being and experience. The entire experience takes place within ourselves as a process of progressive knowing. Treatment consists of a series of steps or layers of thought usually spoken as oral affirmations, for the purpose of bringing about the realization of Truth within the mind.

TALKING TO GOD

Treatment is talking with God, to your subconscious, about yourself. It is suggested that you speak your treatment out loud. This helps keep the mind focused on the job at hand and builds more definite patterns to impress upon the subconscious. Speak definitely, clearly, forcibly and with feeling. Repetition, feeling, frequency and regularity are important factors in implanting ideas within the subconscious. When you reach subconscious conviction, coupled with spiritual realization of good, the treatment is completed; the prayer is answered.

SPONTANEOUS TREATMENT

The many treatments given throughout this book are guides provided for the purpose of helping you give your own treatment. You may use them at first by reading them over as preparation for framing your own treatment. Your treatment should come spontaneously from your own mind. Treatment is a matter of joining your mind with Infinite Mind, and then thinking and speaking as It thinks and speaks through you. Your conscious mind guides and directs the process, and at all times it is consciously aware of what it is thinking and saying, but it also releases itself for larger unfoldment and higher realization than it is capable of by itself.

USE TREATMENT REGULARLY

Start right now. Use Treatment regularly—a general conditioning treatment in the morning upon arising and just before retiring at night, and if possible one or more times during the day. You will find that your life will change for the better in many ways. Overall well-being, as well as the demonstration of specific good, will result from your use of Treatment.

In addition to your general conditioning treatments, you will find occasion for specific treatment about specific matters—a particular condition, situation, circumstance or desire. Use specific treatment to arrive at a realization of good, fulfillment and peace concerning that particular thing. When you do this, what happens will be in accord with what is right and best.

Treatment is for the purpose of bringing our personal will and desire into harmony and accord with Divine Will, by letting it unfold in natural order, without the restriction of human limitation. Treatment is the process of personalizing the Creative Process by universalizing the individual.

Treatment is not the only form of prayer or worship, but it is an all-inclusive technique which incorporates meditation and contemplation within its structure. Your personal treatment comes from within you, and as you progress in its use, the way you treat will be right for you. At the outset, however, the suggestions and complete treatments in each chapter provide good patterns to follow. For further instruction, refer to my earlier book, *Human Problems and How to Solve Them*, page 93.

Personal Science of Mind Treatment for Self-Realization

I move out of the little self into Self-Realization. I am one with the One and only Self. All personal limitation is dissolved as I arise to the true heights within me. "I and my Father are One." (John 1: 30) "He that hath seen me hath seen the Father." (John 14: 9)

I realize the infinite possibilities of my mind and soul. I go forward into the realization of my full potential. I am a whole person: materially, physically, emotionally, mentally, personally, spiritually and cosmically. I am One with the Universe. God is my very being. As I know Him, I know my Self. As I know my Self, I know God. I receive constant inner instruction which guides and enlightens me. I learn the lessons of life on every level. I apply myself, I discipline myself, and I let myself be perfected as I contemplate the beauty and mystery of all being. I am whole. I am free.

As I look upon Him, He looks upon me. I know that He has prepared a place for me within my own heart. I know that where he is, I am also. I am never lost or alone, because my consciousness is One with All That Is.

I am a being of great height and depth. My soul soars to the heavens of enlightenment. My understanding plumbs the hidden meanings of all Creation and all Life. I am wise as Infinite Intelligence is wise. My eyes are open and I see beauty and goodness everywhere. My ears are open to the communications of the still, small voice which constantly instructs and guides me. New horizons beckon to me as I move inward, upward and forward along The Path.

I am a perfect child of God. In all my ways I acknowledge Him, and He directs my paths to the One Path. I draw nigh unto God, and He draws nigh unto me. I dwell in the secret place of the Most High. I abide under the shadow of the Almighty. I am safe and secure. I am strong and whole.

Quietly now, I dwell in the deep silence of His Peace. In the Silence I reach complete Realization. I am One with All that is. I am One with Life, I am One with Truth, I am One with my Self, I am One with the Universe. I am One with God. I am One.

And so it is. Thank you Father.

CHAPTER 15 SUMMARY

1. Science of Mind Treatment helps bring about a change in the consciousness of the individual, which results in a change in his life so that he experiences health, happiness, prosperity and success, and creative achievement.
2. Treatment is the process of integrating the mind mentally, emotionally and spiritually so that its full potential may be realized and utilized.
3. The key to effective treatment is to decide what you want to think about and then concentrate on it in an orderly and disciplined manner.
4. Treatment is the process by which we condition our minds to dwell on the highest possible level.
5. Treatment brings about mental, emotional, psychological and spiritual integration and balance, which permanently elevates the consciousness of the individual.
6. Treatment is the mental, emotional and spiritual process of bringing about a particular desired good, and for sustaining overall good in every part of our being and experience.
7. Treatment is talking *with* God *to* your subconscious *about* yourself.
8. Treatment is joining your mind with Infinite Mind, and then thinking and speaking as It thinks and speaks through you.
9. Treatment is for the purpose of bringing the personal will and desire into harmony and accord with Divine Will by letting it unfold in natural order without the restriction of human limitation.
10. Treatment is the process of personalizing the Creative Process by universalizing the individual.

Chapter 16

How to Develop Your Desired Full Potential

"You think you're pretty good, don't you?" one child taunted another.

"No, I don't," he answered. "Because I know I'm twice as good as I think I am."

Actually we know that we are not twice, but many times better, greater and more capable than our conscious mind is capable of accepting. Science estimates that we use less than ten percent of our capacities and abilities. There are large undiscovered and undeveloped areas within us which have never been probed, and never will be, until we apply the principles of the Science of Mind which we have been discussing throughout this book.

DEVELOPMENT FROM WITHIN

The Science of Mind helps us unlock ourselves from the prison of limited and negative conditioning, by opening our minds to the acceptance of our infinite potential through an expansion of the areas of probability and possibility. As we have seen, this extension of our powers is brought about, not through striving, getting or doing—or even by thinking alone—but by the development of inner areas of being and knowing—vast continents that await our discovery and exploration.

Psychological considerations and techniques for mental and emotional development and conditioning are most important, as is an understanding of the relationship between the conscious and subconscious functions of the mind, all of which have been fully explained in this book. But there is something beyond all of these. It is the desire to find this Something and go all the way with it that makes all the difference. The Science of Mind leads us into the recognition of and identification with our own Inner Being which exists as potential until we consciously become one with it, at which time our potential is released and expressed.

HOW TO GET REALIZATION AND FULFILLMENT

In Chapter 12, Part III, we explained the first ten steps in "The Anatomy of Mental Action," whereby we learned how to engage the conscious mind in thought and by successive steps in the intellectual process, move it along to the attainment of wisdom and its application through understanding. For most people this might seem the ultimate in attainment, but for others of us it is only preparation for the real business of life—the journey into the realization of our full potential, not just as the son of man, but as the Son of God.

We are both. **The son of man is what we presently know. The Son of God is what there is to be known.** The questing mind can never rest while the mountain peaks of the Spirit are there to be scaled.

"Why do you climb that mountain?" the climber is inevitably asked. The answer is always the same, "Because it is there."

YOUR INFINITE POTENTIAL

There is an undeniable thrust which moves us along toward our destiny of complete realization and fulfillment. Sometimes we need to awaken our recognition of it; at other times we just need to go along for the ride. Shakespeare said:

> There's a divinity that shapes our ends,
> Rough-hew them how we will. (*Hamlet*, Act V, scene 2)

He also observed:

> There is a tide in the affairs of men,
> Which, taken at the flood, leads on to fortune;

Omitted, all the voyage of their life
Is bound in shallows and in miseries.

(*Julius Caesar*, Act IV, scene 3)

Emerson recognized this Divine impetus and said that there is that within us which is always moving "better up to best." We can never rest on our laurels. We never "have it made." There is no point at which we can stop or retire. We have within ourselves the capacity to experience the biggest and most perfect expression of all—the Infinite Potential of our own consciousness. As Kipling concludes in his great poem, "L'Envoi":

But each for the joy of the working, and each in his separate star,
Shall draw the Thing as he sees It for the God of Things as They Are!

HOW GOD IS INDIVIDUALIZED IN YOU

We have seen that aims and goals are important—that temporal needs must be met, and that we must make our way and meet our obligations in this world, but we also see that there is Something greater than all of these things—Something which we must find if we are to be whole. Remember, we are not just human beings striving to be good. **We are spiritual beings unfolding into the full expression of That which we really are—God individualized.** The recognition and expression of this potential is our destiny; we cannot escape it. The Science of Mind says, "Let's cooperate with it and assist the process."

THE ANATOMY OF MENTAL ACTION

Let us cooperate with the Father by explaining and developing the remaining ten steps in "The Anatomy of Mental Action" which we started in Part III, Chapter 12:

Vision
Imagination
Intuition
Inspiration
Meditation
Contemplation

Attunement
Awareness
Enlightenment
Illumination

Vision

"Where there is no vision, the people perish." (Pr. 29:18)

True vision is that inner faculty which enables us to see beyond the visible. When Paul says that Faith is the "evidence of things not seen" (Hebrew 11:1) and that "the things which are seen were not made of things which do appear" (Hebrew 11:3), he was indicating that we have a level of perception which, even though it does not deal in tangibles, is much more real than the outer sense of sight. And when he says, "There are . . . celestial bodies and bodies terrestrial" (I Cor. 15:40), he suggests that the two levels of the inner and outer exist even on the physical level of our being.

Vision is the faculty of inner seeing. Visualization, which we discussed in a previous chapter, is a form of vision on the psychological level; goal-setting and achievement aims are a use of vision on the mental level; clairvoyance is vision on the psychic level, but spiritual vision rises above all of these. Spiritual vision is the faculty of "seeing true." This faculty enables us to see the nature of things the way they really are, uninhibited by human limitation and interpretations. It enables us to perceive causes instead of only effects.

God's vision

Vision enables us to see things the way God sees them—whole and perfect. It helps us to see things the way they should be. Functioning as insight, it enables us to understand the "why" of things and of relationships. Vision is complete seeing. Vision is total perception. Vision brings past, present and future into proper relationship and perspective. Vision sees life as an emanation from the Infinite and an extension into eternity.

"I will lift up mine eyes unto the hills from whence cometh my help." (Ps. 121:1) Vision is a natural faculty. The hills are within us. The eyes of total vision are within us. The strength is within us as infinite potential.

Learn to use your capacity for extended seeing. Let your sight be God's vision using your eyes. Look at things from the highest point of view. Stand on raised ground. Establish perspective. Increase your range. Visibility is infinite. We are in the midst of an eternal, infinite picture. Develop peripheral vision. Look around you and see beauty and goodness everywhere and forever. Let your vision come in bright and clear. Make it your own and follow it. You have vision. You are vision.

Imagination

Previously, we dealt with Imagination and its relationship to the other functions of the mental process whereby it is the creative power which gives life and substance to thought. In this regard, imagination is a tool of thought.

Spiritual imagination

In this section on developing our full potential, we are going beyond the scope of our conscious thought, and we are considering imagination as a fountain from which come thoughts, ideas, concepts, plans and pictures of great worth and beauty. Our prior consideration was of imagination as a subconscious mental faculty. In addition to that, it is a superconscious spiritual faculty. As we have said before, there is no limit to the imagination except that placed upon it by our thought and conditioning. Great results can be achieved when the mind forms concepts and dares to imagine that they are true. Now let us see what can happen when we let the imagination form the concept or picture and turn it over to the conscious mind to accept.

Activating imagination

The imagination works both ways: as a receiver and gestator, or as a channel and conductor for emanation from the Infinite Mind. In both instances the individual conscious mind is involved, but in the first instance it activates the imagination, while in the second process, the imagination activates and stimulates the conscious mind, assisting it to rise above itself. In the first process we are using our own mind and imagination to help us accept a desired good. In the second, higher and more extended process, we are letting Imagination itself, an aspect of the One Mind—Divine Intelligence—use our individual intelligence and imagination for purposes of spiritual unfoldment and expansion.

We will see that this process can be encouraged and developed, and it is most important that we do so. Imagination is a gift of God, and anything and everything of God leads us to God if it is properly used. Instruction, guidance, study of Nature and Truth, prayer and meditation are all necessary in developing and sensitizing our consciousness so that Imagination may function through us.

Reality of imagination

Imagination is not detachment from reality. It is Reality itself. True imagination is not fantasizing or making things up. It is the medium through which we accept the reality of Infinite Being and identify ourselves with it. Remember, nothing is too wonderful to happen; nothing is too good to be true.*

Spiritual Imagination is the faculty which lifts us above the imagination.

Intuition

Intuition is direct knowing. It is the process by which we know something without the intellectual process of conscious thought. Just as Spiritual Imagination is the Universal aspect of which individual imagination is a part, so Intuition is an aspect of Divine Mind which functions in the individual mind, and can be developed. The Science of Mind leads to the development of our intuition as the highest of our mental functions, the activity of Mind which lifts us above the mind.

Intuition is spiritual perception. As we recall, Spirit is the Conscious Mind of God—Infinite Intelligence—and individualizes as the conscious mind of man, and functions as intelligence and thought by means of the entire mental, intellectual process with which we have dealt at such length. Part of our purpose has been to teach us how to think truly and clearly in a disciplined and purposeful fashion so that the greatest possible good can be understood and experienced. We have examined in detail the methods of reasoning, and the process and functions of the mind and thought. We

---

*Donald Curtis, *Your Thoughts Can Change Your Life* (Englewood Cliffs, N.J.: Prentice-Hall, Inc., 1961), Chaps. 3 and 9.

have come to understand that man can know God literally and become One with God through his own mind.

Direct knowing

This is true. We now understand this. Now let us do it. Let us go beyond thought. First we must think clearly, then we know. This knowing is intuition, and our use and reliance upon it does not depend upon conscious thought.

"How do you know that?" an astounded husband demands of his wife.

"I don't know—I just know," she affirms. And that settles that. How can you argue with anyone who knows?

Developing intuition

Intuition is knowing without knowing how we know. It is the highest function of the individual mind; Intuition is Divine Mind using individual mind. Intuition is not to be confused with instinct, which is the subconscious reflex of the autonomic nervous system—automatic response in line with the nature of our species. Our instincts are physiological and emotional; intuition is mental and spiritual. Both are important. We don't need to develop instincts; we just need to learn to discipline and control them. On the other hand, even though Intuition is inherent within us, it needs to be developed and used so that it can control us.

When your Intuition speaks to you, listen to it and follow it. It is the voice of the Soul—"the still small voice" that speaks when we become still and listen. In its most common appearance, we call it a "hunch"; in its highest expression, it is the direct influx of Infinite Intelligence from the Mind of God.

We are all inherent mystics with the capacity for this direct knowing. Learn to use your mind effectively as this book instructs, but also learn to unlock yourself from the confines of your mind so that you may hear the Voice of the Silence—Intuition. This book leads us to this level also.

Inspiration

"To inspire" means "to breathe in." Since Spirit is the breath of life, Inspiration is the state and process of being filled with Spirit. Since we know that Spirit is the Conscious Mind of God, when we are inspired we are literally filled with Infinite Intelligence and Power.

Inspiration is that spiritual infusion which lifts us toward the expression of our full potential. Inspiration operates on every level of our being. When we are inspired, we rise above ourselves and are capable of thoughts, insights, expression and actions that we do not rise to at other times. The athlete becomes inspired with the will to win, and "plays over his head," performing better than he knows how to perform, as he drives on to victory. Under inspiration, the artist becomes an instrument in the hand of the Creator, and paints or sculpts a masterpiece before which his own mind is in awe. The composer tunes in on heavenly music when inspired and sets down the notes of a melody so pure and sweet that all who hear it are transported to the same lofty realm.

The speaker, the singer, the actor and the dancer experience flashes or prolonged periods of inspiration when it is as if the words and ideas, the notes, the depth and the movements all come from a level which opens and pours them out unceasingly. Poets and writers all have the experience of feeling, but a pen in the hand of a ready writer sets down the words and phrases in patterns quite beyond our skill or comprehension, as if to shape them for the purposes and designs of a Will above our own. When we read the passage later, we are amazed at what has come through us.

How good shines through you

That is the point: Inspiration is God flowing through us. We make ourselves sensitive and susceptible to inspiration when we maintain order and harmony in our inner and outer lives, and align ourselves with all that is constructive, guarding ourselves from negativity and all destructive influences and tendencies. As we focus our mind upon the good, the true and the beautiful, we become transparencies through which the Light of the Spirit shines and takes form in myriad ways as all that is good. This is Inspiration—"a consummation devoutly to be wished."

Far from being "supernatural," we should think of Inspiration as an inherent part of our true nature as spiritual beings. Is there anything more natural than to be filled with one's self? Since our self is the One Self—All That Is—Inspiration is confirmation and expression of that which we really are.

In this basic and comprehensive book on The Science of Mind, we endeavor to develop and perfect our personal powers on every level of consciousness so that we may always be filled with Inspiration and consciously know it.

Meditation and contemplation

Meditation and contemplation are the means by which we "break through" into higher states of consciousness and evolve into the infinite possibilities of our mind and soul.

Meditation and contemplation are inherent in the process of Science of Mind Treatment, and a natural extension of it. Their practice is essential if we are to develop our full potential.

In the larger sense everything we think, feel, say and do is a prayer. Our life is our real prayer, because it is in the expression of life that we reveal what we really know, feel and experience of God. True prayer is union with God. Prayer must be uttered with body, emotions, mind and soul. We can forget our nothingness when we are immersed in the Oneness, the Wholeness and the Completeness which is God.

Communion

Prayer is for the purpose of joining and unifying the two basic parts of our nature: the human, or external, with the spiritual or internal Reality. In prayer we rise to a realization that the innermost God and the highermost God is One God. In prayer we release our personal limitations into a higher awareness of our Godhood, our true spiritual identity. In the Bible it says, "The effectual fervent prayers of a righteous man availeth much." (James 5: 16) And it also says that the prayer of faith shall save the sick. Prayer is communion with the Divine through positive attention and attunement.

Union

If we would pray for something, if we would ask for something, let us ask for God-realization, let us pray for spiritual understanding, let us pray for guidance, for discipline, for worthiness. All too often people ask for little things—for God to give them a certain object, a certain amount of money, or to bring about a certain circumstance. God is not a messenger boy or a servant. God is the Infinite Reality; and true prayer is joining ourselves in union with the Higher Nature within ourselves. When we do that, all the other things are added unto us.

Realization

Pray for God-realization—to realize the Presence, the Power, the immediacy, the intimacy of God in action through your life. Be still and let the Higher Self, which we know is there, flow through us and instruct us. Let us adopt an attitude of surrender, letting the little self be surrendered into a consciousness of the Greater Self. Then when we are quietly reverent and receptive, the windows of heaven open and pour us out a blessing such that the world is not great enough or big enough to receive.

Inner contact

We receive spiritual understanding in finding that inner contact with Spirit and letting It move through our minds, instructing and guiding us as to the nature of God (Omniscience, Omnipotence, Omnipresence), and instructing us that we are created in His image and likeness. Prayer is a quiet inner time of talking to God and of listening to Him. We don't just talk about God; we experience Him. To experience God is to have the answer to all prayers.

Tennyson said, "More things are wrought by prayer than this world dreams of." Emerson said, "Prayer is the contemplation of the facts of life from the highest point of view."

Voice of the silence

The most practical thing a person can possibly know is how to pray. The sweet communion of prayer brings refilling, regeneration, renewal and uplift as we become one with the Higher Nature, the Higher Self, the Son of God. From this inner contact with Divine Intelligence comes guidance: We somehow know from inner intuition where to go, what to do, and we are given the answer to many things which puzzle the human mind. Simply adopt an attitude of receptivity and personal surrender, and you will experience deep peace and quiet. It is in the silence that the greatest moments come.

HOW TO ACHIEVE YOUR GREATEST EXPERIENCE

In our new state of consciousness which comes through prayer, we become one with the Spirit, which leads us to new understanding. Prayer transforms us: We speak, think, feel and know in a different way. In true prayer we do not seek anything or try to change anything. Prayer is not even for the purpose of humbling ourselves, even though humility is a most wonderful quality of mind and soul. Prayer is for the purpose of experiencing God. This is the altitude of prayer moving us up into Infinite Consciousness.

The mystical way

This union between the Higher Self and the lower self is the essence of the mystical way of life, which is the Spiritual Path which we all seek to follow. The purpose of prayer is to experience God, and for nothing else. So let your prayers be prayers of adoration, prayers of thanksgiving, prayers of recognition and blessing.

Prayer is for the purpose of experiencing this Oneness within ourselves from which all things flow. This will give us inner wisdom—inner vision. A person who is filled with inner vision, a sense of oneness, closeness with God, always has a brightness of eye, a peaceful countenance, and an overall quietude and goodness. When we pray, we travel into the Temple Invisible, surrendering the little self and joining with the Holy Spirit.

MEDITATION IS LISTENING PRAYER

Up until this point, the emphasis of our instruction on prayer and treatment has been upon spoken or self-directed prayer in which we move mentally, emotionally and spiritually toward realization of our Oneness with God and His Presence in and through all of our endeavors. Now we are ready for "listening prayer"—Meditation—in which we still the mind and let God communicate with us. The heights of spiritual experience are reached in silent prayer—Meditation—when we release all else and "Be still and know that I am God" (Psalm 46: 10).

These periods of silence may be combined with and interspersed with your spoken Science of Mind Treatment or other form of prayer, or your silent Meditation may be complete in itself. It is to be remembered that Treatment and Meditation are different aspects of Prayer, and there are techniques to master and follow. All approaches are interrelated and have a common purpose—to consciously contact and activate the Divine Reality within us.

HOW MEDITATION CLEARS THE MIND

Meditation may *seem* to be doing nothing, but this is far from the truth. Meditation is the process by which we clear the mind of all surface and temporal concerns and focus it upon the Infinite and the Eternal—God. Since it is impossible for the mind to know God until God reveals Itself to the mind, Meditation is for the purpose of making the consciousness receptive rather than active. Meditation is not thinking, but it is more than non-thinking; it is conscious non-thinking for the purpose of greater awareness, knowing and being.

In a forthcoming book, we will deal with the specific techniques of Meditation, just as we have dealt with Treatment techniques in this work.

Now, let us conclude by experiencing the effects of Prayer, Treatment, and Meditation: Attunement, Awareness, Enlightenment, Illumination:

ATTUNEMENT

Attunement is at-One-ment—the state of consciousness in which we are actually consciously aware of our Oneness with God. "Tuned in" is the modern phrase for it.

In performing music, we are either in tune or we are not. When we are, the tones are true and clear; when we are not, the discord is ugly and jarring. So it is in life. We must keep our voices and our instruments in tune if the melody of our lives is to be pleasing and harmonious. The mind and heart must first agree with each other, and then when the Soul lets itself be filled with Spirit, the entire orchestra of our being will be in tune.

In his doctrine of Correspondences, Plato asserted that there is a perfect pattern for all things in the Mind of the Infinite. When we maintain harmony and are in tune with that pattern, we will express its perfection. However, if discord and separation develop, we are cut off from the flow of life from the One Source, and we sicken and die. Attunement is maintaining the state of balanced unification by which we know that God's nature is our nature, and they can never be apart.

Become one with the rhythms of nature. Let the air, the water, the earth and all growing things refresh your mind, renew your spirit, and give life and strength to your body. Infinite, eternal life is around us everywhere. Let us attune ourselves to its flow, and move steadily and purposefully with it into eternity.

VIBRATION

When we are in tune with God, we cannot be out of tune with anything. When we vibrate with the One Chord, there can be no discord. When the mind is filled with good, it cannot know anything else. Good is God. God is All-Good. Knowing this is Attunement.

AWARENESS

Awareness is that fine sensitivity of mind which sees true at all times, and perceives the nature of things the way they really are and not the way they appear to be. Awareness is conscious Divine Intelligence. Awareness is knowing that that which is true is true. Awareness is extended consciousness. When one is aware, he is able

> To see a world in a grain of sand
> And a heaven in a wild flower,
> Hold infinity in the palm of your hand
> And eternity in an hour.
> (William Blake, "Auguries of Innocence")

The invisible universe

There are senses beyond the scope of our five physical senses. Through insight, vision, and inner knowing we become aware of a vast Universe of Reality which we cannot see, hear, taste, touch or smell, but which we know is there nevertheless. The more aware we become, the less we rely upon the senses and our resultant thoughts and conclusions to inform us, and the more we go directly to the Source for our instruction and enlightenment. Awareness reveals a world of invisible cause behind all manifestation. Awareness knows that there is more to everything than meets the eye, and that "There are more things in Heaven and earth, Horatio, Than are dreamt of in your philosophy," (*Hamlet*, Act 1, scene 5) and that

> In my Father's house are many mansions; if it were not so, I would have told you. I go to prepare a place for you.
> And if I go and prepare a place for you, I will come again, and receive you unto myself; that where I am, there ye may be also.
> And whither I go ye know and the way ye know. (John 14: 2–4)

Awareness is immersion in eternity and infinity. When we are aware we see the transitory nature of all things. We know that consciousness is the only reality: "Heaven and earth shall pass away; but my words shall not pass away." (Mark 13: 31)

In other words, thinking, feeling, seeing, and experiencing, pleasant though they may be, are but transitory expression of that which has always existed and will endure forever.

Attaining self-development

The powers of discrimination and discernment are sharpened as our awareness grows. We learn to "Judge not according to the appearance, but judge righteous judgment." (John 7: 24) Science of Mind Treatment, with its disciplines and techniques of true prayer, meditation, contemplation, right thinking, and right living, develops our awareness. And as our awareness develops, we become more proficient in these endeavors and move closer to the realization of our full potential.

ENLIGHTENMENT

Enlightenment is a further step along the Golden Bridge* of extended consciousness which unfolds from simple thought, through the 20 points

---

*Donald Curtis, *Your Thoughts Can Change Your Life* (Englewood Cliffs, N.J.: Prentice-Hall, Inc., 1961), Chap. 11.
*Donald Curtis, *Daily Power for Joyful Living* (Englewood Cliffs, N.J.: Prentice-Hall, Inc., 1963), Chap. I.

of our "Anatomy of Mental Action," ending with the final step of Illumination. Each of these steps is a further progression toward spiritual realization.

All steps up to this point can be developed by conscious will and application. As we become proficient on one level, we move on to the next level of consciousness and perfect that. All of our disciplines must be undertaken cheerfully and willingly, with patience and with care.

SELF-IMPROVEMENT THROUGH SELF-UNFOLDMENT

In the process of self-improvement along the spiritual path, we are careful to keep intensive effort and striving at a minimum. Our goal is spiritual perfection, but we do not try to force it. We know that this goal is attained only through a process of natural growth and unfoldment from the center of being. We cannot achieve, know, or have anything unless we first become it. To know God, we must become God, to become Him we must know Him. We start where we are and move through progressive stages of knowing until we discover what we really are.

Knowing that we are God is Enlightenment. **Being** God is Illumination. These achievements are the result of all that has gone before:

> For we know in part, and we prophesy in part. But when that which is perfect is come, then that which is in part shall be done away. When I was a child, I spake as a child, I understood as a child, I thought as a child: but when I became a man, I put away childish things. For now we see through a glass, darkly; but then face to face: now I know in part; but then shall I know even as also I am known. (I Cor. 13: 9–12)

THE UPWARD PATH

There are three basic requirements for one who would attain the heights: Dedication, Discipline and Devotion.

Dedication. First of all, we must be dedicated to the purpose of self-realization. We must believe that it is possible, and make it our guiding influence. We must focus upon it and keep our objective ever before us. We must want to develop and realize our true potential, and be willing to do everything possible and necessary to bring this about.

Discipline. We must make everything subservient to the purposes of the will, which has chosen to follow the Upward Path. Thoughts, feelings, appetites, urges, desires and actions must be rigorously controlled and disciplined so that all of our faculties and energies are free and available for our mental and spiritual disciplines of treatment, prayer, meditation and contemplation. To make full attainment possible, we must provide an overall setting of right living. This takes discipline and control. Each of us alone must decide whether it is worth it. It is never easy; it is often difficult; it is always necessary.

Devotion is the practice of the Presence of God, and the surrender of ourselves completely to the dictates of Divine Will. Jesus gives us the first commandment for devotion:

> The Lord our God is one Lord: And thou shalt love the Lord thy God with all thy heart, And with all thy soul, And with all thy mind, And with all thy strength. (Mark 12: 30)

Devotion is that attitude of consciousness which gives itself completely to God—the only possible attitude for any worshipful observance. Devotion sees God as all that is. This is Enlightenment.

ILLUMINATION

Illumination is the culmination of our mental and spiritual processes. It is the result of focusing our consciousness upon God until we reach complete identification and realization of Reality. Our individual consciousness (the "I," or the "eye") then is illumined by the Light, as complete knowingness of Spirit. We become One with God—a single Universal unit. "The light of the body is the eye: if therefore thine eye be single, thy whole body shall be full of light." (Matt. 6: 22)

THE ONE LIGHT

We are created out of light, energy and intelligence, which are aspects of the One Light—the Word—the Christ—"That was the true Light, which lighteth every man that cometh into the world." (John 1: 9)

> Ye are the light of the world. A city that is set on an hill cannot be hid. Neither do men light a candle, and put it under a

bushel, but on a candlestick; and it giveth light unto all that are in the house. Let your light so shine before men, that they may see your good works, and glorify your Father which is in heaven. (Matt. 5: 14–16)

Since Light is the essence of each of us, the process of evolution and growth through our personal spiritual endeavors leads us back into the Light—Illumination—Realization of the True Self. However, because of the negative conditioning in consciousness of past lives and in this one, we often lose our way and grope around in the darkness of ignorance and despair. "But if thine eye be evil, thy whole body shall be full of darkness. If therefore the light that is in thee be darkness, how great is that darkness." (Matt. 6: 23)

We emerge from the darkness only by developing the various aspects of our full potential which we have been explaining in this and previous chapters. A life lived in dedication, discipline and devotion leads us back into the Light—the realization of the Christ of our own being. This process is called "the Path" or "the Way." It is the choice of each of us whether or not we wish to follow it. There are always teachers along the way to help those who aspire to the heights of Illumination and Self-Realization. The occult axiom affirms, "When the student is ready, the teacher appears."

Jesus was one of the Wayshowers: "I am the way, the truth, and the life: no man cometh unto the Father, but by me." (John 14: 6)

When he says, "I am," he is referring to the Christ within Him and within every man. When he asks his disciples, "Whom say ye that I am?" he is indicating that we will not have arrived at our full potential until we can look within to the true Self and realize, "Thou art the Christ, the Son of the living God." (Matt. 16: 16) When we do this we know that "Blessed art thou . . . for flesh and blood hath not revealed it unto thee, but my Father which is in heaven." (Matt. 16: 17)

The Science of Mind is for the purpose of providing ways and means to learn the lessons of life and to solve its problems in a spiritually scientific way.

In the larger sense, this entire book is a Treatment, in that we have moved through successive stages of understanding ourselves and the application of spiritual principles to every aspect of our lives.

The treatments in each chapter are mind and soul conditioners which develop the consciousness and assist our inner development.

The following treatments deal with the very essence of our being:

Personal Science of Mind Treatment for Personal Growth

I am on an infinite journey of self-development and unfoldment. I live to learn to learn and to grow. I can never stand still. I am ever moving upward into higher levels of understanding and expression. I intend to grow all of my life. I have infinite potential. I am an expanding being. There is no limit to my capacity for knowing and being. I move constantly toward the goal of total being.

Since I can only be what I know, I set about the business of learning more—so that I can be more—so that I may be my highest and best at all times. I have worthy aims and goals. There is much to do, and I accomplish much. I surrender all false ego, and embrace the True Ego, my Selfhood in God. I seek ever to be "my beloved Son in whom I am well pleased." I am a son of God, and my destiny is to know that I am the true Son. Just knowing this makes me grow. As my awareness of Reality grows, I grow with it. I am constantly assuming greater stature. I am a big person in every respect.

I experience constant growth in consciousness. The more my mind grows, the more I know. The more I know, the more I am. The more I am, the greater good I can do. The more good I do, the more I am doing God's work. The more I do God's work, the closer I come to fulfilling my purpose for living. The more aware I become of my purpose and potential, the more I move and grow toward this achievement.

My soul builds more stately mansions in which to dwell. Soul growth is true growth. The size of my soul indicates the amount of Spirit I embody. True growth is at the soul level. My soul is moving ever upward toward its true individuality in the realm of Spirit. My vision is upward. My imagination is rich and fertile with spiritual realization and awareness. I am inspired by the vistas before me. There are new horizons everywhere—beckoning me to climb the mountain tops of realization of my full potential. I move eternally toward this goal.

As I maintain my attunement with the One Life, I am inspired by the magnificent powers that are developing and growing within me. I intuitively perceive the great universe within me. I know much more than I know I know. I am much more than I have ever recognized. I can do much more than I have ever attempted. I grow as I know. Now I know. Thank you, Father.
And so it is.

Personal Science of Mind Treatment to Express My Full Potential

I survey all that is. That is my true potential. I have come to know it. I have taken steps toward attaining it. As I have learned and become more, I now go about the business of giving more. I express my full potential by giving and doing. I let my Infinite Potential pour out into mighty works. The Divine Forces within me flow forth into glorious expression. I express my Self.

My prayers and meditations are expressions of my full potential. As I contemplate the Infinite, I become One with It. That which I contemplate I become. That which I am, I give. I hold nothing back. God has given me all. I give all to Him. My actions, my feelings, my thoughts, my ideas, my perceptions, my recognitions and realizations—all of these are for the expression of my inner potential as it moves outward into form. My extended vision opens my eyes to new and greater areas for expressing my full potential. There is much to do, much to say, much to feel, much to see, much to hear, much to know. I have begun to realize my full potential. Now I must express it. I must be about my Father's business.

I do God's work in this world. I am a thinker. I am a knower. The world changes as I release my wisdom and understanding into it. My ideas, projects and plans express the stature of my full potential. I am a co-creator with God. I have the courage of my convictions. I do that which I know it is right to do. I say that which I have been given to say. I walk the world over with ten-league boots as I move along the path which I must travel. Nothing is too big or too much. I am not interested in how much, but in how well and how good. The standard of excellence is my only standard. God is my only pattern. I live and move and have my being in Him.

Nothing is too good to be true. Nothing is too wonderful to happen. My vision is unlimited. I help others go where I see they must go. My love is warm and all encompassing. I have great love for all people. I encourage them and give them security with my interest and compassion. My heart goes out to all members of God's family. I give all to the glory of God—in and through mankind—as I express my full potential.

And so it is.

SUMMARY OF CHAPTER 16

1. We are many times better, greater, and more capable than our conscious mind now accepts.
2. The Science of Mind opens our minds to our infinite potential through an expansion of the areas of probability and possibility.
3. The real business of life is the realization of our full potential, not just as the son of man but as the Son of God.
4. The son of man is what we know. The Son of God is what there is to be known.
5. There is an undeniable thrust which moves us along toward our destiny of complete realization and fulfillment.
6. We have within us the capacity to express the Infinite Potential of our own consciousness.
7. We are not just human beings striving to be good; we are spiritual beings unfolding into the full expression of That which we really are—God individualized.
8. Higher levels of consciousness have dominion over the lower.
9. Man can know God and become One with Him through his own mind.
10. A life lived in dedication, discipline and devotion leads us into the Light—the realization of the Christ of our own being.

Epilogue

The Science of Mind is dedicated to assisting the spiritual unfoldment of everyone by offering a program of mental, emotional and spiritual instruction, correction, and development which will develop the whole person and enable him to live a richer, fuller life on every level, including the material and the physical. That is the purpose of this book.

The Science of Mind can be thought of as a common sense approach to life which can be understood, used, and practiced by everyone, and from which everyone can benefit. As we have seen, the focus is upon personal development on every level. The Science of Mind teaches self-reliance and personal responsibility. The cause for both the good and the bad experiences of life lies within us, and there is something we can do about it.

That is the underlying theme of this book: *There is something we can do about it.*

THE WAY IS CLEAR FOR YOU

Therefore, if we would move out of the hell of limitation, ignorance and suffering into the heaven of health, happiness, abundance, well-being and understanding, we must develop and follow a way of life which will establish and maintain us in this desired and desirable state. There is no other way. No one can live for us, or learn or grow for us. We must do it by becoming aware of the highest and best that is within, and by being faithful to it and expressing it at all times.

The Science of Mind is a psychological, philosophical and spiritual approach to life that embodies all that is constructive and useful in all three fields, fused together in such a way that they can be applied to human needs and the aspirations of man.

THE KEY YOU CAN TURN FOR ALL GOOD

"The key to every man is his thought," said Emerson. In the Science of Mind we learn to turn that key. We have seen how new attitudes create new conditions. We have found that inner spark which ignites into the sacred flame of our own individuality.

The principles of the Science of Mind and its techniques of Treatment are tried and proved, having helped millions find themselves and move on to freedom and accomplishment, but each one of us who have walked this path and have been helped by it have come to the place where we have had to decide to go all the way with it.

There are no half-way measures. For those who would get out of the tiny prisons which petty thinking, selfishness and stupidity construct, there can be no compromise. We can't get something for nothing. We must do something about ourselves if we would change.

Sometimes we think we can't do anything to help ourselves; the situation seems so hopeless or so desperate. Who says you can't? Of course you can, if you think you can.

WHAT DO YOU NEED TO BE FREE FROM?

What do you need to free yourself from? In what way have you compromised or surrendered? What do you want to do and be? If a change is indicated, why not start by knowing the truth—about yourself—and all things, and letting the truth make you free.

SELF-REALIZATION AND TRUE AWARENESS

Our highest aspiration is to realize the infinite possibilities of our own being. We know that if we truly understand ourselves, we will know all. We intuitively know that since we have always lived, and will live forever, we can experience eternity now. We know we are aware, that we have within us the capacity to move out of:

DEATH into LIFE
DARKNESS into LIGHT
IGNORANCE into ENLIGHTENMENT
CONFUSION into HARMONY
UNREAL into REAL
OLD into NEW
LAW into GRACE
TEMPORAL into ETERNAL
HUMANITY into DIVINITY
FINITE into INFINITE
LIMITED into UNLIMITED
MATERIAL into SPIRITUAL
SELFISHNESS into SELFLESSNESS
VISIBLE into INVISIBLE
HEAD into HEART
FALSE into TRUE
IMPERFECT into PERFECT
EARTH into HEAVEN

YOUR LIFE WITHOUT LIMITATION

Of course, the movement is entirely within our own consciousness. We cannot go anywhere we are not already—if we know it. We cannot know anything which we do not already know—if we know that this is so. There is no limit to our expansion in consciousness when we use the Science of Mind as the Golden Bridge to the Larger Life, and stay there, moving steadily forward toward the limitless horizons of our own spiritual potential. Let this way of life carry you as far as you can go. It has no limits and neither will you, when you follow this initiatory Path to self-mastery and realization of the True Self.

From our previous practice with the treatments in each chapter, we have found that definite results are achieved when we apply ourselves to developing constructive inner mental, emotional and spiritual attitudes. Treatment is the means by which we condition ourselves to actually cause in consciousness the desired good which we wish to experience.

This closing Treatment conditions us to accept the Ultimate of Existence:

Personal Science of Mind Treatment for Your Life Without Limitation

I am a native of Eternity. I have always been, I am now, and I always will be. I am consciously aware of the continuity of all life. I flow with the stream of eternity. I dwell in infinite consciousness which rises above all time and space and yet is one with all time and space.

I am an immortal being, and I express my immortality in the immediacy of the now. I know that to know God is to know Life eternal. God is Life. God has made me in His image and likeness. I am Life—Life abundant, infinite and everlasting. As I die to the old, I am everlastingly resurrected to the new.

> The former things are passed away ... Behold, I make all things new. ... I am Alpha and Omega, the beginning and the end. I will give unto him that is athirst of the fountain of the water of life freely.
>
> He that overcometh shall inherit all things: and I will be his God, and he shall be my son. (Rev. 21: 4–7)

As I die endlessly, I am reborn eternally. There can be no death for that which has no beginning or end. There can only be Life—Life eternal and everlasting. I live foreverbecause the Eternal One lives in me. I am constantly regenerated, renewed and reborn with the Christ.

> I live; yet not I, but Christ *Liveth in me.* (Gal. 2: 20)

> I can do all things *through Christ* which strengtheneth me. (Phil. 4: 13)

> Whosoever drinketh of the water that I shall give him shall never thirst; but the water that I shall give him shall be in him a well of water springing up into everlasting life. (John 4: 14)

> I am the resurrection, and the life; he that believeth in me, though he were dead, yet shall he live. And whosoever liveth and believeth in me shall never die. Believest thou this. (John 11: 25, 6)

I am constantly renewed and strengthened by the Lord—the Life Force within me.

EPILOGUE

> Hast thou not known? Hast thou not heard, that the everlasting God, the LORD, the Creator of the ends of the earth, fainteth not, neither is weary? There is no searching of his understanding. He giveth power to the faint; and to them that have no might he increaseth strength.
>
> Even the youths shall faint and be weary, and the young men shall utterly fail: But they that wait upon the LORD shall renew their strength; they shall mount up with wings as eagles; they shall run, and not be weary; and they shall walk, and not faint. (Isa. 40: 28–31)

Consciousness is the only reality—the Consciousness of the Kingdom. I am reborn.

> Except a man be born of water and of the Spirit, he cannot enter into the kingdom of God. (John 3: 5)

I drink freely of the waters of life:

> Ho, every one that thirsteth, come ye to the waters, and he that hath no money; come ye, buy, and eat; yea, come, buy wine and milk without money and without price. Wherefore do ye spend money for that which is not bread? and your labour for that which satisfieth not? Hearken diligently unto me, and eat ye that which is good, and let your soul delight itself in fatness. Incline your ear, and come unto me: hear, and your soul shall live; and I will make an everlasting covenant with you, even the sure mercies of David. (Isaiah 55: 1–3)

My true home is the kingdom of Heaven.

> And no man hath ascended up to heaven, but he that came down from heaven, even the Son of man which is in heaven. And as Moses lifted up the serpent in the wilderness, even so must the Son of man be lifted up: That whosoever believeth in him should not perish, but have eternal life. For God so loved the world, that he gave his only begotten Son, that whosoever believeth in him should not perish, but have everlasting life. (John 3: 13–16)

The "I" of me is the only "begotten Son." I know this is so.

> Surely goodness and mercy shall follow me all the days of my life: and I will dwell in the house of the LORD for ever. (Psalm 23: 6)

And so it is. Thank you, Father. Amen.

A PERSONAL WORD FROM MELVIN POWERS
PUBLISHER, WILSHIRE BOOK COMPANY

Dear Friend:

My goal is to publish interesting, informative, and inspirational books. You can help me accomplish this by answering the following questions, either by phone or by mail. Or, if convenient for you, I would welcome the opportunity to visit with you in my office and hear your comments in person.

Did you enjoy reading this book? Why?

Would you enjoy reading another similar book?

What idea in the book impressed you the most?

If applicable to your situation, have you incorporated this idea in your daily life?

Is there a chapter that could serve as a theme for an entire book? Please explain.

If you have an idea for a book, I would welcome discussing it with you. If you already have one in progress, write or call me concerning possible publication. I can be reached at (213) 875-1711 or (818) 983-1105.

Sincerely yours,
MELVIN POWERS

12015 Sherman Road
North Hollywood, California 91605

MELVIN POWERS SELF-IMPROVEMENT LIBRARY

ASTROLOGY

___ ASTROLOGY: HOW TO CHART YOUR HOROSCOPE *Max Heindel*	5.00
___ ASTROLOGY AND SEXUAL ANALYSIS *Morris C. Goodman*	5.00
___ ASTROLOGY MADE EASY *Astarte*	5.00
___ ASTROLOGY, ROMANCE, YOU AND THE STARS *Anthony Norvell*	5.00
___ MY WORLD OF ASTROLOGY *Sydney Omarr*	7.00
___ THOUGHT DIAL *Sydney Omarr*	4.00
___ WHAT THE STARS REVEAL ABOUT THE MEN IN YOUR LIFE *Thelma White*	3.00

BRIDGE

___ BRIDGE BIDDING MADE EASY *Edwin B. Kantar*	10.00
___ BRIDGE CONVENTIONS *Edwin B. Kantar*	7.00
___ BRIDGE HUMOR *Edwin B. Kantar*	5.00
___ COMPETITIVE BIDDING IN MODERN BRIDGE *Edgar Kaplan*	7.00
___ DEFENSIVE BRIDGE PLAY COMPLETE *Edwin B. Kantar*	15.00
___ GAMESMAN BRIDGE—Play Better with Kantar *Edwin B. Kantar*	5.00
___ HOW TO IMPROVE YOUR BRIDGE *Alfred Sheinwold*	5.00
___ IMPROVING YOUR BIDDING SKILLS *Edwin B. Kantar*	4.00
___ INTRODUCTION TO DECLARER'S PLAY *Edwin B. Kantar*	5.00
___ INTRODUCTION TO DEFENDER'S PLAY *Edwin B. Kantar*	5.00
___ KANTAR FOR THE DEFENSE *Edwin B. Kantar*	7.00
___ KANTAR FOR THE DEFENSE VOLUME 2 *Edwin B. Kantar*	7.00
___ SHORT CUT TO WINNING BRIDGE *Alfred Sheinwold*	3.00
___ TEST YOUR BRIDGE PLAY *Edwin B. Kantar*	5.00
___ VOLUME 2—TEST YOUR BRIDGE PLAY *Edwin B. Kantar*	5.00
___ WINNING DECLARER PLAY *Dorothy Hayden Truscott*	5.00

BUSINESS, STUDY & REFERENCE

___ CONVERSATION MADE EASY *Elliot Russell*	4.00
___ EXAM SECRET *Dennis B. Jackson*	3.00
___ FIX-IT BOOK *Arthur Symons*	2.00
___ HOW TO DEVELOP A BETTER SPEAKING VOICE *M. Hellier*	4.00
___ HOW TO SELF-PUBLISH YOUR BOOK & MAKE IT A BEST SELLER *Melvin Powers*	10.00
___ INCREASE YOUR LEARNING POWER *Geoffrey A. Dudley*	3.00
___ PRACTICAL GUIDE TO BETTER CONCENTRATION *Melvin Powers*	3.00
___ PRACTICAL GUIDE TO PUBLIC SPEAKING *Maurice Forley*	5.00
___ 7 DAYS TO FASTER READING *William S. Schaill*	5.00
___ SONGWRITERS' RHYMING DICTIONARY *Jane Shaw Whitfield*	7.00
___ SPELLING MADE EASY *Lester D. Basch & Dr. Milton Finkelstein*	3.00
___ STUDENT'S GUIDE TO BETTER GRADES *J. A. Rickard*	3.00
___ TEST YOURSELF—Find Your Hidden Talent *Jack Shafer*	3.00
___ YOUR WILL & WHAT TO DO ABOUT IT *Attorney Samuel G. Kling*	5.00

CALLIGRAPHY

___ ADVANCED CALLIGRAPHY *Katherine Jeffares*	7.00
___ CALLIGRAPHER'S REFERENCE BOOK *Anne Leptich & Jacque Evans*	7.00
___ CALLIGRAPHY—The Art of Beautiful Writing *Katherine Jeffares*	7.00
___ CALLIGRAPHY FOR FUN & PROFIT *Anne Leptich & Jacque Evans*	7.00
___ CALLIGRAPHY MADE EASY *Tina Serafini*	7.00

CHESS & CHECKERS

___ BEGINNER'S GUIDE TO WINNING CHESS *Fred Reinfeld*	5.00
___ CHESS IN TEN EASY LESSONS *Larry Evans*	5.00
___ CHESS MADE EASY *Milton L. Hanauer*	3.00
___ CHESS PROBLEMS FOR BEGINNERS *edited by Fred Reinfeld*	5.00
___ CHESS SECRETS REVEALED *Fred Reinfeld*	2.00
___ CHESS TACTICS FOR BEGINNERS *edited by Fred Reinfeld*	5.00
___ CHESS THEORY & PRACTICE *Morry & Mitchell*	2.00
___ HOW TO WIN AT CHECKERS *Fred Reinfeld*	3.00
___ 1001 BRILLIANT WAYS TO CHECKMATE *Fred Reinfeld*	5.00
___ 1001 WINNING CHESS SACRIFICES & COMBINATIONS *Fred Reinfeld*	5.00

____	SOVIET CHESS *Edited by R. G. Wade*	3.00

COOKERY & HERBS

____	CULPEPER'S HERBAL REMEDIES *Dr. Nicholas Culpeper*	3.00
____	FAST GOURMET COOKBOOK *Poppy Cannon*	2.50
____	GINSENG The Myth & The Truth *Joseph P. Hou*	3.00
____	HEALING POWER OF HERBS *May Bethel*	4.00
____	HEALING POWER OF NATURAL FOODS *May Bethel*	5.00
____	HERB HANDBOOK *Dawn MacLeod*	3.00
____	HERBS FOR HEALTH—How to Grow & Use Them *Louise Evans Doole*	4.00
____	HOME GARDEN COOKBOOK—Delicious Natural Food Recipes *Ken Kraft*	3.00
____	MEDICAL HERBALIST *edited by Dr. J. R. Yemm*	3.00
____	VEGETABLE GARDENING FOR BEGINNERS *Hugh Wiberg*	2.00
____	VEGETABLES FOR TODAY'S GARDENS *R. Milton Carleton*	2.00
____	VEGETARIAN COOKERY *Janet Walker*	4.00
____	VEGETARIAN COOKING MADE EASY & DELECTABLE *Veronica Vezza*	3.00
____	VEGETARIAN DELIGHTS—A Happy Cookbook for Health *K. R. Mehta*	2.00
____	VEGETARIAN GOURMET COOKBOOK *Joyce McKinnel*	3.00

GAMBLING & POKER

____	ADVANCED POKER STRATEGY & WINNING PLAY *A. D. Livingston*	5.00
____	HOW TO WIN AT DICE GAMES *Skip Frey*	3.00
____	HOW TO WIN AT POKER *Terence Reese & Anthony T. Watkins*	5.00
____	WINNING AT CRAPS *Dr. Lloyd T. Commins*	4.00
____	WINNING AT GIN *Chester Wander & Cy Rice*	3.00
____	WINNING AT POKER—An Expert's Guide *John Archer*	5.00
____	WINNING AT 21—An Expert's Guide *John Archer*	5.00
____	WINNING POKER SYSTEMS *Norman Zadeh*	3.00

HEALTH

____	BEE POLLEN *Lynda Lyngheim & Jack Scagnetti*	3.00
____	DR. LINDNER'S SPECIAL WEIGHT CONTROL METHOD *P. G. Lindner, M.D.*	2.00
____	HELP YOURSELF TO BETTER SIGHT *Margaret Darst Corbett*	3.00
____	HOW YOU CAN STOP SMOKING PERMANENTLY *Ernest Caldwell*	3.00
____	MIND OVER PLATTER *Peter G. Lindner, M.D.*	3.00
____	NATURE'S WAY TO NUTRITION & VIBRANT HEALTH *Robert J. Scrutton*	3.00
____	NEW CARBOHYDRATE DIET COUNTER *Patti Lopez-Pereira*	2.00
____	REFLEXOLOGY *Dr. Maybelle Segal*	4.00
____	REFLEXOLOGY FOR GOOD HEALTH *Anna Kaye & Don C. Matchan*	5.00
____	30 DAYS TO BEAUTIFUL LEGS *Dr. Marc Selner*	3.00
____	YOU CAN LEARN TO RELAX *Dr. Samuel Gutwirth*	3.00
____	YOUR ALLERGY—What To Do About It *Allan Knight, M.D.*	3.00

HOBBIES

____	BEACHCOMBING FOR BEGINNERS *Norman Hickin*	2.00
____	BLACKSTONE'S MODERN CARD TRICKS *Harry Blackstone*	5.00
____	BLACKSTONE'S SECRETS OF MAGIC *Harry Blackstone*	5.00
____	COIN COLLECTING FOR BEGINNERS *Burton Hobson & Fred Reinfeld*	5.00
____	ENTERTAINING WITH ESP *Tony 'Doc' Shiels*	2.00
____	400 FASCINATING MAGIC TRICKS YOU CAN DO *Howard Thurston*	4.00
____	HOW I TURN JUNK INTO FUN AND PROFIT *Sari*	3.00
____	HOW TO WRITE A HIT SONG & SELL IT *Tommy Boyce*	7.00
____	JUGGLING MADE EASY *Rudolf Dittrich*	3.00
____	MAGIC FOR ALL AGES *Walter Gibson*	4.00
____	MAGIC MADE EASY *Byron Wels*	2.00
____	STAMP COLLECTING FOR BEGINNERS *Burton Hobson*	3.00

HORSE PLAYERS' WINNING GUIDES

____	BETTING HORSES TO WIN *Les Conklin*	5.00
____	ELIMINATE THE LOSERS *Bob McKnight*	3.00
____	HOW TO PICK WINNING HORSES *Bob McKnight*	5.00
____	HOW TO WIN AT THE RACES *Sam (The Genius) Lewin*	5.00
____	HOW YOU CAN BEAT THE RACES *Jack Kavanagh*	5.00

___	MAKING MONEY AT THE RACES *David Barr*	5.00
___	PAYDAY AT THE RACES *Les Conklin*	5.00
___	SMART HANDICAPPING MADE EASY *William Bauman*	5.00
___	SUCCESS AT THE HARNESS RACES *Barry Meadow*	5.00
___	WINNING AT THE HARNESS RACES—An Expert's Guide *Nick Cammarano*	5.00

HUMOR

___	HOW TO FLATTEN YOUR TUSH *Coach Marge Reardon*	2.00
___	HOW TO MAKE LOVE TO YOURSELF *Ron Stevens & Joy Grdnic*	3.00
___	JOKE TELLER'S HANDBOOK *Bob Orben*	5.00
___	JOKES FOR ALL OCCASIONS *Al Schock*	5.00
___	2000 NEW LAUGHS FOR SPEAKERS *Bob Orben*	5.00
___	2,500 JOKES TO START 'EM LAUGHING *Bob Orben*	5.00

HYPNOTISM

___	ADVANCED TECHNIQUES OF HYPNOSIS *Melvin Powers*	3.00
___	BRAINWASHING AND THE CULTS *Paul A. Verdier, Ph.D.*	3.00
___	CHILDBIRTH WITH HYPNOSIS *William S. Kroger, M.D.*	5.00
___	HOW TO SOLVE Your Sex Problems with Self-Hypnosis *Frank S. Caprio, M.D.*	5.00
___	HOW TO STOP SMOKING THRU SELF-HYPNOSIS *Leslie M. LeCron*	3.00
___	HOW TO USE AUTO-SUGGESTION EFFECTIVELY *John Duckworth*	3.00
___	HOW YOU CAN BOWL BETTER USING SELF-HYPNOSIS *Jack Heise*	4.00
___	HOW YOU CAN PLAY BETTER GOLF USING SELF-HYPNOSIS *Jack Heise*	3.00
___	HYPNOSIS AND SELF-HYPNOSIS *Bernard Hollander, M.D.*	5.00
___	HYPNOTISM (Originally published in 1893) *Carl Sextus*	5.00
___	HYPNOTISM & PSYCHIC PHENOMENA *Simeon Edmunds*	4.00
___	HYPNOTISM MADE EASY *Dr. Ralph Winn*	3.00
___	HYPNOTISM MADE PRACTICAL *Louis Orton*	5.00
___	HYPNOTISM REVEALED *Melvin Powers*	3.00
___	HYPNOTISM TODAY *Leslie LeCron and Jean Bordeaux, Ph.D.*	5.00
___	MODERN HYPNOSIS *Lesley Kuhn & Salvatore Russo, Ph.D.*	5.00
___	NEW CONCEPTS OF HYPNOSIS *Bernard C. Gindes, M.D.*	7.00
___	NEW SELF-HYPNOSIS *Paul Adams*	7.00
___	POST-HYPNOTIC INSTRUCTIONS—Suggestions for Therapy *Arnold Furst*	5.00
___	PRACTICAL GUIDE TO SELF-HYPNOSIS *Melvin Powers*	3.00
___	PRACTICAL HYPNOTISM *Philip Magonet, M.D.*	3.00
___	SECRETS OF HYPNOTISM *S. J. Van Pelt, M.D.*	5.00
___	SELF-HYPNOSIS A Conditioned-Response Technique *Laurence Sparks*	7.00
___	SELF-HYPNOSIS Its Theory, Technique & Application *Melvin Powers*	3.00
___	THERAPY THROUGH HYPNOSIS *edited by Raphael H. Rhodes*	5.00

JUDAICA

___	SERVICE OF THE HEART *Evelyn Garfiel, Ph.D.*	7.00
___	STORY OF ISRAEL IN COINS *Jean & Maurice Gould*	2.00
___	STORY OF ISRAEL IN STAMPS *Maxim & Gabriel Shamir*	1.00
___	TONGUE OF THE PROPHETS *Robert St. John*	7.00

JUST FOR WOMEN

___	COSMOPOLITAN'S GUIDE TO MARVELOUS MEN Fwd. by *Helen Gurley Brown*	3.00
___	COSMOPOLITAN'S HANG-UP HANDBOOK Foreword by *Helen Gurley Brown*	4.00
___	COSMOPOLITAN'S LOVE BOOK—A Guide to Ecstasy in Bed	7.00
___	COSMOPOLITAN'S NEW ETIQUETTE GUIDE Fwd. by *Helen Gurley Brown*	4.00
___	I AM A COMPLEAT WOMAN *Doris Hagopian & Karen O'Connor Sweeney*	3.00
___	JUST FOR WOMEN—A Guide to the Female Body *Richard E. Sand, M.D.*	5.00
___	NEW APPROACHES TO SEX IN MARRIAGE *John E. Eichenlaub, M.D.*	3.00
___	SEXUALLY ADEQUATE FEMALE *Frank S. Caprio, M.D.*	3.00
___	SEXUALLY FULFILLED WOMAN *Dr. Rachel Copelan*	5.00
___	YOUR FIRST YEAR OF MARRIAGE *Dr. Tom McGinnis*	3.00

MARRIAGE, SEX & PARENTHOOD

___	ABILITY TO LOVE *Dr. Allan Fromme*	7.00
___	GUIDE TO SUCCESSFUL MARRIAGE *Drs. Albert Ellis & Robert Harper*	7.00
___	HOW TO RAISE AN EMOTIONALLY HEALTHY, HAPPY CHILD *A. Ellis*	5.00

	SEX WITHOUT GUILT *Albert Ellis, Ph.D.*	5.00
	SEXUALLY ADEQUATE MALE *Frank S. Caprio, M.D.*	3.00
	SEXUALLY FULFILLED MAN *Dr. Rachel Copelan*	5.00
	STAYING IN LOVE *Dr. Norton F. Kristy*	7.00

MELVIN POWERS' MAIL ORDER LIBRARY

	HOW TO GET RICH IN MAIL ORDER *Melvin Powers*	20.00
	HOW TO WRITE A GOOD ADVERTISEMENT *Victor O. Schwab*	20.00
	MAIL ORDER MADE EASY *J. Frank Brumbaugh*	20.00

METAPHYSICS & OCCULT

	BOOK OF TALISMANS, AMULETS & ZODIACAL GEMS *William Pavitt*	7.00
	CONCENTRATION—A Guide to Mental Mastery *Mouni Sadhu*	5.00
	EXTRA-TERRESTRIAL INTELLIGENCE—The First Encounter	6.00
	FORTUNE TELLING WITH CARDS *P. Foli*	5.00
	HOW TO INTERPRET DREAMS, OMENS & FORTUNE TELLING SIGNS *Gettings*	5.00
	HOW TO UNDERSTAND YOUR DREAMS *Geoffrey A. Dudley*	3.00
	ILLUSTRATED YOGA *William Zorn*	3.00
	IN DAYS OF GREAT PEACE *Mouni Sadhu*	3.00
	LSD—THE AGE OF MIND *Bernard Roseman*	2.00
	MAGICIAN—His Training and Work *W. E. Butler*	3.00
	MEDITATION *Mouni Sadhu*	7.00
	MODERN NUMEROLOGY *Morris C. Goodman*	5.00
	NUMEROLOGY—ITS FACTS AND SECRETS *Ariel Yvon Taylor*	3.00
	NUMEROLOGY MADE EASY *W. Mykian*	5.00
	PALMISTRY MADE EASY *Fred Gettings*	5.00
	PALMISTRY MADE PRACTICAL *Elizabeth Daniels Squire*	5.00
	PALMISTRY SECRETS REVEALED *Henry Frith*	4.00
	PROPHECY IN OUR TIME *Martin Ebon*	2.50
	SUPERSTITION—Are You Superstitious? *Eric Maple*	2.00
	TAROT *Mouni Sadhu*	10.00
	TAROT OF THE BOHEMIANS *Papus*	7.00
	WAYS TO SELF-REALIZATION *Mouni Sadhu*	7.00
	WITCHCRAFT, MAGIC & OCCULTISM—A Fascinating History *W. B. Crow*	7.00
	WITCHCRAFT—THE SIXTH SENSE *Justine Glass*	7.00
	WORLD OF PSYCHIC RESEARCH *Hereward Carrington*	2.00

SELF-HELP & INSPIRATIONAL

	CHARISMA How To Get "That Special Magic" *Marcia Grad*	7.00
	DAILY POWER FOR JOYFUL LIVING *Dr. Donald Curtis*	5.00
	DYNAMIC THINKING *Melvin Powers*	5.00
	GREATEST POWER IN THE UNIVERSE *U. S. Andersen*	7.00
	GROW RICH WHILE YOU SLEEP *Ben Sweetland*	7.00
	GROWTH THROUGH REASON *Albert Ellis, Ph.D.*	7.00
	GUIDE TO PERSONAL HAPPINESS *Albert Ellis, Ph.D. & Irving Becker, Ed. D.*	7.00
	HANDWRITING ANALYSIS MADE EASY *John Marley*	5.00
	HANDWRITING TELLS *Nadya Olyanova*	7.00
	HELPING YOURSELF WITH APPLIED PSYCHOLOGY *R. Henderson*	2.00
	HOW TO ATTRACT GOOD LUCK *A. H. Z. Carr*	5.00
	HOW TO BE GREAT *Dr. Donald Curtis*	5.00
	HOW TO DEVELOP A WINNING PERSONALITY *Martin Panzer*	5.00
	HOW TO DEVELOP AN EXCEPTIONAL MEMORY *Young & Gibson*	5.00
	HOW TO LIVE WITH A NEUROTIC *Albert Ellis, Ph. D.*	5.00
	HOW TO OVERCOME YOUR FEARS *M. P. Leahy, M.D.*	3.00
	HOW TO SUCCEED *Brian Adams*	7.00
	HUMAN PROBLEMS & HOW TO SOLVE THEM *Dr. Donald Curtis*	5.00
	I CAN *Ben Sweetland*	7.00
	I WILL *Ben Sweetland*	3.00
	KNIGHT IN THE RUSTY ARMOR *Robert Fisher*	10.00
	LEFT-HANDED PEOPLE *Michael Barsley*	5.00
	MAGIC IN YOUR MIND *U. S. Andersen*	7.00

___	MAGIC OF THINKING BIG *Dr. David J. Schwartz*	3.00
___	MAGIC OF THINKING SUCCESS *Dr. David J. Schwartz*	7.00
___	MAGIC POWER OF YOUR MIND *Walter M. Germain*	7.00
___	MENTAL POWER THROUGH SLEEP SUGGESTION *Melvin Powers*	3.00
___	NEVER UNDERESTIMATE THE SELLING POWER OF A WOMAN *Dottie Walters*	7.00
___	NEW GUIDE TO RATIONAL LIVING *Albert Ellis, Ph.D. & R. Harper, Ph.D.*	7.00
___	PROJECT YOU *A Manual of Rational Assertiveness Training Paris & Casey*	6.00
___	PSYCHO-CYBERNETICS *Maxwell Maltz, M.D.*	5.00
___	PSYCHOLOGY OF HANDWRITING *Nadya Olyanova*	7.00
___	SALES CYBERNETICS *Brian Adams*	7.00
___	SCIENCE OF MIND IN DAILY LIVING *Dr. Donald Curtis*	7.00
___	SECRET OF SECRETS *U. S. Andersen*	7.00
___	SECRET POWER OF THE PYRAMIDS *U. S. Andersen*	7.00
___	SELF-THERAPY FOR THE STUTTERER *Malcolm Frazer*	3.00
___	SUCCESS-CYBERNETICS *U. S. Andersen*	6.00
___	10 DAYS TO A GREAT NEW LIFE *William E. Edwards*	3.00
___	THINK AND GROW RICH *Napoleon Hill*	7.00
___	THINK YOUR WAY TO SUCCESS *Dr. Lew Losoncy*	5.00
___	THREE MAGIC WORDS *U. S. Andersen*	7.00
___	TREASURY OF COMFORT *edited by Rabbi Sidney Greenberg*	5.00
___	TREASURY OF THE ART OF LIVING *Sidney S. Greenberg*	5.00
___	WHAT YOUR HANDWRITING REVEALS *Albert E. Hughes*	3.00
___	YOUR SUBCONSCIOUS POWER *Charles M. Simmons*	7.00
___	YOUR THOUGHTS CAN CHANGE YOUR LIFE *Dr. Donald Curtis*	7.00

SPORTS

___	BICYCLING FOR FUN AND GOOD HEALTH *Kenneth E. Luther*	2.00
___	BILLIARDS—Pocket • Carom • Three Cushion *Clive Cottingham, Jr.*	5.00
___	CAMPING-OUT 101 Ideas & Activities *Bruno Knobel*	2.00
___	COMPLETE GUIDE TO FISHING *Vlad Evanoff*	2.00
___	HOW TO IMPROVE YOUR RACQUETBALL *Lubarsky Kaufman & Scagnetti*	5.00
___	HOW TO WIN AT POCKET BILLIARDS *Edward D. Knuchell*	5.00
___	JOY OF WALKING *Jack Scagnetti*	3.00
___	LEARNING & TEACHING SOCCER SKILLS *Eric Worthington*	3.00
___	MOTORCYCLING FOR BEGINNERS *I. G. Edmonds*	3.00
___	RACQUETBALL FOR WOMEN *Toni Hudson, Jack Scagnetti & Vince Rondone*	3.00
___	RACQUETBALL MADE EASY *Steve Lubarsky, Rod Delson & Jack Scagnetti*	5.00
___	SECRET OF BOWLING STRIKES *Dawson Taylor*	5.00
___	SECRET OF PERFECT PUTTING *Horton Smith & Dawson Taylor*	5.00
___	SOCCER—The Game & How to Play It *Gary Rosenthal*	5.00
___	STARTING SOCCER *Edward F. Dolan, Jr.*	3.00

TENNIS LOVERS' LIBRARY

___	BEGINNER'S GUIDE TO WINNING TENNIS *Helen Hull Jacobs*	2.00
___	HOW TO IMPROVE YOUR TENNIS—Style, Strategy & Analysis *C. Wilson*	2.00
___	PSYCH YOURSELF TO BETTER TENNIS *Dr. Walter A. Luszki*	2.00
___	TENNIS FOR BEGINNERS, *Dr. H. A. Murray*	2.00
___	TENNIS MADE EASY *Joel Brecheen*	4.00
___	WEEKEND TENNIS—How to Have Fun & Win at the Same Time *Bill Talbert*	3.00
___	WINNING WITH PERCENTAGE TENNIS—Smart Strategy *Jack Lowe*	2.00

WILSHIRE PET LIBRARY

___	DOG OBEDIENCE TRAINING *Gust Kessopulos*	5.00
___	DOG TRAINING MADE EASY & FUN *John W. Kellogg*	3.00
___	HOW TO BRING UP YOUR PET DOG *Kurt Unkelbach*	2.00
___	HOW TO RAISE & TRAIN YOUR PUPPY *Jeff Griffen*	5.00

The books listed above can be obtained from your book dealer or directly from Melvin Powers. When ordering, please remit $1.00 postage for the first book and 50¢ for each additional book.

Melvin Powers
12015 Sherman Road, No. Hollywood, California 91605

YOUR THOUGHTS CAN CHANGE YOUR LIFE
By Dr. Donald Curtis

Contents:
1. Where Do We Go from Here? 2. The Art of Sitting Loose 3. Something Wonderful Is About to Happen 4. The Universe is a Very Big Place 5. One with All Life 6. Why Are We Alive? 7. Hitch Your Wagon to a Star 8. God Cannot Say No 9. Nothing Is Too Good to Be True 10. The Time is Now; The Place is Here 11. On the Threshold of Great Experience 12. Get Out and Get Going 13. How to Build a Better Life 14. Life is a Daily Proposition
240 Pages... $7.50 Postpaid

HUMAN PROBLEMS AND HOW TO SOLVE THEM
by Dr. Donald Curtis

Contents:
1. You Can Be as Happy as You Want to Be 2. How to Stop Hurting 3. The Richest Man in the World 4. You're in the Driver's Seat 5. How to Make Your Life a Hit 6. "Be Thou Made Whole!" 7. God has had His Arm Around You for a Long Time 8. Your Magnificent Potential 9. "I Never Met a Man I Didn't Like" 10. You are a Wonderful Person 11. How to Be a Winner 12. "The Truth Shall Make You Free"
224 Pages... $5.50 Postpaid

DAILY POWER FOR JOYFUL LIVING
by Dr. Donald Curtis

Contents:
1. LIVING: Your Golden Bridge to Life 2. SELF: How to Make The Most of Yourself 3. PEOPLE: "... all the World Art Queer Save Thee and Me..." 4. WORK: Thank God for Work! 5. FAMILY: The Keystone of Society 6. TODAY: The Best Day You Have Ever Had 7. THE WORLD: This Great Big Beautiful World 8. COUNTRY: "My Country 'Tis of Thee!" 9. MIND: "As a Man Thinketh..." 10. BODY: The Temple of the Spirit 11. HEALTH: The Secret of Vital Health 12. TIME: All the Time There Is 13. POSSESSIONS: "What Doth it Profit a Man...?" 14. MONEY: How to Have Financial Security 15. PLAY: Life Is a Ball 16. RESPONSIBILITY: "To Thine Own Self Be True..." 17. EDUCATION: Toward Becoming a Whole Person 18. PROBLEMS: A New Way to Solve Old Problems 19. LOVE: "...Makes the World Go Around" 20. FAITH: "The Substance of Things Hoped for..." 21. BEAUTY: "...A Joy Forever" 22. SLEEP: To Sleep, Perchance To Dream 23. PERSONALITY AND GOD: "...In Our Image, After Our Likeness..." 24. PROSPERITY: The Law of Increase 25. SELF-DISCOVERY AND SELF-EXPRESSION: The "Father's Business" 26. ATTITUDES AND HABITS: "Every Day in Every Way..." 27. AIMS AND GOALS: The Art of Standing Tall 28. RELIGION: Something to Live by 29. PRAYER AND TREATMENT: "Teach Us to Pray" 30. AGE: Breaking the Age Barrier 31. ETERNAL LIFE: The Great Adventure 366 Personal Daily Affirmations
256 Pages... $5.50 Postpaid

A NEW GUIDE TO RATIONAL LIVING
by Albert Ellis, Ph.D. & Robert A. Harper, Ph.D.

Contents:
1. How Far Can You Go With Self-Analysis? 2. You Feel the Way You Think 3. Feeling Well by Thinking Straight 4. How You Create Your Feelings 5. Thinking Yourself Out of Emotional Disturbances 6. Recognizing and Attacking Neurotic Behavior 7. Overcoming the Influences of the Past 8. Does Reason Always Prove Reasonable? 9. Refusing to Feel Desperately Unhappy 10. Tackling Dire Needs for Approval 11. Eradicating Dire Fears of Failure 12. How to Stop Blaming and Start Living 13. How to Feel Undepressed though Frustrated 14. Controlling your Own Destiny 15. Conquering Anxiety 16. Acquiring Self-discipline 17. Rewriting Your Personal History 18. Accepting Reality 19. Overcoming Inertia and Getting Creatively Absorbed 20. Living Rationally in an Irrational World 21. Rational-Emotive Therapy or Rational Behavior Training Updated
256 Pages... $7.50 Postpaid

The books listed above can be obtained from your book dealer or directly from Melvin Powers.

Melvin Powers
12015 Sherman Road, No. Hollywood, California 91605